Growing for Justice

Growing for Justice

A Developmental Continuum of Leadership Capacities and Practices

Eleanor Drago-Severson

Jessica Blum-DeStefano

Deborah Brooks Lawrence

A joint publication with Learning Forward.

FOR INFORMATION:

Corwin

A SAGE Company

2455 Teller Road

Thousand Oaks, California 91320

(800) 233-9936

www.corwin.com

SAGE Publications Ltd.

1 Oliver's Yard

55 City Road

London EC1Y 1SP

United Kingdom

SAGE Publications India Pvt. Ltd.

Unit No 323-333, Third Floor, F-Block

International Trade Tower Nehru Place

New Delhi 110 019

India

SAGE Publications Asia-Pacific Pte. Ltd.

18 Cross Street #10-10/11/12

China Square Central

Singapore 048423

President: Mike Soules

Vice President and
  Editorial Director: Monica Eckman

Program Director and Publisher: Dan Alpert

Content Development
  Manager: Lucas Schleicher

Content Development Editor: Mia Rodriguez

Senior Editorial Assistant: Natalie Delpino

Production Editor: Tori Mirsadjadi

Copy Editor: Diana Breti

Typesetter: C&M Digitals (P) Ltd.

Cover Designer: Candice Harman

Marketing Manager: Melissa Duclos

ISBN 978-1-0718-1889-3

This book is printed on acid-free paper.

23 24 25 26 27 10 9 8 7 6 5 4 3 2 1

CONTENTS

ACKNOWLEDGMENTS

In the flush of love's light we dare be brave
> —Maya Angelou, "Touched by an Angel"

At its heart, this is a book that pays forward gifts. Gifts of self and wisdom from the generous and brilliant participants who opened their hearts and minds to us so that we could learn from and share their wisdom, experiences, practices, and insights with all who are reading and benefiting from this book. These are gifts of light, love, and reciprocal learning from the dedicated students, educators, leaders, and colleagues we have had the honor of working with in the field as well as gifts of support from cherished teachers and loved ones—those still walking beside us and those we carry inside of us and always will. We hope that every single person—and there are many—who has helped bring this book into being feels our deep and enduring gratitude. We want also—together and individually—to make special mention of the contributions of a few particular people and groups. Your care and generosity infuse the pages that follow.

First and of course, we want to thank—infinitely and effusively—the fifty extraordinary, courageous, and inspirational leaders who opened their hearts and busy calendars to us in this research. You filled us up to the brim and beyond with your thoughtfulness, generosity, and passion. We carry your priceless stories with us each and every day. It is an honor to share your insights and introspections—and *you*—with the world. Although we cannot mention your names here, please know that they are written in our hearts.

We would also like to express our tremendous admiration and appreciation for Professor Robert Kegan, whose creation and articulation of constructive-developmental theory, wisdom, and visionary leadership continue to inform, inspire, and guide our work, research, and teaching. We truly stand humbly on the shoulders of a giant, a light.

To Dan Alpert, Lucas Schleicher, Mia Rodriguez, Tori Mirsadjadi, Diana Breti, Natalie Delpino, Melissa Duclos, and all on the Corwin team: Thank you for your faith and enduring confidence in this work, your patience, your longstanding support, your wise feedback, and your expert shepherding. We feel so well held in your hands and are so grateful for your partnership and collaboration.

We thank from deep in heart Suzanne Bouffard and all our friends at Learning Forward for their continued support and championing over the years and for the treasured opportunity to share our work with their esteemed book club. What an honor!

We hope, too, that Nancy Popp, Gabriella Oldham, Katie Embree, Christy Joswick O'Connor, Georgina Duff, Katherine Seol, Pierre Faller, Barbara Rappaport, David Severson, Rachel Harari, Lucy Tam, Amy Deiner, Hyunjin Choi, and Pat Maslin-Ostrowski know and feel our heartfelt gratitude. We also want to express sincere and deep gratitude for the many students, faculty, and administration at Teachers College, Columbia University, Harvard's Graduate School of Education, and Bank Street College of Education who continue to influence us and what we are able to share. You teach us, lift us, and inspire us.

In addition, we want to express our enduring gratitude for and to the droves of dedicated educators who have generously shared their stories, thinking, and experiences with us and for the trust they place in us—in general and in our research, university courses, workshops, institutes, coaching, and professional learning initiatives in schools, districts, and other organizations. Learning with and from you continues to be a tremendous gift, which we cherish. We are so grateful for you and for all you teach us. Your wisdom and generosity of heart and mind inspire.

DEBORAH'S PERSONAL ACKNOWLEDGMENTS

It is with admiration and grace that I thank all who participated in this project not only for trusting in the process, but also for giving and engaging with unbounded fidelity that is the core of this work.

It is with immediate and immense gratitude that I thank Ellie Drago-Severson and Jessica Blum-DeStefano for inviting me on this journey rife with an anticipation of learning with a true sense of wholeness.

All that I have done and will do is irrevocably tied to my family. I thank my husband, Jerry Lawrence, the keeper of my eternal love, for always being my knight in shining armor. I thank our daughter, Samantha Brooke Lawrence, for being our guardian angel, and I thank our grandchildren, Sydney and Joy, for always trying to hold onto patience and waiting until we can play again in full force.

I am paying my gratitude forward to thank all of the education practitioners, parents, and guardians who will embrace this work as a viable resource.

I thank all in my company now and all who have come before me in service to the legacy of equity.

JESSICA'S PERSONAL ACKNOWLEDGMENTS

I would like to honor all whose support, challenge, love, trust, experience, and relationship have made this moment—and the many gifts in my life—possible. You're all in there and will always be a part of me. For example, I couldn't possibly imagine better parents, a more loving sister, a more perfect partner, a more supportive family and network, or more energizing students and colleagues. And my kids! Well, you are my heartbeat. I love every single bit of you with every bit of me. Thank you for being exactly who you are.

It's also imperative here to name my bursting-full appreciation and love for Ellie and Deb, my cotravelers on this journey. You are my forever teachers, friends, thought partners, and extended family—and your superpowers synergize and astound. What an adventure we've been on together—and that's made it all the more meaningful.

ELLIE'S PERSONAL ACKNOWLEDGMENTS

I would like to honor all in my life whose support, love, care, presence, trust, and courage help me to grow; touch my heart; and help me to become better, to give more, and to be. These relationships are many and are blessings every single day. I offer my love and heartfelt gratitude to my family, friends, colleagues, and collaborators for their care, love, presence, supports, and stretching, which have strengthened me, helping me grow to be able to make the contributions I am able to make. Each of you has powerfully influenced my life, and therefore this work, in important, impossible-to-describe, and inspiring ways. I know that I am who I am, and who I am growing to become, because of all of you.

I begin with heartfelt appreciation for family-friends, extended networks of family-work friends, colleagues, and partners in thought who have contributed to this book in meaningful and different ways because of their influence and presence in my life. I trust you know in your heart what an honor it is to collaborate with you, to know you, and how much I admire all you give every day to make this world a better place. I trust you know why I mention you here. Though I express gratitude for you on this page, I hope you feel my deep loving gratitude and love each and every day and know that I carry you in my heart: Richard Ackerman, Mary Anton-Oldenburg, Bill Baldwin, Ira Bogotch, Ken Bonamo, Judith Brady, Maria Broderick, Tashia Brown, Tom Buffett, Kirsten Busch, Robb Clouse, Christine Chavez, Chris Coughlin, Jerry Crisci, Tracy Crow, Jeannie Crowley, Mary Czajkowski, Kathy De la Garza, Sharon DeLorenzo, Lauren Drapek, Eleanor Duckworth, David Eddy Spicer, Jane Ellison, Katie Embree, Rafaela Espinal, Melissa Feinberg,

Brenda Garcia, Monica George-Fields, Felix Gil, Chris Griffen, Rochelle Hauge, Thomas Hagerman, Jen Hefner, Rochelle Herring Fred-Ted Hill, Sharon Hill, Trish Iasiello, Tom James, Susan Moore Johnson, Anne Jones, Christy Joswick-O'Connor, Mara Koeke, India Koopman, Jed Lippard, Andy Malone, Andrew Mandel, Neville Marks, Victoria Marsick, Pat Maslin-Ostrowski, David McCallum, Kathleen McCartney, Edgar McIntosh, Ann Meyer, Ailene Altman Mitchell, Peter Neaman, Ella O'Connor, Liam O'Connor, Anie O'Gorman, Drew Patrick, Ray Pappalardi, Brian Perkins, Lisa Pilaski, Julie Porter, Eric Rauschenbach, Steve Silverman, Sue Steubner, Maria Stile, Meghan Troy, Chris Welch, Marion Wilson, William Yang, Jeff Young, and all leaders in the Scarsdale Administrative Council family. Special gratitude for all of these friends, colleagues, and fellow admirers of Auguste Rodin's *The Thinker*. Thank you for your courageous leadership and for modeling the importance of deep thinking, profound pondering, and heart-felt care for all. I have had the honor and privilege of longer-term relationships with these leaders and many leaders and educators who serve—with heart and soul—in a variety of organizations in order to build a better world for children, adults, and communities. I am grateful for all that you teach me as we strive together to enhance conditions that support adult growth, leadership development, and social justice.

I share my sincere and deep gratitude for these organizations and the giving and dedicated people within them: Berkeley Heights Public Schools, Bronxville Public School District, the Chicago Public Schools, District 31, the New York City Department of Education and its offices and districts, the Cahn Fellows Program, Learning Forward, Florham Park Public Schools, Summit Public Schools, Middle School 88, Minds at Work, Teach for America, New Visions Charter Schools, the School Leaders Network, the Near East South Asian Council of Overseas Schools (NESA), Lexington Public School District, Scarsdale Public School District, and the network, district, and school leaders in New York State.

I want to offer a little extra-special and deep gratitude for two of my many teachers and mentors. For more than thirty years, I have benefited tremendously from the teachings, insights, and cherished friendship of Professor Howard Gardner of Harvard's Graduate School of Education. Thank you for so generously and selflessly sharing your wisdom with the world and with me. I am very grateful for your friendship and leadership and for the gift that is you. Thank you so very, very much from my heart.

For more than thirty years, I have been truly blessed with the precious gift of learning from, with, and alongside Professor Robert Kegan of Harvard's Graduate School of Education. During these years, I have been a beneficiary of Bob's extraordinary gifts as magnanimous leader, master teacher, trusted advisor, wise mentor, thought partner and collaborator in research, treasured colleague, and cherished friend. I have benefited from how you, Bob, exquisitely and ingeniously create holding environments. I thank you from my heart for developing your theory—a generative gift to this world—and for the ways that you have altered the course of my life and the contributions I am able to make. Thank *you* for all of that and for teaching and modeling how to really—*really*—hold people and to support development. I hope that in your big heart you feel my deepest gratitude as I work to pay forward your gifts with those in my care. Thank you from all of me for all that you are and for helping me to become who I am becoming. You are inspiration, gift, and light.

It's hard to find words to express my deepest appreciation to Jess and Deb, cobuilders of bridges, cotravelers in this learning journey—and in life, dear teachers, cherished friends, and thought partners. We *live* the power of we, and for that and so much more I am deeply grateful. Thank you, Jess and Deb, for your trust, generosity, love, and all you teach me.

It is very important to acknowledge and offer immeasurable gratitude for my beginnings. My tender expressions of love and gratitude go to those who most shaped my life and what I am able to offer in support to others—my parents. My late father, Dr. Rosario Drago, and my late mother, Mrs. Betty Brisgal Drago, have been and continue to be lights, guides, lifelong teachers, and friends. Although they have passed from this world into the next, they live each day so brightly in my life, my work, what I can give, and in who I am in this world. With extraordinary love, wisdom, joy, exemplary hard work, and care, my parents modeled *how* to love, give, learn, care, and lead. Their teachings continue to fuel and to hold me. Their love, courage, and presence strengthen and live within me.

I thank my six siblings and their families for their love, for their presence, and for their enduring support. Thank you for your love, your faith in me, and for all that you teach me.

And now, I will *try* to express my deepest and enormous gratitude to you, beautiful, generous, wise, David Severson. You, Daye, are my light, loving husband, precious soul mate, best friend, North Star, and cherished, brilliant, sage teacher. How does one thank the sun for its light, its warmth, its giving, and its nurturing? Thank you from my soul for pouring your love into me and for all of the many, many ways you help me grow each and every day—and year. Although it's difficult to find words to express my enormous love and gratitude, somehow in your gigantic, compassionate heart and brilliant mind I hope you know and feel how very grateful I am for the enduring blessing and treasured gift of *you* in my life, David. Your generosity, your courage, your strength, goodness, love, care, and compassion inspire me every day.

Thank you from my soul for the tremendous love, generosity, tender support, and deep care you give and that inspire—in the truest sense of the word, meaning to breathe life into—others and me. Sweet Daye-Love, please feel deeply appreciated for being truly exquisite, giving you. No words could ever truly capture the breadth of my soul-felt gratitude, heartfelt respect, and love for you. Somehow, though, I hope you know. Thank you for showing me the way, for teaching me how to be better, and for belaying me. Thank you for your extraordinary love, sacrifices, and compromises that you so generously give each and every day. You are my kitchen cabinet, Love.

Thank you for the gift of you, your loving companionship, and your cherished friendship every step in our journey. Thank you for believing in me—and in us—and the work we do *together* each day, Star. The contributions we make, we make *together*. You are the brightest light in my life. You are my treasured love, angel, and cherished touchstone. I love you and I thank you from the deepest parts of me. I thank God for all blessings—and especially for bringing us together.

ABOUT THE AUTHORS

Eleanor Drago-Severson, EdD, is professor of education leadership and adult learning and leadership at Teachers College, Columbia University. A developmental psychologist, Ellie teaches, conducts research, and serves as a consultant—to school and district leaders, systems leaders, and teacher leaders in public, charter, and private schools and systems—on professional and personal growth and learning; leadership development; and coaching and mentoring. She is also an internationally certified developmental coach who works with leaders to build internal capacity, lead on behalf of social justice, and grow systemwide capacity.

For more than three decades, Ellie's research, teaching, and partnerships in the field have sought—synergistically—to explore and extend the possibilities of adult development and developmental leadership as levers for internal capacity building at the individual, team, organizational, and societal levels. Her work explores interconnected streams that focus on internal capacities and educational leaders' practice on behalf of social justice; a developmental approach to feedback; pressing challenges faced by leaders nationally and internationally; leadership preparation and development; a learning-oriented model for leadership development; teaming across and within systems; supporting diverse adult English language learners and those who serve them; and growing teacher leadership. Consonant with the urgent conversations about transforming schools, systems, and society as more learning- and equity-oriented contexts, her work foregrounds *how* we can support leaders' internal capacity building in schools, organizations, and leadership preparation programs. Ellie loves opportunities to accompany school leaders in their vital work—and never takes it for granted. Instead, she considers it a gift.

At Teachers College, Ellie is director of the PhD Program in Educational Leadership; teaches aspiring and practicing principals in the Summer Principals Academy, aspiring superintendents in the Urban Education Leaders Program, and leaders from a variety of different sectors in the Accelerated Education Guided Intensive Study (AEGIS) Program; and also coaches leaders in the Cahn Fellows Program for Distinguished Leaders and in her private coaching practice. She also serves as faculty director and cofacilitator of the Leadership Institutes for School Change at Teachers College. Ellie is author of the best-selling books *Helping Teachers Learn: Principal Leadership for Adult Growth and Development* (Corwin, 2004) and *Leading Adult Learning: Supporting Adult Development in Our Schools* (Corwin/The National Staff Development Council, 2009), as well as *Becoming Adult Learners: Principles and Practice for Effective Development* (Teachers College Press, 2004) and *Helping Educators Grow: Strategies and Practices for Leadership Development* (Harvard Education Press, 2012). She is also a coauthor of *Learning for Leadership: Developmental Strategies for Building Capacity in Our Schools* (Corwin, 2013), *Reach the Highest Standard in Professional Learning: Learning Designs* (Learning Forward & Corwin, 2014), *Tell Me So I Can Hear You: A Developmental Approach to Feedback for Educators* (Harvard Education Press, 2016), and *Leading Change Together: Developing Educator Capacity Within Schools and Systems* (ASCD, 2018).

Ellie's work has earned awards from the Spencer Foundation, the Klingenstein Foundation, and Harvard, where she served on the faculty for eight years and was awarded the Morningstar Award for Excellence in Teaching and the Dean's Award for Excellent Teaching. Most recently, Ellie received three outstanding teaching awards from Columbia University. She has earned degrees from Long Island University (BA) and Harvard University (EdM, EdD, and post-doctoral fellowship). Ellie grew up in the Bronx and is very grateful for the way in which it and that community has shaped her life.

Jessica Blum-DeStefano, PhD, is an instructor and advisor in the Leadership Department at Bank Street College of Education, where she teaches adult development and qualitative research methods. Her teaching, scholarship, and approach to leadership foreground the power of growth and interconnection—especially as they relate to individual perspective transformation, authentic collaboration, and capacity building systemwide. Toward these ends, her work is inspired by an interdisciplinary tapestry of ideas—including adult developmental theories, social justice frameworks, the history and philosophy of education, organizational studies, student voice, and qualitative/mixed-methods research—as well as the nine rewarding years she spent as a teacher and school administrator in K–12 alternative education settings. Jessica earned her PhD in education leadership from Teachers College, Columbia University, and holds additional degrees from Emory University (BA), Hofstra University (MA), and Teachers College (MPhil). Jessica is a coauthor of *Learning for Leadership: Developmental Strategies for Building Capacity in Our Schools* (Corwin, 2013), *Tell Me So I Can Hear You: A Developmental Approach to Feedback for Educators* (Harvard Education Press, 2016), and *Leading Change Together: Developing Educator Capacity Within Schools and Systems* (ASCD, 2018). She is also the cofacilitator of the Leadership Institutes for School Change at Teachers College, Columbia University.

Deborah Brooks Lawrence, EdD, is a native New Yorker who believes that equitable access to viable resources will pave the road for universal recognition and sustainability of human rights, and as educators we, without question, need to prepare all of our practitioners and students to embrace the possibilities of equitable opportunity. This is couched in her witness to, and participation in, the civil rights and women's movements as well as her firsthand witness to apartheid and Nyerere's pan-Africanism. It is through this inclusive lens that she weaves theory, research, advocacy, and practice in her current role as a city research scientist with the City of New York. Alongside her current role, Deborah was a teaching fellow in educational leadership and development for the Summer Principals Academy at Columbia University, she cotaught a dissertation research course at Teachers College, Columbia University, and designed and teaches a course on the historical and philosophical foundations of education at Bank Street College of Education. Prior to this work, Deborah taught logic and rhetoric for Antioch College's NY Extension, taught in a charter elementary school, and was the founding director of the only supplemental educational program to mandate parents' attendance to learn and discover alongside their children. Deborah's scope of work includes interim director of ReServe (an organization for retired individuals); education director of in-school, out-of-school, and after-school programs throughout NYC for a large nonprofit; work on tolerance with the United Nations Association of the United States of America (UNA-USA); and pivotal work with immigrant populations, disenfranchised adults, marginalized children and families, and education and child welfare practitioners. She is the coauthor of *Inherited Wisdom: Drawing on the Lessons of Formerly Enslaved Ancestors to Lift up Black Youth* (Cognella, 2022).

CHAPTER 1

....

INTRODUCING A DEVELOPMENTAL MODEL FOR JUSTICE-CENTERING EDUCATIONAL LEADERSHIP

Social justice: it's on everyone's mind these days. From political pundits to teacher educators, from school principals to parents, and from political scientists to car salespeople, everyone has an opinion on social justice ... But what exactly is social justice? And ... what does social justice have to do with education?

—Sonia Nieto (2010, p. ix)

A goal. A process. A commitment. Social justice is everywhere—and in everything—because of the inescapable *in*justice that permeates daily life. Yet, as esteemed author and Professor Emerita Sonia Nieto wrote more than a decade ago—in the epigraph above that feels both prescient and fresh—the ubiquity of social justice in modern discourse does not presume a shared definition of the concept, nor a common understanding of the underlying imperatives. Nor does it offer a clear blueprint for action for educational leaders committed to social justice in their classrooms, schools, districts, organizations, and communities.

As nearly any justice-minded principal, coach, teacher, superintendent, team leader, consultant, or teacher educator could likely attest, supporting aspiring and practicing educators in their social justice work (writ large) means finding ways to support adults along a vast continuum of experiences, understandings, and capacities. Even when educators enter into their work with deep and professed commitments to social justice, they will often orient to—and enact—these commitments in markedly different ways, for many different reasons (e.g., personal positionality, lived experience with privilege and oppression, familiarity with social justice concepts, time spent in their professional roles). Seeing into and honoring this expansive diversity while pushing forward the urgent work at hand can be a real challenge without a roadmap for making sense of it—especially because doing so also requires simultaneous *inner* work and reflection. No matter a leader's readiness and know-how, there is always more to learn, unlearn, and do—within and without. So, how might leaders committed to social justice support the growth and contributions of others while also developing their *own* capacities to engage, appreciate, understand, connect, and lead for change and transformation? This question inspires the heart of our study.

The developmental model we present in this book is based on research with fifty diverse educational leaders in different roles from across the United States, in addition to our combined decades of teaching and leading in schools and university educator preparation programs. It offers, we hope, one promising mapping of overlapping, synergistic, and increasingly expansive justice-centering practices in education, and it connects growth along this continuum to specific developmental capacities leaders need on the inside to enter into and engage most effectively in different domains. As such, we offer our model as an invitation to consider pressing aspects of social justice leadership on multiple but complementary levels.

Toward this end, you may find it helpful to hold the following questions in heart and mind as you read the chapters ahead:

- How might ideas from this book inform your work supporting others as they develop as educational advocates and allies?

- How might the many different stories shared by the leaders who participated in our study resonate with, be different from, and/or reflect your own leadership journey?

- How might the focal ideas, stories, and practices help you recognize and address areas for needed growth—in yourself and/or others—that can limit or even impede impact and contributions?

- How might the trajectory of learning, growth, and action detailed across the chapters that follow help you see into yourself and others in ways that celebrate the gifts, brilliance, passion, dedication, and love educators can bring to this work?

Although there are, of course, many lenses through which to explore social justice leadership in education and in the world, we hope that introducing an adult developmental lens to the discourse adds something new to the conversation and to our collective leadership toolboxes. In honor of and in solidarity with the teachers, administrators, students, parents, researchers, policymakers, activists, and leaders from around the world and across time who have been working to cultivate more equitable, liberatory educational systems from different vantage points, understandings, and roles, we offer this book, humbly, as one new thread in the rich tapestry of scholarship dedicated to fundamental human dignity and potential, and to education as one promising lever for real change and progress.

OUR TEAM: A PURPOSEFUL COMING TOGETHER

We—Deborah, Jessica, and Ellie—have had the gift of knowing and loving each other for more than a decade. We have grown closer and closer over years—caring for and about each other's families and loved ones, accompanying each other through sorrows, joys, celebrations, and life's milestones. We have been learners and teachers together in leadership preparation programs—and in life. We have deep respect for each other and share with compassionate honesty and kind frankness. These and other aspects of our relationship have made this book better.

We are a cross-cultural team who—together—have engaged in much thinking, dreaming, and collaborating in this project and others. We have the deepest respect for each other as human beings, scholars, friends, and givers. We are three cisgender, heterosexual, married women, each in a different decade of life. Deborah self-identifies as Black. Jessica and Ellie self-identify as white. Each of us teaches at a university, and our teaching centers on supporting all adults, especially practicing and aspiring leaders and teachers. Our deep collaboration and friendship continue to inspire us, expand our individual and collective fields of vision, and inform our work together and in the world. Our deep and ongoing conversations about our own identities, stories, experiences, theories, and ideas about justice, race, education, and more enrich our lives and the pages of this book.

LEARNING FROM FIFTY LEADERS

In a similar way, the fifty educational leaders we learned from in our study all shared an underlying commitment to social justice while holding incredible but different capacities and understandings. Although no one person had all the answers or solutions, their experiences—together—helped paint a composite portrait of real-life leaders in education, at this moment in history, making sense of and enacting their commitments. Receiving and paying forward their powerful and deeply personal, front-line sharings has been an honor of the greatest kind, and we extend our most enduring and heartfelt gratitude to each of them for their generosity, insight, courage, compassion, passion, and expertise. This book is a tribute to them, and we hope that their stories help surface new points of entry into advocacy (for more and more people!), deepen understandings of leadership terrain already traversed, and point us toward horizons of justice yet unexplored—in ourselves, each other, schools, and society. We thank you, sincerely, for thinking, dreaming, and exploring with us, and we welcome you wholeheartedly to this book.

CONTEXT AND MOTIVATION FOR THIS BOOK: WHY A DEVELOPMENTAL LENS? WHY NOW?

Philosophically speaking, this project has been in development all our lives. More formally, though, we began some conceptual writing about the connection between adult development and social justice leadership during the lead up to the 2016 election, with the idea that we could share some of the ways a developmental lens had been helping us and the graduate students in our leadership classes make sense of the phenomena unfolding—especially since it seemed a lens largely missing from wider analyses. Atop these conceptual explorations, we dreamed of doing a more empirical study that asked, "How, if at all, might educational leaders' different developmental capacities influence their leadership on behalf of social justice?"

Over the next few years—backdropped and further fueled by the tumultuous and tragic events across the United States and the world—we learned from leaders up and down the educational system who shared a commitment to social justice as a core value but spoke from a diverse array of roles, positionalities, identities, and geographies. Through in-depth interview conversations, we explored important and pressing questions like the following:

- How were leaders making sense of and approaching pressing social justice challenges?

- What internal capacities helped them lead in the ways that felt most important and urgent to them?

- What did we—and the world—need to learn from them?

We conducted our first interviews as the Trump administration was nearing its midpoint, and we continued learning from leaders through the 2020 election and as COVID-19 first grew from a distant worry to an inescapable, worldwide pandemic. As such, our learning cannot be disentangled from the time in which it took place—a time marked by deep polarization; the traumatic and increasingly public killings of Black men and women at the hands of law enforcement; deadly alt-right rallies and the January 6th insurrection at the Capitol; social and legal battles over fundamental LGBTQIA+ rights and protections; surging transphobia, Islamophobia, xenophobia, antisemitism, and anti-immigration sentiment; hate crimes against the Asian American and Pacific Islander (AAPI) community; the separation of children and parents at the border; mounting economic, healthcare, educational, and social inequities further exacerbated by the pandemic; and human rights crises and climate disasters that seemed to come in relentless waves of hurt and sorrow.

As we continued to think about, discuss, and learn from the wisdom leaders shared with us in their interviews, our own analytic processes continued to be informed by the times. We couldn't help, for instance, but feel the fury of the backlash against both the Black Lives Matter movement and the increasingly mainstream (but still too slow) acknowledgment of systemic racism in the politicized campaign against Critical Race Theory as well as the reignited curriculum wars and book bannings. We couldn't help but feel the weight of the war in Ukraine, the terror of the shootings in Buffalo and Uvalde, and the implications of the Supreme Court overturning *Roe v. Wade*. We had no choice but to carry with us the grief of our own pandemic losses and goodbyes and those of our students and loved ones. There were too, too many. It is into this painful context that we offer this book, not as panacea, but as testament to the potential—and hope—of human growth and development amidst and in spite of the tragedies of the world.

Most specifically, this is a book about the promise and possibilities of development and its relationship to growing as justice-centered leaders. Though distinct from the concept of *conscientization* pioneered by renowned Brazilian educator and philosopher Paulo Freire—who wrote and taught powerfully about the importance of developing critical consciousness (i.e., deepening one's awareness of inequities, biases, assumptions, and oppressive systems as a lever for change)—the trajectory of development and practice we describe in this book is likewise aimed at, as Freire (1970/2000) described it, "the pursuit of a fuller humanity" through internal learning, growth, and transformation (p. 47). More specifically, we use constructive-developmental theory (Drago-Severson, 2004a, 2004b, 2009, 2012, 2016; Drago-Severson & Blum-DeStefano, 2016, 2017, 2018; Drago-Severson, Blum-DeStefano, & Asghar, 2013; Kegan, 1982, 1994; Kegan & Lahey, 2009, 2016) as an organizing lens to consider the relationship between leaders' inner meaning making and external action—particularly as it relates to their efforts as advocates for justice in schools and the education sector.

Constructive-Developmental Theory: Previewing an Integrative Lens

An integrative theory of human development that recognizes identity as inherently sociocultural, constructive-developmental theory highlights adulthood as a potentially rich time of growth and change, rather than a static period in which development is "done" or complete. More specifically, the theory posits that adults actively *construct* their experiences at all times—and that the complexities of these constructions can continue to *develop* when we benefit from appropriate supports and challenges. Drawing from decades of research with thousands of adults from around the world (Kegan, 1982, 1994; Kegan & Lahey, 2009, 2016), the theory outlines four distinct stages of meaning making—the instrumental, socializing, self-authoring, and self-transforming—which we call *ways of knowing* (Drago-Severson, 2004b, 2009, 2012; Drago-Severson & Blum-DeStefano, 2016, 2018, 2019; Drago-Severson et al., 2013). Taken together, these ways of knowing describe a cumulative (but not essentializing or normative) directionality to development, while honoring the complexities and socially embedded nature of human identity.

Briefly, what we refer to as a way of knowing is an internal meaning-making system or developmental orientation to the world. In Chapter 2, we will discuss constructive-developmental theory in greater depth. For now, though, we offer what follows as an orienting preview.

In this book we will use the terms *way of knowing, meaning-making system,* and *developmental orientation* interchangeably. Like any system, a way of knowing has both strengths and areas for growth, which we refer to as "growing edges." As mentioned, this theory identifies four ways of knowing in adulthood. As a person grows from one way of knowing to the next, they increase their cognitive, affective or emotional, interpersonal, and intrapersonal capacities that enable them to better manage the complexities of living, leading, learning, and teaching (Drago-Severson, 2004b, 2009, 2012; Drago-Severson & Blum-DeStefano, 2016, 2018). Next, we share some of the main characteristics of each way of knowing, which we discuss in more detail in Chapter 2.

Adults with an instrumental way of knowing have concrete, right/wrong orientations to leadership and the world. They view things through the prism of their inherited worldviews and personal needs. When we say *inherited* worldviews, we are referring to ideas consciously or unconsciously passed down from others—including families, teachers, curricula, and the media—that can go unquestioned without conscious examination. We want to emphasize that we all have these kinds of constructions to varying degrees at different points in our lives. Part of growth, as we're defining it here, involves coming to more consciously understand and take a perspective on these imprinted influences—carrying forward the things that still serve us well and strengthen who we want to be and renegotiating those that may no longer fit our needs, values, or aspirations. It is also important to know that, although adults with an instrumental way of knowing can be kind and intelligent, they have not yet developed the internal capacity to more fully take others' perspectives or to see beyond the bounds of the constructions and worldviews they see as "right" or even universal.

Adults with a socializing way of knowing *have* developed this capacity, and accordingly orient strongly to valued others'—and society's—opinions and assessments of them. This capacity allows them, generally speaking, to tune in effectively to emotional states. Reality for socializing knowers is co-constructed—and having the approval of authorities, supervisors, and valued others is essential to adults with this way of knowing. They need it to feel whole and in balance. Because socializing knowers remain largely "run" by their relationships in the psychological sense (i.e., their relationships feel so close up, embedded, and immediate that socializing knowers cannot yet stand outside of them or take a greater perspective on their influence), it tends to be a developmental stretch to engage in conflict and/or take a strong stand for what they believe in when they sense others may disagree.

Growing into a self-authoring way of knowing involves building even more internal capacity to take a reflective perspective on external expectations, others' judgments, and important relationships. Self-authoring knowers also have a corresponding capacity to author—and advocate for—their own values, internal standards, and beliefs. Like adults with any way of knowing, self-authoring knowers still have growing edges and can benefit from internal growth. One important growing edge for them is developing the capacity to critique their own ideologies and to recognize the bounds of their personal value systems (i.e., seeing how they are still necessarily partial, incomplete, and influenced in unconscious ways).

Like self-authoring adults, self-transforming knowers have personally generated philosophies and value systems, yet they are no longer "run" by them in the ways just described. Instead, self-transforming knowers have the internal capacity to recognize that they have multiple self-systems—and some of them are more fully developed than others. In light of this, they are constantly seeking to grow parts of themselves through intimate connection—in the psychological sense—with others. In fact, from their perspective, mutuality and interconnection are ongoing prerequisites for reflection, renegotiation, self-growth, and the evolution of communities. We will dive more deeply into these ways of knowing in Chapter 2 and will highlight their connections to justice-centering educational leadership throughout the book.

Although individuals are, of course, infinitely complex and multidimensional—and bring *all* of their intersecting identities, experiences, abilities, and rich fullness to their work—we hope that foregrounding the connection between leaders' internal, developmental capacities and the different strengths and foci they can bring to practice as justice-centering leaders helps give shape and form to at least some of the space between the world as it is and the world as it could be. For instance,

- What might educators need to be able to know and do—internally and externally—to more effectively teach and lead for justice?
- Where might different people find new ways into justice-centering education—and opportunities to grow their impact?

What Does it Take—Internally—to Engage in Social Justice Work?

As Bobbie Harro (2013) wrote when describing the cycle of liberation in her widely cited piece in *Readings for Diversity and Social Justice*, moving toward emancipatory action—and breaking free from inherited and oppressive norms—is a *process*, often a cyclical one, that requires ongoing investment, learning, time, and persistence. As Harro recognized, "many people who want to overcome oppression do not start in the critical transforming stage, but as they proceed in their efforts, it becomes necessary for them to move to that level for success" (p. 619). Indeed, although Harro's cycle illuminates some of what the most successful advocates, organizers, and leaders do to precipitate greater change and liberation (e.g., influencing policy, sharing power, supporting healing), less is known about what it takes—internally—for leaders to actually be able to engage most effectively in such practices or how they grow toward and into these ways of working over time. What specific internal capacities might help serve as entry points—or stepping stones—for leaders as they build their practice as justice-centering leaders? This, we feel, is where constructive-developmental theory—and the stories from the leaders in this book—may be of particular, practical value.

By offering a granular portrait of what it looks like, sounds like, and feels like to care deeply about justice from different developmental points along the continuum—as well as a deep dive into the iterative and often painful experience of developmental *stretching* that can accompany the exhilaration and responsibility of growing as justice-centering educational leaders—our book adds something new to both the social justice literatures and our understanding of developmental theory and its applications. We offer it with deep love and respect for each of the leaders who shared such important parts of their hearts, lives, sense making, and selves with us. Their stories are acts of loving care. We also offer this book with deep admiration and respect for you—and for the hard work of the heart you give every day in pursuit of a future big enough to hold everyone with dignity, equity, and tenderness.

WHAT DO WE MEAN BY JUSTICE-CENTERING EDUCATIONAL LEADERSHIP?

Throughout history, the idea of justice has been pursued from many diverse epistemological, cultural, and intersectional standpoints (Reisch, 2014; Sen, 2009)—and informed by varied philosophical, political, religious, empirical, and theoretical strands of thought. Today, along distinct but interrelated axes of *in*justice (Fraser, 2019)—including racial, economic, carceral, medical, environmental, reproductive, social, and educational—people around the world continue to fight for systems and societies that foreground dignity and liberation.

Yet, there remains no universal approach to justice, nor consensus even around its definition (Adams, 2014). In fact some, like the American philosopher Richard Rorty (1998), propose thinking of the concept in the plural (i.e., as *justices*).

Thinking About (In)Justice in Education

The same holds true, it seems, about the role of justice in education. As Maurianne Adams (2014), an early advocate for social justice as an academic discipline in the education field, explained, the robust literatures about social justice in schools are "rooted in and nourished by multiple historical and interdisciplinary traditions" (p. 257). Much justice-centering teaching and leading today, for instance, draw from and build upon pathfinding ideas about multiculturalism, ethnic studies, progressivism, anti-racism, culturally responsive/sustaining practices, inclusion, critical studies, restorative approaches, and more. Though diverse in focus and application, social justice efforts in education generally share a common commitment to recognizing and addressing systemic inequities in schools and society and to foregrounding education as one promising lever for critical learning, resistance, agency, and change (e.g., Adams, Blumenfeld, Castañeda, Hackman, Peters, & Zúñiga, 2013; Apple, 2018; Au, 2018; Ayers, 2008; DeMatthews, 2018; Dover, 2013; Giroux, 2016; Grant, 2012; Irby, 2021; Jean-Marie, Normore, & Brooks, 2009; Keenan, 2017; Khalifa, 2018; Kumashiro, 2015; Love, 2019; Muhammad, Dunmeyer, Starks, & Sealy-Ruiz, 2020; Nieto, 2010; Welton & Diem, 2022; Young, O'Doherty, & Cunningham, 2022).

Today, as more and more schools are folding social justice into their strategic visions—or, alternatively, crafting "anti-woke" policies to deliberately limit or even prevent vital discussions of race, racism, gender identity, sexual orientation, history, and current events—it seems more clear than ever that people's understandings of justice are deeply influenced by the positions they inhabit on earth (i.e., geographic, temporal, cultural, racial, economic, developmental, intersectional). The stakes also remain incredibly high. The highest, really, as they concern children's lives.

So what does it mean to center justice as an educational leader amid all of this urgency and complexity? By "justice-centering educational leadership," we mean leadership that holds justice (along multiple dimensions) as central to—and inseparable from—the work of caring for, joining, championing, and guiding any group, team, faculty, school, district, or organization. It is not, in other words, an add-on or side project distinct from or running in parallel to academic learning and professional supervision. Also, though we recognize that leaders will orient to and understand justice in different ways—and can bring different foci, passions, capacities, sensitivities, and expertise to their work—we focus in this book on a diverse group of educators who have already expressed a commitment to addressing the roots and manifestations of harm and oppression as they surface in schools and society. In other words, this is a book about the different ways educators who *want* to lead on behalf of social justice are trying to do so—and the different developmental supports and challenges that have helped them grow in and expand their practice. It is not, in other words, a book about how to *convince* someone that justice matters in education. That said, a developmental lens may hold promise for understanding why people come to think the way they do, as every belief system is ultimately a construction and a product of a universe of influences.

Here and throughout this book, we are using *justice-centering leadership* as an umbrella term (along with *social justice leadership* and *leadership on behalf of social justice*) to cover but not conflate the many different areas of focus the leaders in our study prioritized—such as anti-racism, support for emergent multilingual learners and students with physical and learning disabilities/variations, authentic collaboration with parents and families, greater support and care for LGBTQIA+ students, more equitable resources and learning opportunities, scaffolding for economic mobility, the importance of representation in school staffing and admin- istration, culturally responsive and inclusive curricula and pedagogies, DEI coaching and training, and holistic support for children *and* adults. We use the term also as a way of emphasizing the collectivity required to move the needle toward greater justice. With so many roots and branches of justice (and injustice) to address—and so many imperatives connected to race; culture; gender; sexual orientation; religion; immigration sta- tus; socioeconomic status (SES); linguistic, physical, and neurological diversity; and the intersections of these and all dimensions of identity— *everyone* is needed.

As we will say more about next, in the preview of our developmental model, we share our mapping not with the intention that everyone should be able— today—to engage full speed ahead in every way in each of the four domains we describe. Rather, we hope that our model helps bring new clarity to potential points of entry (for self and others), as well as areas of strength and needed growth. As you will see, when we talk about "entry points" into justice-centering educational leadership, we are referring to the different— and each very important—layers of justice-centering practice that adults can most readily engage with, depending on their ways of knowing and internal capacities. Although leaders can, of course, continue to grow and enrich their practices in the different domains once they've "entered" them, effectively engaging in each subsequent layer requires new internal capacities. Because so much of development can happen under the surface, we hope that bring- ing the connections between leaders' internal capacities and their justice- centering practices into more conscious awareness creates a roadmap of sorts for meeting people where they are *and* stretching forward. As one of the lead- ers in our study put it, it's about "owning the things we need to grow in, but also owning our gifts."

Before journeying forward, and as a way of framing what follows, we invite you to consider the following reflective questions.

PREVIEWING OUR DEVELOPMENTAL MODEL FOR JUSTICE-CENTERING EDUCATIONAL LEADERSHIP

As we listened carefully during the interviews, it became clear that—in their thinking and acting—leaders were describing four qualitatively distinct domains of justice-centering practice in education that felt implicitly connected to the ways of knowing as outlined in constructive-developmental theory. More specifically, and when considered collectively, the leaders spoke passionately about their efforts, successes, joys, and struggles across four domains:

- the **concrete** domain, which is characterized by an individual's tangible action steps, often in response to specific needs;

- the **interpersonal** domain, which foregrounds the emotional, relational labor essential for strengthening bonds, belonging, and inclusion between people and groups;

- the **system-focused** domain, which involves the purposeful alignment of efforts and initiatives within a school or educational organization, in keeping with a leader's guiding vision or value system; and

- the **interconnecting** domain, which, while less commonly surfaced in our study, is distinguished by an emphasis on *inter*dependence—of schools and broader social systems, of people across roles and positionalities— and the need for coalition when leading for justice and change.

By articulating these different but overlapping domains of practice and focus, our model parallels other lenses and theories that recognize racism and oppression as operating on multiple levels simultaneously (e.g., we are thinking here about individual, organizational, and structural/systemic factors [Bonilla-Silva, 1997; Kendi, 2019; López, 2000] as well as the "four I's of oppression": ideological, institutional, interpersonal, and internalized [John Bell, n.d.]). Distinct from these other important frameworks, however, our model emphasizes how effective action within each distinct but cumulative

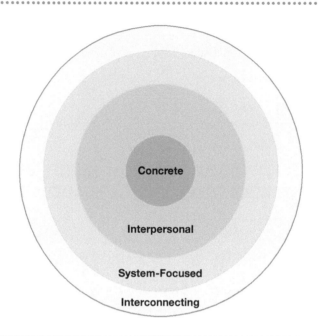

domain is connected to leaders' *internal capacities*. Much like the ways of knowing themselves—or the rings of a tree, and as illustrated in Figure 1.1— we see these domains as increasingly expansive approaches to justice-centering leadership, with each new, mutually reinforcing layer reflecting an expanded scope of vision, understanding, and locus of control and agency.

Importantly, while we connect the different domains—or layers—of our model with specific developmental capacities that provide a readiness for effective engagement in each, the domains in our model are not directly *correlative* with ways of knowing. In other words, there is not a simple 1:1 relationship between leaders' developmental capacities and the approaches they took to center justice in the field, as leaders bring—along with their internal ways of making meaning—the sum total of *all* of their experiences, learnings, position-alities, knowings, and not knowings. That said, we do hope that these four domains of practice nonetheless provide a helpful organizing framework for seeing into the strengths and growing edges of aspiring and practicing leaders working to center justice, as well as the differentiated supports and challenges they may need as they grow these parts of their practice and themselves.

When thinking about how the different domains of leadership practice inter-sect and overlap—*and* connect to developmental capacities—we find it help-ful to turn the concentric circles in Figure 1.1 on their sides, as we have in Figure 1.2. Seeing the domains in this three-dimensional way helps illustrate a few key features of our model.

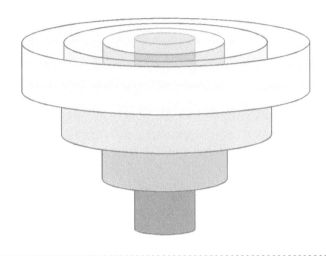

First, visualizing the domains of practice as stacked, interlocking cylinders—that cover increasingly more "ground" as they get wider—helps underscore *the expanding scope of focus foregrounded in each layer.* Moving from the concrete, to the interpersonal, to the system-focused, to the interconnecting domain means aiming one's justice-centering efforts at an ever-wider expanse of practice and impact (i.e., from individual actions, to interactions with others, to the entirety of an organization or sector, to the relationships between groups and systems). Although each area of focus is necessary and important, if a leader only has the capacity to engage within one or some of the cylinders, other critical facets of justice-centering leadership can be unintentionally left out without purposeful attention.

Toward a similar end, the fact that the thinner cylinders at the center continue to run through and inside of the wider ones serves as a reminder that *moving from one domain to the next doesn't mean leaving the earlier ones behind.* The domains are not "stages" of justice-centering leadership, but rather *layers*—although they do imply an order of sorts, as filling up one's capacity in one layer serves as a prerequisite for moving to the next (i.e., a leader can't just skip ahead, as the capacities that came before are embedded in and part of the wider ring). Put another way, each consecutive layer fits within and becomes a part of those that follow.

Moreover, as the heights of the different cylinders suggest, *there is also room to grow "vertically" within each domain*—to infuse a specific layer of practice with greater richness and intentionality as one grows and develops over time. In fact, and as you will see in Chapters 3 to 6, even though leaders require certain developmental capacities to first enter into and engage with each new layer, educators can continue to strengthen their practice in the innermost domains as these cylinders become incorporated into the larger, more encompassing ones layered overtop.

As an illustration of growing within the concrete domain, please consider the distinction between enacting a tangible kindness—like offering to tutor someone—as a reaction to an immediate problem (e.g., "This student is in distress because of their grade, so I'm going to give up my time after school and help them.") and engaging in that same concrete action with an understanding of, say, the interpersonal complexities and power dynamics of tutoring, or with a critical eye toward how corporate curriculum design, testing culture, and sociocultural and historical factors may also be at play. Although the offer to serve as a tutor could look the same from the outside even when approached in these different ways, and could feel just as meaningful to the beneficiary, the thinking and meaning making *underlying* the offer can be qualitatively distinct. These are the kinds of internal shifts we are most interested in exploring and describing in this book. The ability to grow within and across different domains is also why you will see many of the leaders in our study appear in different chapters—as they were able to draw on different parts of themselves (and their constellation of internal capacities) at different times.

Finally, we hope that our three-dimensional view helps illustrate how *effective engagement in each domain isn't automatically accessible to leaders,* even though understanding the developmental arc of practice can give directionality and purpose to leaders' efforts. Rather, engaging meaningfully in each new layer requires ongoing learning and growth. For instance, although the opportunity to make concrete contributions—at any point in time—rests on the ground floor of our model, so to speak, and can serve as an entry point or area of focus open to all, contributing most meaningfully in consecutive domains requires iterative "jumps" in capacity and perspective taking. Put another way, growing from one domain to the next requires ongoing developmental stretching, both up and out.

With their generous and courageous sharing, the leaders in our study actually helped map out the ways development (i.e., internal growth) can help leaders become more effective within and especially *across* domains of justice-centering leadership. In the chapters that follow, rich stories from the leaders in our study help answer the following questions:

- What did it look like, sound like, and feel like for leaders to bring a growing edge into conscious awareness?

- How did they find ways to expand their thinking and acting when they bumped into the "border" of one domain and wanted to grow toward the next?

- What supports and challenges best helped them in the moment and over time?

By sharing leaders' stories of stretching and growing, our model also details a continuum of developmental supports and challenges that—like the promising practices in each domain—can carry through a leader's journey and be deepened, enriched, and revisited over time. Figure 1.3 is a preview of another key focus in Chapters 3 to 6: the stretches that helped leaders grow between domains. The figure's wave-like background echoes the movement involved in increasing our internal cognitive, emotional, intrapersonal, and interpersonal capacities—iteratively—as we grow and benefit from differentiated supports and challenges.

Ultimately, by linking justice-centering leadership practices in different, cumulative domains to particular developmental capacities—and mapping out layered stretches forward—our model provides a map with many different entry points for educators, much to celebrate, and clear pathways for growth. The powerful practices, strategies, and experiences highlighted throughout this book underscore the vast range of possibilities, contributions, and areas of focus for justice-centering leaders today and—we hope—spark visions of ways that you, and those in your care, might continue to give, grow, and lead. There are, after all, so many needed, synergistic ways to center justice—and we offer all that follows with the hope, promise, and wonder of connecting people and practices across the system.

FIGURE 1.3 A PREVIEW OF A CONTINUUM OF DEVELOPMENTAL STRETCHES FOR GROWTH FOR JUSTICE-CENTERING EDUCATIONAL LEADERS

| Ongoing learning about history, (in)equity, and identity | Scaffolding for engaging in necessary conflict and difficult conversations | Practice inviting others more fully into one's vision and leadership | Thought partnership and company while continuing to explore paradoxes and possibilities of justice and identity |
| Opportunities to connect and build relationships across lines of difference | Encouragement from valued others to share one's authentic thinking, feeling, and ideas | Deep engagement with others who have shared/similar values to examine beliefs and explore the incompleteness of one's expertise | Support in turning back toward concrete action amid multiple, competing possibilities |

IMAGE SOURCE: istock.com/Lesikvit

THE RESEARCH INFORMING THIS BOOK: METHODS

To gather the data and stories that informed our developmental model of justice-centering leadership, we engaged in two in-depth interviews with fifty educational leaders from various roles, backgrounds, and geographic regions in the United States.

Two Sets of In-Depth Interviews With Fifty Leaders

The first set of interviews—which we conducted with leaders over the phone for 90–120 minutes—was aimed at exploring leaders' thinking, feeling, and practice about social justice. We asked questions like the following:

- How do you define social justice?

- What brought you to this work?

- What is most important to you about social justice leadership? Most satisfying? Hardest?

- What kinds of practices/initiatives are you are engaging in as you lead on behalf of social justice?

- How do you go about supporting others' social justice–oriented work?

- What is working well? What is challenging?

- What do you want to get better at?

- What supports have been most helpful to you?

The second set of interviews involved semi-clinical, developmental assessments called subject-object interviews (SOIs; Lahey, Souvaine, Kegan, Goodman, & Felix, 1988/2011). Using a protocol tested and refined since 1988, the SOIs—which lasted about 90 minutes—aimed to pinpoint, with a relatively high degree of accuracy, the contours of a person's meaning-making system or way of knowing at the time. We hired a nationally recognized, independent expert not on our research team to administer and score the SOIs, so that we would not know participants' "scores" as we engaged in the first phase of data collection and analysis. For a subset of the SOI interviews, we also hired additional, outside scorers to help strengthen the validity of our interpretations and deepen our sense of leaders' scores and ways of knowing. In total, and as we worked to integrate learnings from both sets of interviews, we drew from more than 200 hours of leaders' conversation, reflection, and sharing.

ATTENDING TO VALIDITY AND DEEPENING ANALYSES

Throughout the study, we attended to descriptive, interpretive, and theoretical validity (Maxwell, 2013) to the best of our ability. More specifically, we did this by paying careful and mindful attention to our own identities as researchers on a cross-cultural team. As you may recall, we are three cisgender, heterosexual women, each in a different decade of life; two of us identify as white and one of us identifies as Black. In purposeful ways that we feel expanded our collective field of vision, we coupled our analyses with ongoing discussions about our own identities, stories, theories, and ideas about justice, race, education, and more. We feel strongly that these experiences of authentically coming together enriched both the process and the outcome of our work.

By way of example, we would like to make transparent here how—in addition to exploring how a developmental lens could illuminate relevant patterns in leaders' experiences—a significant focus of our analytic discussions involved reflecting on the study design and the instrumentation itself. Specifically, we found it vital to recognize that, although the semi-clinical, SOIs provided us with very important snapshots of participants' meaning making about particular issues at a given moment in time, these interviews are ultimately interpretive tools, influenced and informed—as all research is—by the lens and epistemological orientations of the tool design and the analysts interpreting the data.

We made the conscious decision, therefore, to consider participants' *most expansive* range of making meaning—as evidenced across *both* sets of interviews—when linking their justice-centering leadership practice with underlying developmental capacities in the chapters ahead. Recognizing that the complexity and fluidity of human development is nearly impossible to truly pin down or capture in a raw score, we also want to give you a sense of the overall range and frequency of leaders' ways of knowing, as measured by the SOIs. Accordingly, in Figure 1.4, we provide an overview of the developmental scores that served as a general barometer and jumping off point for our analyses.

FIGURE 1.4 OVERVIEW OF THE SUBJECT-OBJECT INTERVIEW (SOI) RESULTS

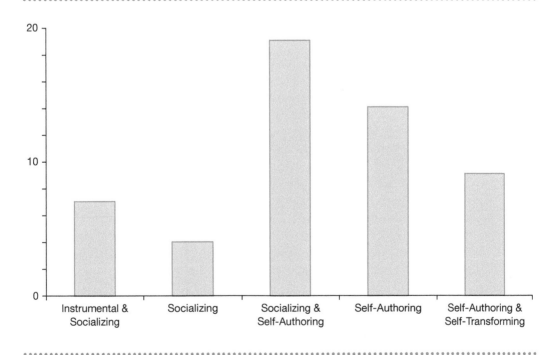

As you can see in Figure 1.4, the largest number of leaders in our sample made meaning with a mix of both the socializing and self-authoring ways of knowing (i.e., they had, to different degrees, elements of both meaning-making systems operating simultaneously), followed by leaders who seemed to be operating firmly as self-authoring knowers. A few of the participants in our study were making meaning most fully as socializing knowers, while some seemed to be moving between the instrumental and the socializing ways of knowing. Finally, as revealed in the last column, we were also able to identify a group of leaders who were growing beyond the self-authoring way of knowing toward a more self-transforming way of making meaning. Because, in some cases, additional data from our qualitative interviews helped us see even more deeply into leaders' meaning making at the time, we share this overview without linking individual scores to specific individuals. As mentioned earlier, because leaders making meaning with more complex ways of knowing are better equipped—on the inside—to engage within and across more of the domains, you will see many of the leaders appear in multiple chapters, as they foreground different aspects of their practice.

INTRODUCING THE LEADERS IN OUR STUDY

As we move closer to sharing the stories, insights, joys, struggles, and triumphs of the leaders in our study, you might be wondering, "Who are these people? How did you pick them, and why are their stories important?" As we shared earlier, learning from these leaders—listening open-heartedly and with deep gratitude to their experiences, wonderings, insights, and hopes—has been, for us, a humbling honor. We feel confident that you, too, will feel wise for getting to "know" them through this book.

As you will soon see in Table 1.1, we were privileged to learn from a diverse group of teachers, administrators, former leadership students, professionals in the field we met through professional development work, educators recommended to us by trusted colleagues, and even people who reached out to us after reading some of our earlier pieces about the connection between adult development and social justice leadership. Our primary selection criterion for inclusion in this particular research study was that each participant had an explicit, espoused commitment to social justice. Our hope was not, per se, to generate a book of best practices culled from the most successful, most accomplished justice-centering leaders out there (although we do, we are happy to report, get to recount *many* promising strategies and approaches!). Rather, we were interested in learning from leaders across the *widest possible range* of perspectives, identities, experiences, roles, geographies, and ways of knowing that we could at the time.

For this reason, and as you can see in the list below and in Table 1.1, the leaders in our study were diverse across a number of metrics:

- *role* (e.g., principal, assistant principal, dean, teacher leader, assistant superintendent, former superintendent, teacher educator, central office/district-level leader, curriculum leader, consultant, coach, head of school, early childhood director, ESL coordinator, director of culture/language, admissions director, educational technologist, social worker, counselor, department chair, regional- /national-level leader, nonprofit leader)

- *organization/school type* (charter, public, independent; urban, suburban, rural; nonprofit)

- *race* (thirty-one people of color, including seventeen who identified as Black and/or African or Caribbean American, seven who identified as Latinx and/or Afro-Latinx, two who identified as Asian American, three who identified as bi- or multiracial, one who identified as Iranian American, and one who identified as Egyptian American; nineteen identified as white)

- *gender identity* (nineteen identified as men and thirty-one as women, with no participants identifying as nonbinary or transgender)

- *sexual orientation* (four participants self-identified as gay/queer)

- *age* (early thirties to seventies)

- *experience in education* (nine years to multiple decades)

- *religion* (Christian, Jewish, Muslim, Buddhist, agnostic, atheist)

- *location* (Arizona, California, Connecticut, Illinois, Indiana, Louisiana, Maryland, Mississippi, New Jersey, New York, North Carolina, Rhode Island, Tennessee, Texas, Washington, and Washington D.C., with a large number of people [n = 32] from the Tri-State area, as we began sampling by tapping our own networks of professional contacts. For this reason, many of the examples reflect the perspectives of participants in the Northeastern United States)

In addition to spotlighting many different dimensions of diversity the leaders brought so generously to our study, the list also reveals some of the broader limitations of our sampling, as it raises the ever-important question of, "Whose perspective is missing?" We recognize, for instance, that—because of the limits of our networks at the time—we were unable to benefit from the perspectives of any educators who identified primarily as Native American/Indigenous or South Asian, as just two examples of cultural groups under- or unrepresented. While a few of the leaders in our study described personal experiences within the special education system, none explicitly identified as differently abled, disabled, or neurodiverse. In addition, to our knowledge, none of our participants identified as nonbinary, transgender, or gender expansive/nonconforming, although we remain indebted to the students and colleagues who continue to teach us about and share these parts of their personal experiences. Your trust and collaboration also infuse these pages.

We likewise think it's very important to share a bit about our choices around language and naming different aspects of identity. Recognizing the complexity and deeply personal nature of who people "are," we list—in Table 1.1—the identifiers leaders *chose* to share with us in their interviews, as a way of honoring their specific words and choices at the time. That is why, in some cases, we use different terms (i.e., African American or Black, Latino or Latinx) to refer to race, and why certain identifiers (e.g., marital status, age, parenthood, sexual orientation, religious affiliation, years in education) appear inconsistently in the table. We thank you for honoring, as we do, the parts of themselves leaders felt most important to name and center.

In keeping with the most recent guidelines articulated by the Associated Press and our publisher, Corwin, when using participants' self-selected racial, cultural, and ethnic identifiers, we capitalize names of minoritized groups to honor and convey the shared sense of history and identity implied. Although there are different opinions on the current decision to leave "white" in lowercase, we do so now in keeping with current journalistic standards and with the understanding that language conventions are both evolving and important to name, as they carry significant weight. In addition, we intentionally use "they/their" as gender-neutral singular pronouns when describing unnamed individuals in illustrative examples (i.e., rather than "he or she" or "his or her"), to move our language beyond binary constructs. Later in the book, we also use the term *BIPOC*—meaning Black, Indigenous, and people of color—as an umbrella term to acknowledge the cultural and experiential diversity of different groups, as well as the solidary that can exist between communities of color.

Also, in most cases, the names that appear in Table 1.1 and throughout the book are pseudonyms. These were often selected with care and intention by the participants to honor family, heroes, and ancestors. This, again, is the reason the names sometimes take different formats.

We have also been careful to remove any identifying information about people's schools, organizations, and colleagues from the text and quotes. In some cases, participants opted to use their real names—as Brent did—because it felt important and/or more comfortable. As Brent explained his decision,

> To be honest, I'd like you to keep it as is. I spent a long time trying to be someone I wasn't, and I really value owning who I am now, and so part of me wants you to just call me Brent. This is who I am, and I'm totally comfortable with . . . everything I've said, even if it's challenging.

We trust and hope, as you get to know each of the inspiring leaders and people—who, like Brent, gave so generously of their time, expertise, hearts, wisdom, and personal journeys to make this book possible—that you will love and admire them as much as we do. What we share here is their gift to you.

TABLE 1.1   OVERVIEW OF THE LEADERS WHO PARTICIPATED IN THE
            STUDY

NAME/ PSEUDONYM	SELF-IDENTIFIED DEMOGRAPHICS	PROFESSIONAL ROLE/REGION
Adam	white, male, cisgender, forty-four years old father, married	assistant superintendent; suburban Northeast
Amaia	Mexican American female, eleventh year in education	teacher leader/coach, charter school; urban Northeast
Angela	thirty-one years old, African American with West Indian heritage, female, Christian, heterosexual, ninth year in education	district-level teacher development and evaluation coach, former teacher; urban Northeast
Bernard	fifty-seven years old, African American/Black, male, father	teacher educator, former principal/superintendent; urban Northeast
Brent	white, gay male, married, mid-thirties	assistant principal; urban Northeast
Brooke	white, cisgender female, late forties, gay, married	interim independent school head; suburban Northeast
Carter	thirty-one years old, white, male, cisgender, recently engaged	high school principal; urban Northeast
Celine	female, multiracial, partnered, mother, daughter of Chinese immigrant, physically and emotionally able, survivor	regional leader of national nonprofit; Mid-Atlantic
Charlotte	white, woman, married, thirty-three years in education	district-level leader (teacher leadership focus); urban Northeast
Cheryl	white, woman, wife, mother, eighteen years in education	district-level school improvement leader; urban Northeast
Christopher	forties, Christian, African American male, married, father	leader in national nonprofit philanthropic organization, focus on principal development and support; Northeast
D.	forty years old, Latino, first generation American, married with two kids	teacher leader; urban Northeast
Dana	African American male, father	elementary teacher leader; suburban Northeast
Donald	white, Jewish, married to a woman, seventy-five years old	retired high school teacher leader, higher ed; West Coast

(Continued)

(Continued)

NAME/ PSEUDONYM	SELF-IDENTIFIED DEMOGRAPHICS	PROFESSIONAL ROLE/REGION
Dr. B	forty-one years old, African American female, divorced, mother	teacher educator, former principal; Southwest
Elena	Latin American, born and raised in Dominican Republic, forty-five years old, mother	assistant principal, PK–5, ELL focus; urban Northeast
Ella	thirty-four years old, African American, woman, not married	director of culture/language learning, charter school; urban Northeast
Evan	white, cisgender male, thirty-six years old, thirteen years in education	district-level curriculum leader; urban Northeast
Gabriel	thirty-seven years old, African American male, married, father	CEO of a reading-focused institute, former principal; South
Harris	forty-eight years old, white, male, gay	principal, high school for English language learners; urban Northeast
Hazel	Filipino American, daughter of Filipino immigrants, married	college persistence counselor; Southwest
Henrietta	white, female, grew up on a farm, married	co-founder of education nonprofit company; Southeast
Ian	thirty-one years old, white, cisgender male	elementary teacher leader; urban Northeast
Irene	white, female, fifty-six years old, Jewish, mother left Vienna 1939, married, mother	director of admissions and enrollment, independent school; Northeast
Jack	Eastern European/Slavic, immigrant, fifty-four years old, male	assistant principal, former principal; urban Northeast
James	Hispanic, mixed race, male, born-again Christian	teacher leader, middle school department chair; suburban Northeast
Janae	Black, woman, mother	leader in national nonprofit philanthropic organization with education focus; Northeast
Jean-Claude	Asian American, male, forties, strongly identifies with values of his progressive West Coast city	district-level leader, coordinator of curriculum and teacher leadership; West Coast

NAME/ PSEUDONYM	SELF-IDENTIFIED DEMOGRAPHICS	PROFESSIONAL ROLE/REGION
Joyce	Caribbean African American woman, early thirties, single, Pentecostal, daughter to Jamaican immigrants	educational consultant; Northeast, national, and international
Kathy	white, woman	teacher leader; suburban Northeast
Kristina	Black woman, native of a Southern city well-known for its civil rights history, from a faith-driven family, married	consultant; South
Ladan Jahani	Iranian American, straight, female, partnered, thirty-nine years old, bilingual	social worker in a transfer high school; urban Northeast
Lee	forty years old, white, cisgender gay male, partnered, Jewish	national-level nonprofit leader; Northeast
Linda	Black, woman	educational consultant, former principal; Northeast
Lisa	thirty-seven years old, Black of Haitian descent, female, single, seventeen years in education	early childhood center director; Northeast
Loile	thirty-four years old, African American, cisgender female, Black woman of Caribbean/Jamaican descent, single	district-level leader, former principal; urban Northeast
Luz	Black Afro-Latina, cisgender woman, twenty years in education	high school principal; urban Northeast
Margot	white-presenting, multiracial	assistant superintendent; urban Northwest
May	white, woman, thirteenth year in education	academic dean in charter middle school; Northeast
Micki	Black, woman, fifties	assistant principal/dean of students, alternative school; Southwest
Nat	thirty years old, tenth year in education, Puerto Rican woman, cisgender (she/her), heterosexual, single	STEAM ed technologist, independent elementary school; Northeast
Nick	forty-one years old, white, male, heterosexual	independent lower school head; mid-Atlantic

(Continued)

(Continued)

NAME/ PSEUDONYM	SELF-IDENTIFIED DEMOGRAPHICS	PROFESSIONAL ROLE/REGION
Norma	thirty-two years old, white, cisgender woman, married, eleventh year in education, grew up in the South and Midwest with a single mother in a low-SES household, lived abroad (South Africa)	dean/ESL coordinator; Midwest
Rana	Egyptian American, Muslim woman	head of independent school; urban Midwest
Serena	thirty-one years old, cisgender, Caribbean American, woman	central office special education leader; urban Northeast
Shokry	thirty-four years old, mixed race Egyptian and Dominican, "American-ish," Northeastern person of color	educational consultant; Northeast, national, international
Sylvia	thirty-eight years old, Puerto Rican, woman, Christian, mother	district-level teacher support administrator; urban Northeast
Thea	Black woman, married, tenth year in education	district-level leader with teacher leadership focus; urban Northeast
Yaacov	Orthodox Jewish father and husband, thirty-two years old, nine years in education	teacher leader, charter middle school coordinator; urban Northeast
Zora	African American woman (she/her), heterosexual, grew up in low-income community, experienced economic mobility, mother, wife	founder and CEO of nonprofit with national reach; urban Midwest

LOOKING BACK AND AHEAD: THE ORGANIZATION OF THIS BOOK

In this chapter, Chapter 1, we foregrounded social justice as *the* imperative of education—and educational leadership—today. After setting the stage in relation to the urgency of this work—and honoring the long, rich, and varied justice efforts of educators, researchers, scholars, and activists from across time and around the world—we shared how understanding the arc of leaders' diverse ways of knowing, as outlined by constructive-developmental theory, can add something new and vital to these conversations. In effect, this chapter opened a new window into *how* to develop and support social justice leaders along a continuum of experiences and understandings—and made explicit the connection between leaders' internal capacities and their effectiveness in different, layered domains.

Toward this end, this chapter introduced our developmental model for justice-centering educational leadership practice and learning. More specifically, we began to discuss how the four distinct but cumulative domains in the model—the concrete, interpersonal, system-focused, and interconnecting—can offer different entry points and growing paths for leaders with different ways of knowing. As we will continue to explore throughout the book, understanding the developmental underpinnings—and prerequisites—of engaging most successfully in these layers can help leaders even more intentionally differentiate supports and challenges, for both self and others.

In addition to framing and introducing our model, we also shared a little about ourselves and what brought us together to collaborate on this dream project. Likewise, we introduced the fifty diverse educational leaders—from across the United States—who so generously made this book possible by sharing their wisdom, stories, and experiences with us in interviews. We began this study and end it with tremendous, heartfelt gratitude to each and all of them for opening their hearts and minds to us so that we could share with you their life experiences, strengths of practice, growing edges, courage—and inspiration.

In Chapter 2, we will offer a deep dive into constructive-developmental theory (Drago-Severson, 2004b, 2009, 2012, 2016; Kegan, 1982, 1994, 2000; Kegan & Lahey, 2009, 2016) as one promising lens for considering social justice capacity building. Although our prior research has highlighted many important applications and dimensions of constructive-developmental theory (e.g., for collaboration, feedback, designing professional learning, mindfulness, supervision), in this book we introduce the newest extensions and implications of the theory—particularly as they relate to justice-centering educational leadership and leading for social justice in schools and society.

Specifically, we will dive deeply into the four ways of knowing most commonly found in adulthood—the instrumental, socializing, self-authoring, and self-transforming—and consider them, holistically, as an integrative meta-story of learning and growth, both in general and especially as it relates to leading on behalf of equity or justice. Understanding the different ways of knowing as part of a cumulative continuum can help you see more deeply into your own and others' developmental strengths and growing edges—and the different supports and challenges that can scaffold growth as justice-centering leaders.

In Chapters 3 through 6, we offer leaders' stories and lived experiences of justice-centering educational leadership in each of the four domains of our model—the concrete, interpersonal, system-focused, and interconnecting. Each chapter also foregrounds how the internal capacities connected to a particular way of knowing can serve as an entry point for the featured domain of practice. For example, we explore how

- instrumental capacities can serve leaders well in the concrete layer (Chapter 3),

- socializing capacities can enhance and enrich leaders' work in the interpersonal domain (Chapter 4),

- self-authoring capacities are needed to most effectively engage in the system-focused level (Chapter 5), and

- self-transforming capacities allow for fuller engagement as interconnecting leaders—bringing together individuals, systems, and domains (Chapter 6).

In addition to spotlighting areas of focus and strength in the different domains—and celebrating them—each chapter also describes leaders' experiences of growing toward the next layer of practice, including the stretches and experiences they found most helpful as they grew.

In Chapter 7, we will look back on and bring together the many different ideas covered in this book and offer stories, metaphors, and tools for launching forward. In particular, we will present a full and synthesized version of our model, invite you to engage in some additional reflective opportunities to connect big ideas to your practice and experience, and provide opportunities for action planning and future application.

Most important, as you move through every chapter, we invite you to hold, carry forward, and share whatever feels most relevant to *you*—for the fullness, complexity, and potential of your own growth and the growth of those in your care.

A REFLECTIVE INVITATION

Before journeying forward into the next chapter—in which we will dive even more deeply into constructive-developmental theory as an integrative lens—we want to invite you to consider a series of centering questions. Often, we've found, it can be helpful to begin by reflecting privately (by either free writing or free thinking) about some or all of these questions and then sharing your reflections with a partner or several partners.

1. After reading this chapter, what is top of mind and/or heart for you?

2. At this time, how do you define social justice?

3. What, in your experience, does it mean to lead on behalf of—or center—justice in education?

4. What do you consider to be two or three of your bigger strengths as a justice-centering leader?

5. What is one practice you engage in on a regular basis (by yourself or with colleagues) to support justice in your workplace? How is it working at this time?

6. What are two or three of your biggest, personal hopes for learning in reading this book?

7. What, at this time, are you most curious about after reading this chapter?

8. Now that you've had a preview of ways of knowing, what do you see as some of your bigger developmental strengths? How do these show up in your day-to-day care for others? For yourself in your leadership?

9. What do you consider to be your own growing edges or areas for growth?

10. What feels like your most pressing challenge in your justice-centering leadership right now?

11. What is something you'd like to grow about your justice-centering leadership—or get better at?

12. What is something you'd like to grow in your workplace culture, especially with respect to justice, diversity, and equity-focused learning, teaching, and leading?

13. What are some of your burning questions at this time?

14. After reading this chapter, what is something you'd like to think more deeply about? Do differently? Learn more about?

CHAPTER 2

····························

CONSTRUCTIVE-DEVELOPMENTAL THEORY

A New Lens on Social Justice Capacity Building

There is no question that the work of school leadership is challenging or that achieving high-quality education for all children in schools is strongly tied to the capacity of education leaders.

—Michelle Young, Ann O'Doherty, and
Kathleen Cunningham (2022, p. 1)

As leadership scholars Michelle Young, Ann O'Doherty, and Kathleen Cunningham (2022) argue in their book, *Redesigning Educational Leadership Preparation for Equity*, educational leaders require sophisticated capacities to meet the urgencies and imperatives of educating for greater justice and equity. Yet, what *are* these capacities—and how do leaders develop them? Although research is beginning to surface factors that can influence the knowledge, skills, and dispositions educational leaders bring to social justice practice—such as race, culture and identity, lived experience, and explicit training (Bonilla-Silva, 2010; Brooks, 2016; Rubie-Davies, 2008; Sleeter, 2016)—less is known about the role that leaders' *internal, developmental capacities* play in this important dimension of their leadership. As the collective body of social justice scholarship makes clear, it is not just what educators *do* in classrooms, schools, and districts that counts, but also their *thinking, feeling,* and *sensemaking* that matters for effective practice (e.g., Cherng & Halpin, 2016; Crowley, 2016; Gooden & O'Doherty,

2015; Khalifa, 2018; Pollock, Deckman, Mira, & Shalaby, 2010; Sleeter, 2016; Sue, 2010; Zembylas, 2010).

In this chapter, we dive deeply into constructive-developmental theory (Drago-Severson, 2004a, 2004b, 2009, 2012, 2016; Drago-Severson & Blum-DeStefano, 2016, 2017, 2018, 2019; Kegan, 1982, 1994, 2000; Kegan & Lahey, 2009, 2016) as one promising lens for considering social justice capacity building *on the inside*—as well as the connection between inner meaning making and external action. Like theories of racial and social identity development, constructive-developmental theory posits that development progresses in a cumulative though fluid order—like a building wave—with gradual movement from one way of knowing (or meaning making system) to the next reflecting increases in a person's cognitive, affective, interpersonal, and intrapersonal capacities (Drago-Severson, 2009, 2012). As we will discuss, growing our ways of knowing involves changes in what we know, how we know it, and how we understand ourselves and others. We have also found in our research that ways of knowing hold implications for how leaders—and adults across all levels of the educational system—orient to and understand equity and diversity and what it means (from their perspectives) to lead for social justice.

GROWTH—AND GIFTS—ACROSS THE LIFESPAN

One of the gifts of constructive-developmental theory is that it helps us to look closely at an individual's meaning making system—or how they take in and make sense of their experiences. It also gives us a language to discuss things that we may have observed before but could not name. There's a whole internal system that exists in each of us, and it can be incredibly powerful and helpful to understand that we might have different internal capacities than our neighbors. Understanding this can also, we hope, help more people find ways into the vital work of centering justice in schools and society—and grow their practice with even greater intentionality.

In this spirit of finding new entry points—and new possibilities and pathways for growth—constructive-developmental theory also serves as an important reminder that, as adults, our learning journeys are never "done." Despite the care and attention educators often devote to child and adolescent development, it is only fairly recently that the education sector has begun to recognize the parallel importance of supporting *adult* learning and development—because of its inherent value *and* its promising link to improved student outcomes and experiences (Donaldson, 2008; Gill, 2019; Grissom, Egalite, & Lindsay, 2021; Guskey, 1999; Leithwood & Louis, 2012; Mizell, 2007; Wagner, 2007).

Just a few decades ago, adulthood was conceptualized as a life stage in which brain development was largely complete (Kegan & Lahey, 2009, 2016). We certainly understand that, by age 25, certain parts of the human brain have likely reached a maturity of sorts, but could you imagine if adults *really* stopped developing with so much potential life ahead? Fortunately, recent advances in psychology and neuroscience suggest an incredible range of neural plasticity in the adult brain, as well as a general increase in mental complexity as we age (Immordino-Yang, 2015; Immordino-Yang & Knecht, 2020; Immordino-Yang et al., 2018; Johnson, 2022; Kegan & Lahey, 2016; Rock, 2010; Rock & Grant, 2016; Rock & Page, 2009). We see this as the best news, in that all of us—everyone—can keep learning and growing.

As the educators in our graduate classes and professional development institutes often attest, there seems to be a shared sense in schools that adults can—and must—keep learning new facts and information, but there is also a unique exasperation that can bubble up when working with adults who don't meet expectations or seem to push back against very important requests and nonnegotiables, especially when it comes to (in)equity. Given educators' positions of great responsibility, we completely understand (and have certainly shared at times) the impulse to ask, "Shouldn't you know or be able to do this already? Aren't you a *grown up*?" Or, "If you know X to be true, how come you can't do Y?" And the fact is, sometimes people can't—yet. *But,* and we want to underline this, we can continue to grow *if* we have *both* supports and appropriate pushes or developmental stretching, and in this there is great hope. This matters in general—and it matters for justice-centering leadership and social justice in particular.

Without diminishing the urgency, we have come to see constructive-developmental theory as an underutilized roadmap for seeing into, reframing, and addressing resistance; better understanding the gap that can exist between knowing and doing; and (re)investing in human potential. For example, though not a guarantee of any particular moral commitment, value stance, or political leaning, developing in the ways described in this chapter and book can help educators bring a greater *readiness* to equity learning—including the intrapersonal reflection, emotional vulnerability, critical humility, and intellectual flexibility required to embrace discomfort and more transformative possibilities. Letting go of old ways of thinking and seeing is never easy. Development, however, can arm leaders with the prerequisite capacities needed to risk real change—in themselves, in their practice, and in the world. As leadership scholars Karen Osterman and Robert Kottkamp (1993) reminded us long ago, real change in organizations truly does begin with us.

Ultimately, and as we will continue to explore, constructive-developmental theory can help us differentiate the supports and challenges we offer to each other as we work to manage complexity, examine assumptions, and more fully center justice in schools and society. It can, as one leader recently shared with us after learning about these ideas, "help infuse a compassionate, purposeful pause" between one's first reactions and external responses. It can also, as Robert Kegan (1982) argued when first articulating the theory, help us move "further into life, [and] closer to those we live with" with our new understandings because "what the eye sees better the heart feels more deeply" (p. 16). We hope that—by making more visible some of the under-the-surface aspects of developmental diversity—the explorations in this chapter can, indeed, help us look about and within with ever more compassionate ways of seeing, feeling, connecting, and being.

THE ROOTS AND BRANCHES OF CONSTRUCTIVE-DEVELOPMENTAL THEORY

The Roots: An Expansively Inclusive, Integrative Lens

Pioneered by developmental psychologist Robert Kegan (1982, 1994, 2000) and extended into schools by professor and leadership scholar Eleanor Drago-Severson (1996, 2004b, 2009, 2012), constructive-developmental theory draws from more than forty-five years of research about how people learn and grow—and posits a shape and trajectory of development across the lifespan that traverses cultures and continents (e.g., Basseches, 1984; Baxter-Magolda, 1992, 2009; Belenky et al., 1997; Drago-Severson, 1996, 2004a, 2004b, 2009, 2012, 2016; Drago-Severson & Blum-DeStefano, 2016, 2018; Kegan, 1982, 1994, 2000; Kegan & Lahey, 2009, 2016; Knefelkamp & David-Lang, 2000; Kohlberg, 1969, 1984; Perry, 1970; Piaget, 1952).

In pursuit of a kind of "metapsychology" (Kegan, 1982, p. 14) that would break down some of the intellectual silos between academic studies and clinical practice, Kegan—when first articulating the theory in the early 1980s—strove to look *across* prominent theories of development at the time to more holistically describe the "fundamental motion" of life or, more specifically, what he called the "evolution of meaning" (p. 15). Integrating biological, cognitive, psychological, social, and affective lines of study and thought—and drawing on insights from Jean Piaget, Lawrence Kohlberg, Jane Loevinger, Abraham Maslow, David McClelland, and Erik Erikson (as well as many lessons about the human experience from poetry, literature, the visual arts, and spiritual thinkers)—Kegan worked to bring together the principles of *constructivism* and *developmentalism,* which were regularly discussed in the field but typically considered separately.

By bringing these two big areas of focus together (and hence the hyphenated term *constructive-developmental*), Kegan helped foreground the idea that although all people actively *construct* their realities—meaning that their ways of seeing, feeling, thinking about, and understanding the world all stem from their personal interpretations of the phenomena around them (as opposed to, say, there being one objective truth)—the complexity of these constructions can continue to *develop* when people benefit from the right combination of supports and challenges. In other words, even though people construct their worlds in one way one day, they are still free to construct—and make sense of—their experiences differently tomorrow, and also the day after that, and the day after that, too.

This, as we will continue to discuss throughout this chapter and book, is all possible provided that growth-enhancing conditions exist. Importantly, constructive-developmental theory helps us see that adults will need *different* kinds of supports and challenges—or developmental stretching—to grow. We offer our deep and sincere gratitude to and for Robert Kegan for underscoring this foundational developmental insight for the world.

The Branches: Theoretical Extensions and Connections

Today, constructive-developmental theory has been studied and applied across sectors—and tested with thousands of adults from around the globe. In our own teaching and research, for instance, we have found constructive-developmental theory to be an incredibly powerful lens for enhancing school leadership, leadership development, collaboration, feedback, coaching, mindfulness, supervision, and the design of professional learning experiences, just to name a few (e.g., Drago-Severson, 1996, 2004b, 2009, 2012, 2016; Drago-Severson & Blum-DeStefano, 2016, 2017, 2018, 2019; Drago-Severson, Blum-DeStefano, & Asghar, 2013; Drago-Severson, Roy, & von Frank, 2015). Although we certainly would not argue that constructive-developmental theory, as a singular lens, explains *all* of experience, we do find the theory flexible, fluid, and epistemologically roomy enough to serve as one organizing, integrative framework for many diverse and distinct streams of thought and areas of focus. Constructive-developmental theory's capacity to bring and hold together ideas from different fields has felt especially important and exciting as we explored its applicability as a lens for growing social justice leaders (Drago-Severson, Blum-DeStefano, & Brooks Lawrence, 2020, 2021, 2022).

More specifically, as we re-immersed ourselves in the literatures about identity, development, and justice in schools and society, we were eager, like Kegan, to look *across* academic, psychological, and critical theories—and we sought to cast an even wider net in relation to the ideas and lenses that could inform our theoretical perspective. With an eye out for potential connections, parallels, synergies, and discrepancies, we looked to the following (by way of a few examples):

- different pathways and conceptualizations of racial identity development (e.g., Crenshaw, 1989, 1991, 2013, 2017; Cross, 1995; DiAngelo, 2018, 2021; Helms, 2020; Holvino, 2012; Singh, 2019; Tatum, 2013, 2017; Wijeyesinghe & Jackson, 2012);

- the process of conscientization (Freire, 1970/2000);

- diverse cultural and epistemological conceptualizations of knowledge and selfhood (e.g., Merriam & Associates, 2007);

- frameworks for developing racial literacy and engaging in conversations about race and identity (e.g., Magee, 2019; Price-Dennis & Sealy-Ruiz, 2021; Singleton, 2014; Vulchi & Guo, 2019);

- women of color feminisms and threshold theorizing (e.g., Anzaldúa, 2002, 2015; Collins, 2022; Keating, 2013);

- the directionality of social movements and advocacy (e.g., Almeida, 2019; Harro, 2013; Staggenborg, 2016); and

- articulations of culturally responsive/sustaining teaching and leading (e.g., DeMatthews, 2018; Gay, 2010; Khalifa, 2018; Khalifa, Gooden, & Davis, 2016; Ladson-Billings, 1995a, 1995b; Ladson-Billings & Tate, 1995; Muhammad, 2020; Paris & Alim, 2017).

Although each of these important areas of study reveals different and vitally essential aspects of life, teaching, leadership, and experience—and, together, they represent just the tip of the proverbial iceberg when it comes to the vast universe of ideas, lenses, and thinkers important to cover and consider within and beyond these disciplinary foci—looking across different literatures helped us to recognize the ways constructive-developmental theory could potentially serve as one integrative *meta-story* of development that could weave together key parts of justice-centering leadership and offer a kind of sequence and pathway toward growing one's capacities and greater effectiveness. Just like people, theories can also grow to hold and include more!

In particular, we found that constructive-developmental theory offers a clear and simple language for naming—and bringing together—some of the important concepts that run across different theories and approaches. Though certainly not the *only* words or terms we could use, we once again recognized, in different parts of the social justice literature, the importance of both *constructivism* and *developmentalism*—as well as the vital role of *perspective taking* (on self, others, history, the educational system, and society) when leading for greater equity, inclusion, and justice.

For example, Glenn Singleton's (2014) pioneering work around *Courageous Conversations* has made mainstream the idea that people often, and sometimes unknowingly, enter into conversations about race, identity, and social justice with different epistemological and affective constructions—namely emotional, intellectual, moral, and/or action-oriented "compass points" (p. 29). Likewise, theories of racial and social identity development (e.g., Cross, 1995; Helms, 2020; Singh, 2019; Tatum, 2013, 2017; Wijeyesinghe & Jackson, 2012) illustrate how disentangling oneself from—and taking greater perspective on—externally imposed, hegemonic narratives about one's racial group and developing a positive racial identity is an ongoing process that will develop and unfold differently for different people at different times, just as the trajectory will be different for people of color and white people in a racist society. Both bodies of literature underscore how bringing under-the-surface, less-visible orientations into more conscious awareness—for individuals and groups—can help people more intentionally come together and scaffold justice work, as it presupposes the need for different entry points, supports, and contexts for ongoing learning.

Likewise, in *The Inner Work of Racial Justice*, law professor and restorative facilitator Rhonda Magee (2019) makes a compelling case for mindful practices as a way to continually see race, history, and identity "through a wider aperture" (p. 114). By recognizing race as a construct, she argues, and by examining our own constructions as engineered (rather than absolute or universal), we can begin to deconstruct and reconstruct historical and personal understandings in ways that wake up "a new power for navigating the world" with and for one another (p. 37). Doing this inner work, she explains, is intimately connected to the broader healing action that is or is not possible in society.

Although constructive-developmental theory may use different terminology and framing than some of the theorists above, running underneath and through the different lenses, we argue, is an emphasis on expanding one's capacities and consciousness as a vehicle for more transformative action (i.e., moving from the local and immediate to broader and ever more inclusive ranges of vision, agency, and understanding; moving away from the unconscious acceptance of societal expectations toward more interconnected understandings of self, society, and the world). As we will discuss next, constructive-developmental theory gives further shape and form to these developmental processes, as it is predicated on the idea that as we grow through the different ways of knowing, we are actually shifting—in a particular order—the balance between what we are run by, in the psychological sense, and what we can actively take a perspective on and hold out as object about ourselves, others, and society. When we shift our *subject-object balance* in these ways, we are less controlled by unconscious assumptions, worldviews, norms, and patterns of acting and feeling that no longer serve us or others well—and we are more free to be the biggest versions of ourselves.

THE SHAPE—AND PACE—OF GROWTH

When Kegan (1982) first visualized constructive-developmental theory, he depicted it as a helix, with development involving the gradual movement upward and back and forth along a spiral. There is so much we love about this shape. The implied flex of a helix, like a spring, mirrors the ways we can sometimes stretch up toward greater capacities (especially with help) and also those times when we may fall back and feel more compressed, unable or uninvited to lead (for any variety of reasons) with our most complex ways of being in the world. Often, when teaching about constructive-developmental theory, we like to encourage educators to imagine the helix as a spiral staircase: Moving "up" doesn't make you an intrinsically better or more valuable person, but it *does* give you a different view of the world and yourself. It also helps capture the idea that, no matter where you are on the "staircase," you can look back to remember what it was like to be standing on a prior step, and you can look up—even if you can't yet peek fully around the bends and curves of the steps ahead—to see what it looks like to demonstrate capacities you might not yet have. As we gain perspective, we are able to see more, without and within.

Building on and expanding these ideas, we have come to see the shape of constructive-developmental theory more like a *gyre*—a conical helix—in which each upward return on the spiral not only moves higher, but also gets bigger, as it holds more. We see this particular kind of spiral—which we depict in Figure 2.1—like a fractal, a special kind of *growing shape* that is mirrored on the smallest and largest of scales in the world around us, in the swirls of shells and ancient fossils, the expanses of distant galaxies, and the precision of mathematical proportions found all throughout nature.

FIGURE 2.1   THE PATHWAY AND SHAPE OF DEVELOPMENT AS
             VISUALIZED IN CONSTRUCTIVE-DEVELOPMENTAL THEORY

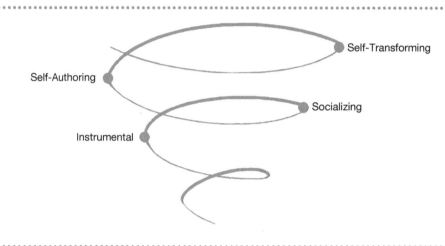

Perhaps most importantly, the gyre makes clear that development is not a linear process, but rather iterative and cyclical. As we grow, we revisit different tensions—between self and other, thinking and feeling, learning and unlearning, knowing and doing—again and again and with new eyes. You might relate, for example, to the experience shared by many people of redefining the boundaries and parameters of adulthood as you move through it. It's so easy to feel like a "real adult" as one first reaches different milestones and lives through life-shaping events, only to look back later at your younger self and think, "Ahh, if I only knew then what I know now. *This here* is adulthood." And then to repeat the process again (and again)! The same holds true, we find, for explorations of self, identity, and justice. As we grow and learn, we come to see these parts of ourselves and experiences from new heights and different vantage points, and in ways that help us build on, extend, and redefine what we'd come to know before.

Growing on Our Own Timelines

The way you grow old is kind of like an onion or like the rings inside a tree trunk or like my little wooden dolls that fit one inside the other, each year inside the next one.

—Sandra Cisneros, "Eleven" (1991, pp. 6–7)

Of course, development—as we're talking about it here—doesn't happen with the snap of a finger. It is a process that unfolds over time and with incredible variation within and across people. Much like running a marathon—during which athletes adjust their pace to sprint forward, hold steady, or fall back to recharge as needed—development is a process of continual motion, the pace of which is nonetheless interactive with and continually influenced by circumstances both external and internal.

Central, however, to constructive-developmental theory is the idea that, at different points in life, adults tend to spend significant time in or around particular ways of knowing. In the next section, we will dive more deeply into the four ways of knowing most common in adulthood, which we refer to as the instrumental, socializing, self-authoring, and self-transforming. Before doing so, though, we want to recognize them here as pause points—or plateaus—that punctuate the developmental gyre (quite literally in this case, since they are "dots" on Figure 2.1). Because human beings cannot keep growing (or running, as in a marathon) infinitely uphill, we tend to find temporary "evolutionary truces," as Kegan (1982, p. 28) called them, or adaptive balances that let us rest, in the psychological sense, as we grow into a way of knowing that suits us well. We call this match between a person's meaning making and the demands of the world around them "goodness of fit" (Drago-Severson, 2009, p. 310). When a way of knowing helps us navigate the challenges and opportunities of our current life circumstances, there is less pressure for change. However, when the limits of our current capacities bump up against external demands that outpace our knowing and doing (as can often happen when working to center justice as a leader), we can find ourselves growing—or wanting to grow—in ways that help us reach a new, more complex balance or plateau.

For this reason, and as we depict in Figure 2.2, moving from one way of knowing to the next isn't a simple or even straightforward jump "up" or ahead. Like the Xs on the diagram, adults can spend a good deal of time *in between* any two ways of knowing, when the earlier way of making meaning is gradually becoming incorporated into the next. For example, as you can see in Figure 2.2, there are three Xs in the space between the socializing and the self-authoring ways of knowing. Growing from one way of knowing to another is a *process*, and in that process of growth there are increases in one's cognitive, affective, intrapersonal, and interpersonal *internal* capacities. Like the beautiful image of aging *as the accumulation of layers of years* that author and Presidential Medal of Arts winner Sandra Cisneros (1991) helped capture in her short story, "Eleven," each new way of knowing incorporates the former into its more expansive system as one grows—from one X on the gyre to the next.

Again, the pace of these transitions is different for everyone and can be different even for the same person at different times in their lives. The hopefulness, though, is that we can all keep growing. And, sometimes people can surprise us by showing us new capacities, understandings, and previously unseen sides of themselves.

FIGURE 2.2   THE WAYS OF KNOWING AND TRANSITIONAL PHASES

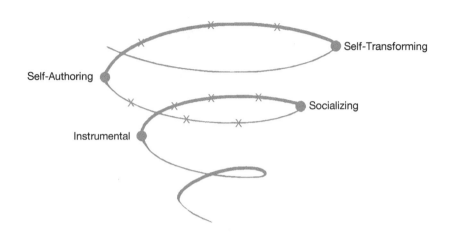

About Growing and Bamboo

Of course, there are certain situations, life events, and experiences that can slow down our growth—and others that can accelerate it. Just as we can care for bamboo for days, weeks, months, and even years and it may look like nothing is happening, all of a sudden, bamboo plants can grow many feet. Sometimes that is what it feels like when we notice new capacities in ourselves or others for the first time. We can look back at our old selves and recognize how much we've grown, on the inside, and see with fresh eyes the new selves we've become and are in the process of becoming.

In the next section, we will continue to explore the different ways of knowing and their connections to justice-centering leadership. First, though, we invite you to engage with the following reflective prompts. We offer them as opportunities to pause and consider your own experiences, as well as what's at the top of your mind and heart right now. You might want to respond to them privately first and then engage in dialogue with a partner and/or group of colleagues.

REFLECTIVE INVITATION

1. What does growth look like for you? What does it feel like? How would you draw it, describe it, or define it?

2. What theories/theorists of growth and development have most influenced your understanding of how people learn and change?

3. Which ideas resonate most for you so far?

4. What questions are you holding?

5. What, if anything, does not coincide with your own thinking and feeling about development?

6. How, if at all, do the ideas presented so far connect to other frameworks that you use in your leadership, your justice-centering leadership, and your life to understand yourself and others?

WAYS OF KNOWING

The only true voyage of discovery . . . would be not to visit strange lands but to possess other eyes, to behold the universe through the eyes of another, of a hundred others, to behold the hundred universes that each of them beholds, that each of them is.

—Marcel Proust, *Remembrance of Things Past*

As we have begun to explore, a way of knowing—according to constructive-developmental theory—is a developmental meaning making system that underlies and informs how someone sees, understands, feels about, and orients to the world. Put another way, it's the (often unconscious) internal lens through which a person filters all of life's experiences. Understanding the different ways of knowing more common in adulthood (i.e., the instrumental, socializing, self-authoring, and self-transforming) can help us recognize how our own and others' actions are fueled in large part by our current cognitive, emotional, interpersonal, and intrapersonal capacities. In the case of justice-centering leadership, for instance, familiarizing ourselves with the ways of knowing can help us better pinpoint some of the reasons *why* educational leaders may orient to and conceptualize their work differently. In addition, it can help us to understand better why some colleagues *can* do certain things (e.g., take a strong stand on behalf of a personal belief system—even when facing resistance), and others cannot yet do this. Because in any team, organization, or system, developmental diversity will exist. *How* we engage with ourselves and each other will vary qualitatively, and the kinds of supports and stretching we will need to grow on the inside will as well. As such, understanding ways of knowing also helps us carve out pathways for desired learning and growth.

Importantly, although each way of knowing has common strengths and growing edges that live under the surface in our meaning making, the way people "wear" ways of knowing—on the outside—can be as infinitely diverse and unique as the people making meaning with them.

More specifically, a person's way of knowing is *not* correlated with intelligence, kindness, personality, happiness, belief system, or leadership style

(Kegan, Broderick, Drago-Severson, Helsing, Popp, & Portnow, 2001). A person can be incredibly intelligent, happy or unhappy, introverted or extroverted, and make meaning with an instrumental, socializing, self-authoring, or self-transforming way of knowing. Research with people from around the world has also shown that ways of knowing are *not* dictated by race, gender, sexual orientation, age, religion, culture, socioeconomic status, or any other element of our personal identities. People from all walks of life can make meaning with any of the ways of knowing we will describe. It is also the case, though, and very important to underscore, that the supports and challenges we experience in life—which in turn influence our development—*are* intimately connected to the many intersections of our identities, as are the capacities we are encouraged (or not) to bring to our relationships and professional work. We discuss this confluence and interrelationship, briefly, next.

ON HIGHWAYS AND INTERSECTIONALITY

As pioneering scholar and civil rights advocate Kimberlé Crenshaw (1989, 1991, 2013, 2017) demonstrated in her powerful articulations of intersectionality, people live lives not just in one domain of identity, but at the intersections of all of the different parts of their being, both internally and externally defined. And, especially for people living, learning, and leading from multiply marginalized positionalities, the impact of oppressions can be magnified exponentially. As Crenshaw (2017) explained,

> Intersectionality is a lens through which you can see where power comes and collides, where it interlocks and intersects. It's not simply that there's a race problem here, a gender problem here, and a class or [LGBTQ] problem there. Many times that framework erases what happens to people who are subject to all of these things. (paragraph 4)

Yet, just as research has begun to explore how race- *and* gender-based trauma, alongside poverty, can complicate development and thriving for the most vulnerable and marginalized in communities without additional support (e.g., Bridwell, 2013), so too have people speaking and leading from the intersections of oppression (e.g., as Black women) proven to be some of the most wise, needed, and prescient guides for transformation and justice, both historically and today (see Collins, 2022; Muhammad, Dunmeyer, Starks, & Sealey-Ruiz, 2020; Love, 2019). Development, in other words, is *not* predetermined by identity, although identity—along with many other aspects of experience (such as family, culture, education, resources, location, and community)—provides significant context *for* development, in that it can influence the supports, challenges, and opportunities people receive (or not) in the outside world. When thinking about greater justice, then, both in schools and out—as well as development and the human journey of becoming—there exists a call to look, as clearly as possible, at *all* the factors that influence a person's experiences and life chances over time and to make more visible those parts of experience that can be hidden or obscured, even as things are in flux all around us.

Put another way, when thinking about all the complex, moving parts of development for the people in any team, group, faculty, community, or world, growth in motion can be likened to driving on a mega highway where all different kinds of vehicles are moving at various speeds, eager and ready to get to their destinations. It can be hard, sometimes (and especially when you're in the midst of it), to know or guess where someone else is heading or from whence they came—although it's clear that people are going all kinds of places at many different speeds for many different reasons.

For any one person, it is an exercise in *readiness* to get to a place other than the one you left. However, as you move, you hold onto what you know about the last place you were, adding a layer of understanding of what is to come. This is not a tangential journey of learning and discovery. It is fluid and incremental—and personal—such as when construction pylons are before you and your travel on the highway suddenly becomes a bit slower, allowing for convergence into fewer lanes. For some, this can be a most frustrating delay. For others, it can become an opportunity to take advantage of the slower pace to enjoy a more detailed view of the environment—so much so that when you reach your entry ramp, you do so with a greater appreciation of the uniqueness of the journey.

Sometimes, in development, slowing down is speeding up. At other times, we are ready to rev our engines. Understanding more about adult development and ways of knowing, we hope, can help us see more deeply into the pacing of another's journey and be of good company along the way.

DIFFERENTIATION IS ESSENTIAL

As we will continue to explore, understanding adults' different ways of knowing can help us *differentiate* the kinds of developmental supports and challenges we offer to those in our care as we work to build the internal capacity needed in individuals, schools, and systems to more effectively center justice and human dignity. We truly hope that, in this complicated and complex world, appreciating and deepening our understanding of developmental diversity can help us see ever-greater promise in ourselves and each other and flourish forward.

As illustrated in both Figure 2.1 and 2.2, there are four ways of knowing most commonly found in adulthood—the instrumental, socializing, self-authoring, and self-transforming. Each has strengths and limitations—gifts and growing edges. Currently, research suggests that the socializing way of knowing remains the most common among adults (Kegan & Lahey, 2016; Officer, 2018; Thoma, Caretta-Weyer, Schumacher, Warm, Hall, Hamstra, & ICBME Collaborators, 2021), although more and more people are gradually developing higher-order capacities as a result of the increasing complexities and demands of modern life (e.g., expanded access to information and technology, increasing awareness of systemic inequities, shifting professional norms toward greater collaboration, proliferation of new media).

For example, the fourth way of knowing—the self-transforming—was rather rare just a few decades ago. In the mid-90s, according to meta-analyses (Kegan, 1994), only 3–5 percent of adults in the United States were making meaning with some form of this way of knowing. Today, that number has jumped to approximately 8–11 percent, which amounts to nearly 40 million people in this country alone making meaning with self-transforming capacities (Kegan, 2013, 2018).

In the next sections, we turn to describing the strengths and growing edges of the different ways of knowing. As you read, we invite you to consider the ideas on multiple levels, as encouraged in the reflective invitation that follows. We offer these questions as opportunities to pause and consider your own experiences, as well as what's top of mind and in your heart right now. You might want to respond to them privately first and then engage in dialogue with a partner and/or group of colleagues.

REFLECTIVE INVITATION

1. How, if at all, might you see yourself in one or more of the ways of knowing? Your colleagues and other important people in your life?

2. What questions and/or insights come up for you?

3. What do you see as some of the bigger implications for practice?

THE INSTRUMENTAL WAY OF KNOWING: PRIORITIZING CONCRETE, RIGHT/WRONG ACTIONS FOR TEACHING AND LEADING

Developmental Strengths

Adults with an instrumental way of knowing can bring many strengths to their work, teaching, leading, and relationships, including deep content expertise, tremendous work ethics, a strong sense of right and wrong, great loyalty, and even genuine commitment to social justice. In the psychological sense, instrumental knowers are able to hold out their impulses as "object," meaning that they can reflect on their impulses, take a perspective on them, control them, and manage them. Because of this, instrumental knowers can be quite purposeful and deliberate in their actions and in taking steps to reach their goals.

Perhaps most characteristically, instrumental knowers orient to the world and their work in concrete, dualistic ways (i.e., "Is this right or wrong?")—and through the filter of how things will impact them, personally. As depicted in Figure 2.3, we sometimes find it helpful to think of the instrumental way of knowing as a "me" orientation. This is not because instrumental knowers are selfish or self-centered (they are not!), but because they have not yet grown the capacity to see the world more fully through others' eyes. Internally, they are still subject to (or run by) their own individual needs, interests, and understandings of how the world works. So, for instrumental knowers, new initiatives, ideas, and ways of working tend to be filtered through the lens of personal impact. "What would this mean for me?" is a question often at the fore. Or, from their particular perspective and vantage point, "How does this align (or not) with what's *right*?"

FIGURE 2.3   THE INSTRUMENTAL WAY OF KNOWING AND GROWING STEPS JUST BEYOND

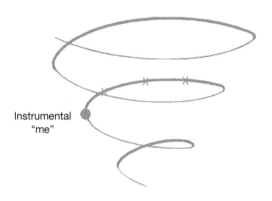

Instrumental
"me"

Growing Edges and Developmental Stretches

Although, again, instrumental knowers can care deeply about equity and justice—especially if these values are part of how they understand doing "right" or being "good" in the world—a growing edge of a "me"-focused orientation (when it is at the fore or running the show psychologically) is the tendency to generalize one's personal worldview as if it should be universally applicable to others, regardless of circumstance, positionality, or experience. Here, for instance, you could call to mind educators who, with the best of intentions, uncritically teach or lead in the ways *they* found most helpful—guided by the idea that there's a particular right way to be a teacher or leader and that changing that way would somehow be wrong or harmful.

Similarly, instrumental knowers tend to demonstrate kindness or compassion by treating others as they would like to be treated, often through concrete demonstrations of care (e.g., giving tangible items, direct expressions of support, doing things for others). Although this echoes the golden rule of "do unto others as you would have them do unto you," when educators act with the assumption that students, families, colleagues, and community members feel just as they would in a particular situation—rather than, say, seeking to really join others in their feeling and experience—it can limit, or even negate, the impact of intended kindnesses. Moving toward an internal world of feelings is a growing edge for adults with this developmental orientation. Similarly, they have not yet grown to have the internal capacity to stand in someone else's shoes—so to speak—or to deeply take on another person's perspective and consider it.

Another expression—and growing edge—of instrumental knowers' more concrete, right/wrong orientations is a generalized struggle with abstraction and uncertainty. Because there is not yet room for much "gray" in instrumental knowers' constructions of the world, they can struggle when there's not a clear answer or one correct solution, action, or directive to solve complex challenges (like social justice). Without the capacity yet to really critically examine the worldviews they've inherited and grown up with, they can also seem quite fixed in their convictions and decisions. From their view, if everyone would just do the right thing, there wouldn't be a problem.

Here, for instance, we are reminded of a teacher who recently confided to us that he wished his administration would just tell him what he needs to do to "get equity right." "Give me rubrics, or directions, or a blueprint I can follow," he explained. "I need that! If they would just tell me I would do it."

Of course, even though there are many powerful models, resources, books, articles, and curricula that could absolutely help educators learn about and scaffold justice-centering practice, supporting instrumental knowers means both providing these just-right supports *and* helping them stretch to explore some of the less visible, less tangible elements of looking beyond oneself and seeing more deeply into others.

In Chapter 3, we will dive deeply into ways leaders can bring and apply the internal capacities connected to an instrumental way of knowing to their justice-centering educational leadership practice—as well as the developmental supports and stretches that helped leaders continue to expand their approaches and understandings.

THE SOCIALIZING WAY OF KNOWING: FOREGROUNDING THE AFFECTIVE, RELATIONAL DIMENSIONS OF TEACHING AND LEADING

Developmental Strengths

Educators who make meaning with a socializing way of knowing have grown the internal capacity to more fully recognize and take into account others' feelings and experiences. As such, they can bring great relational strengths and sensitivities to their teaching and leading—in general and for justice. In a snapshot, adults with a socializing way of knowing often orient strongly to the inner world of feelings, and they can bring great capacities for loving, caring, and joining *with* other people. Socializing knowers want very much to make people feel valued and celebrated. Moving up and out on the developmental gyre beyond the instrumental way of knowing, they have also grown to take a perspective on the fact that there is no one, universal way to live, learn, teach, or lead—and they are no longer run by their individual wants and needs in the psychological sense.

That said, without the anchor of an instrumental knower's certainty, socializing knowers tend to orient strongly to others' expectations of them—so much so that, as depicted in Figure 2.4, we often describe the socializing way of knowing as a "you" orientation. Whereas before socializing knowers could look to the "rules" for the "right" way to think, feel, and act, they now turn outward, to valued others like family, friends, partners, colleagues, supervisors, and even societal norms, to co-construct new understandings, expectations, and definitions. Although socializing knowers can care deeply about others in their wholeness and complexity—and also justice—they have not yet developed the capacity to disentangle their own sense of self from their perceptions of how others see them. It's as if they are saying, often and unconsciously, "What you think of me, I think of me." It's almost as though other people serve as mirrors to how these knowers see themselves.

FIGURE 2.4   THE SOCIALIZING WAY OF KNOWING AND GROWING STEPS JUST BEYOND

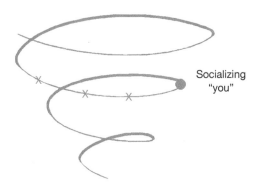

Growing Edges and Developmental Stretches

Psychologically speaking, socializing knowers are run by others' opinions and assessments of them because others play such a large role in their very understandings of self. Because of this, exposing inner uncertainties and vulnerabilities and engaging in conflict can leave socializing knowers feeling very distressed and even torn apart. When it comes to sensitive and sometimes difficult conversations about race, equity, and identity, for instance, socializing knowers may struggle to take risks or engage fully for fear of jeopardizing relationships. "What would happen if I shared what I was really thinking and feeling?" stands out here as a representative question. "If I say something, will I disappoint you?" is another.

By way of a more specific example, a school principal recently shared with us her struggle to confront colleagues she felt weren't buying into or respecting the school's equity efforts. "I'm ashamed to say that I often avoid those conversations, or kind of talk around them," she confided. "I know I need to speak up, and I'm working up to it, but I'm afraid that if I say something to them directly, they'll undermine me with my other teachers. They have a lot of influence. How can I lead the school without my relationships?"

Because the socializing way of knowing remains the most common in adulthood, understanding and honoring the qualitative experience of adults who make meaning in this way can be an especially powerful support for their social justice capacity building. For example, socializing knowers will often feel supported when mentors, supervisors, and trusted others make them feel valued as they are learning. By coupling constructive feedback with affirmations of confidence and care and encouraging socializing knowers to begin to look within, share their thinking and feeling, and more fully stand in their own truths, leaders can help socializing knowers feel secure in their professional relationships while trying on new capacities. Creating these kinds of relationships and spaces for socializing knowers can help them—over time—to share their perspectives and build their own internal benchmark of judgment and standards.

In Chapter 4, we will take an even deeper dive into the strengths and growing edges that educators demonstrating socializing capacities can bring to their justice-centering leadership, as well as the experiences that helped them stretch forward.

THE SELF-AUTHORING WAY OF KNOWING: DECIDING FOR ONESELF—AND ADVOCATING FOR—WHAT'S MOST IMPORTANT

Developmental Strengths

Growing from a socializing to a self-authoring way of knowing involves moving up even "higher" on the developmental gyre to be able to take a new perspective on—and not be run by—one's relationships and other people's feelings. It's not that self-authoring leaders care less about other people than socializing knowers (remember, their socializing capacities are still there, operating as part of a larger meaning making system), but rather that they've now grown the internal capacity to consider others' expectations, assessments, feedback, and ideas in relation to their *own*.

More specifically, the shift from the socializing to the self-authoring way of knowing involves transitioning from being made up by people or judgments *outside of oneself* to being able, on the inside, to author one's own values, standards, and long-term purposes. In fact, for self-authoring knowers, leading, teaching, and living in accordance with self-determined values and standards is of the utmost importance—so much so that, as we depict in Figure 2.5, we often think of this way of knowing as an "I" orientation.

FIGURE 2.5   THE SELF-AUTHORING WAY OF KNOWING AND GROWING STEPS JUST BEYOND

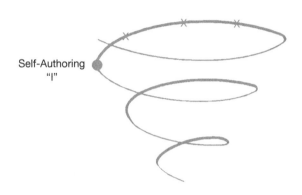

Self-Authoring "I"

For self-authoring leaders, questions at the fore include, "Am I living up to my own values and standards for performance?" and "Am I demonstrating my competencies to the best of my ability?" Even though, like instrumental knowers, self-authoring knowers—from the outside—can seem quite resolute in a particular position or ideology, their sense of assurance is qualitatively different because the *source* of their certainty is different. Self-authoring knowers have come to see their position not as "the one right way" for everyone, but as a personally significant value system carefully curated over time. In other words, self-authoring knowers recognize that people will have different opinions, orientations, and ideas about teaching, leading, and living—but they've developed a personal philosophy, vision, or way of working that they've decided, strongly, is the best for *them*.

Because of this, self-authoring knowers have grown the internal capacity to think systemically about larger organizational challenges and the roles they can play, and they can engage in necessary conflict without feeling torn apart. Even when self-authoring leaders hold collaboration and relationships as core values (and many do), they are able to speak their truths, challenge authority, and stand up for things that feel important to them and others. It is almost as if, we like to say, self-authoring knowers have grown a developmental *suit of armor* that nurtures and protects important capacities for leadership, advocacy, and promoting social justice.

For example, we were recently talking with an assistant principal about the current political challenges she was facing in her district regarding curriculum and equity learning. "I will never, *ever* do anything that undermines the dignity of my students, particularly my students of color," she explained. "That is just way too important to me personally and professionally, and I *will* find a way to make sure they feel seen, represented, and valued in our curricula. I'm willing to take the heat."

Growing Edges and Developmental Stretches

Although, like this assistant principal, self-authoring knowers can feel more comfortable advocating for their beliefs—as well as their students, colleagues, and themselves—they have not yet, psychologically speaking, grown the capacity to see into and critique the ideologies and value systems they hold so close or to see the inevitable partiality of their perspectives. Just as a suit of armor can serve as a protective shield when charging into (metaphorical) battle, so too can it block out different ways of thinking—and even possibilities for more inclusive connections and initiatives.

Accordingly, to be of good developmental support to self-authoring adults, it can be helpful to encourage them—not to let go of their convictions, but to consider them through an increasingly wider lens, and as part of a larger constellation of "best" practices.

In Chapter 5, we further explore how the capacities associated with a self-authoring way of knowing have served justice-centering leaders, as well as the supports and stretches that have helped them continue to grow on the inside and to enhance their practice even more.

THE SELF-TRANSFORMING WAY OF KNOWING: SEEING DEEPER INTO ONESELF, OTHERS, AND INTERCONNECTION

Developmental Strengths

Like self-authoring knowers, self-transforming adults have the internal capacity to take a firm stand on their values and principles. However, they have also grown to recognize the necessity of regularly looking *beyond* themselves—of opening up their metaphorical suits of armor to explore an ever-wider spectrum of points of view, possibilities, and ideas. Just as developing self-authoring capacities involves a turn back on the gyre toward the individualistic side of meaning making, but with new perspectives and capacities (i.e., the difference between "me" and "I"), growing toward a self-transforming way of knowing involves a more inclusive revisiting of a collective orientation to the world—in this case, moving from the socializing "you" in Figure 2.4 to a self-transforming "we," as depicted in Figure 2.6.

FIGURE 2.6   THE SELF-TRANSFORMING WAY OF KNOWING AND
             GROWING STEPS JUST BEFORE

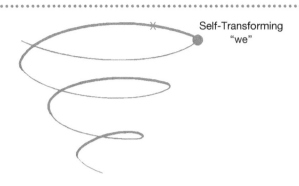

Self-Transforming
"we"

In fact, as we illustrate in Figures 2.7 and 2.8, depicting development as a gyre or helix also helps make explicit the cyclical tension—a kind of dance, so to speak—that persists throughout life between filling up and focusing within, on the individual self, and situating and understanding that self as part of a larger whole or collective. As we shared earlier, development—in and across many different domains—is made up of just this kind of revisiting and re-exploration.

Because of their enhanced capacity to look both without and within, self-transforming knowers orient to interconnection and psychological intimacy as a way of enhancing their self-understanding and the collective reach of leadership and justice efforts. More specifically, adults with self-transforming capacities recognize plurality as a necessary support to and component of human progress. And they aspire, continually, to explore and grow the many different parts of their identities, understandings, and ways of being in the world. For the most part, they do this

FIGURE 2.7   REVISITING, IN A DEVELOPMENTAL SENSE, THE CORE
             TENSION BETWEEN THE INDIVIDUAL AND THE
             COLLECTIVE

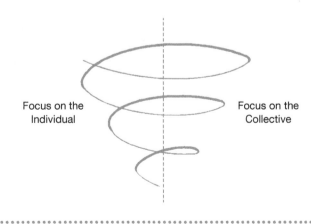

Focus on the
Individual

Focus on the
Collective

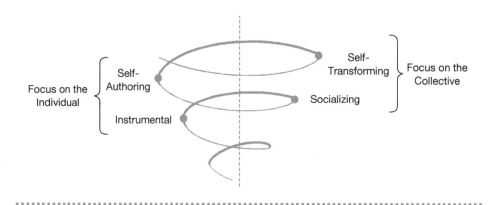

by being in relationships with others. Questions now at the fore include, "How can we learn from each other and grow together?" and "How can I develop more parts of myself—and help others do the same—through mutual collaboration?"

Growing Edges and Developmental Stretches

Toward these ends, self-transforming adults often seek out others with whom they can engage in deep dialogue—especially about the paradoxes, complexities, and inconsistencies all around and within themselves. However, it can be harder for self-transforming knowers to turn back toward concrete action amid many competing tensions and possibilities, especially with their new, internal capacities that enable them to think and feel that any solution is only partial and/or temporary. It can also—especially without an awareness of development and developmental diversity—be a lonely way of knowing to inhabit.

As another assistant principal recently shared, she finds it difficult to stretch and grow in the ways she'd like to on the job because she's so busy caring for other people's learning needs. "I can't often be on *my* growing edge," she confided. "While it gives me a lot of joy to hold and care for others, sometimes it's harder to find people to connect with in the way I'd like to." She also felt confined by what she experienced as restrictive professional norms in her building that made it harder to bring her fullness and complexity to work. "I often think about the parts of me that aren't allowed on the job," she explained. "Why is that?"

As we will continue to explore in Chapter 6 and throughout this book, the capacities connected to a self-transforming way of knowing can help leaders bring important—and frequently less understood and demonstrated—capacities to their justice-centering work. Seeing more deeply into the experience of making meaning in this way, as we will explore, also raises important questions about some of the structural and organizational conditions that could make the education sector even more supportive of interconnection and mutuality.

Now that we have explored all four of the ways of knowing more commonly found in adulthood as a cumulative progression—or evolving story—of development, we invite you to engage with the following reflective invitation, to connect big ideas from this section to your personal experience. You might want to respond to them privately first and then engage in dialogue with a partner and/or group of colleagues.

REFLECTIVE INVITATION

1. What do you see as your developmental strengths? Your growing edges?

2. What kinds of supports do you have to help you to exercise justice-centering leadership?

3. What kinds of supports do you *wish* you had to further grow your practice?

4. What might help you—if you feel the need to or the desire—to move to the next layer of capacities?

HOLDING ENVIRONMENTS FOR WHOLE PEOPLE

Recently, we received one of the most precious compliments we could imagine when a school leader said to us, "I feel like I can tell you anything—that you understand, see, and value me." Perhaps, more than anything else, it is our hope that, in exploring constructive-developmental theory and its extensions, we can share one more lens for looking deeply into ourselves and others—into the gifts, vulnerabilities, and beautiful potentialities we each carry within us, as well as our growing edges—and to help everyone feel more recognized and cherished. Although no two people enter into equity conversations from exactly the same spot—and, as you know, there exists a vast continuum of understandings, experiences, commitments, and orientations to justice-centering leadership influenced by all of our intersectional identities, experiences, and constructions—we truly believe that everyone is needed.

Though development—as we've outlined and defined it in this chapter—is certainly not a guarantee of effectiveness in or even commitment to justice-centering educational leadership, we feel that the different internal capacities we've been exploring in our discussion of ways of knowing can serve as prerequisites that help leaders more readily enter into and make contributions in different domains of justice-centering leadership. These internal capacities can, we argue, help us be more open to learning, to being in relationship, to reassessing former certainties, and to seeing how things—and people—connect, diverge, and overlap.

In the next four chapters, we will learn from leaders making meaning all across the developmental expanse depicted in Figure 2.8, and we will zoom in on four qualitatively distinct areas of justice-centering leadership practice: the concrete, the interpersonal, the system-focused, and the interconnecting. Through the real-life stories, reflections, and experiences of leaders from across the country, we will make further connections between these different layers of practice and the internal, developmental capacities they brought to their justice-centering work.

Ultimately, we hope these explorations will help further illustrate how all educators—no matter their ways of knowing—can benefit from just-right combinations of developmental supports and stretches when growing as individuals and justice-centering leaders. Just like the youngest of humans, who thrive best in holding environments and nurturing relationships that hold them closely enough to feel safe and offer gentle release to encourage new development (Drago-Severson, 2004a, 2004b, 2009, 2012; Kegan, 1982, 1994, 2000; Winnicott, 1965), adults can benefit from individualized care and attention that honors all of who they are throughout their lives.

The Origins and Three Functions of a Holding Environment

By way of further context, the term *holding environment* was originally employed by pediatrician and psychoanalyst Donald Winnicott (1965) to describe the different forms of physical and psychological holding infants need from birth into toddlerhood. Extending Winnicott's concept of a holding environment to adult development, it becomes clear that good holding environments serve three important functions.

First, a good holding environment must hold well, meaning recognizing, confirming, and accepting who someone is and how they go about making meaning in the world. We often refer to this function as *meeting people where they are*. We are not, it is important to underscore, dismissing the urgencies of our world—nor the urgent need for progress. Rather, we emphasize this kind of deep seeing and understanding as a first step to making change possible.

Second, when a person is ready to try growing beyond or outside of their current meaning making, a good holding environment needs to "let go," permitting and even encouraging a person's growth. This second function of the holding environment emphasizes the importance of stretching—and differentiating our stretches depending on one's way of knowing.

Third, a good holding environment for adult development "sticks around" to provide continuity and stability, even as those within it continue to grow and evolve. By this, we mean caring for and continuing to be present for people as they—and we—are changing.

Powerfully, a holding environment can be a relationship, a team, a family (broadly defined), a coalition, an organization, and/or a system. Good holding environments—in any of these forms—can help us grow. They can help us to feel well held as we benefit from the just right (i.e., developmentally appropriate) supports and stretches we've been highlighting in this chapter. Doing so will help us to grow—individually and collectively—as we strive to meet the pressing urgencies of justice *together* in our world today.

We hold as a mantra the idea that *growth happens at the intersection of support and challenge*, as people really do need both. Too much support can obscure the need for change. Too much challenge can block or slow down progress. But just the right amount of both? Well, that's where the magic happens.

It's equally important to underscore that like most things—the things that seem to *really* matter in life—we need to be patient with ourselves as we practice offering the appropriate mix of supports and stretching for others and for ourselves. We've found it helpful to think about it as building our developmental muscles. How do we get in shape psychologically and physically? We work at it. We try.

Toward this end, in Table 2.1, we provide an overview of the orienting concerns of adults with different ways of knowing and zoom in on key supports and stretches that can help you meet educators where they are. After all, both are needed to nurture growth.

TABLE 2.1 WAYS OF KNOWING, ORIENTING CONCERNS, AND SUPPORTS AND STRETCHES FOR GROWTH

WAY OF KNOWING	ORIENTING CONCERNS	SUPPORTS AND STRETCHES FOR GROWTH
Instrumental *"What does this mean for me?"* *"Is this right or wrong?"* *"What, exactly, do I need to do?"*	• Orients to and is run by own needs and inherited worldviews. • Filters experience through the lens of personal impact. • Understands the world in concrete, dualistic terms. • Sees others as helpers or obstacles for meeting goals and needs. • Does not yet have the capacity for abstract thinking in the psychological sense.	Supports: • Concrete models, examples, rubrics, protocols, resources, and readings. • Discussions about what went right and wrong. • Timelines with clear action steps and measurable deliverables.

(Continued)

(Continued)

WAY OF KNOWING	ORIENTING CONCERNS	SUPPORTS AND STRETCHES FOR GROWTH
Instrumental (Continued)	• Is most concerned with tangible consequences of own and others' actions. • Makes decisions based on what the self will acquire and on following the rules.	**Stretches:** • Managing leadership or teaching challenges that do not have a clear answer or solution. • Making abstract connections. • Seeing things from another's point of view. • Looking beyond own understandings of the "right" thing to do and how things "are."
Socializing *"What you think of me, I think of me."* *"What would happen if I shared what I was really thinking and feeling?"*	• Orients to inner states (feelings). • Is "run" by valued others' expectations, assessments, and opinions. • Adopts others' standards, values, and judgments. • Feels responsible for others' feelings and holds others responsible for one's own.	**Supports:** • Demonstrations of appreciation. • Affirmation of what's going well (e.g., hard work, effort, progress). • Recognition of growth and contributions. • Feeling accepted as a person and a colleague. **Stretches:** • Encouragement to share authentic thoughts and feelings. • Taking in—or giving—critical feedback without feeling torn apart. • Engaging in difficult conversations with valued others or supervisors. • Turning toward conflict and high-risk situations with support.
Self-Authoring *"Am I living up to my own values and standards for performance?"*	• Orients to internally curated values and systems of belief. • Evaluates criticism according to own standards. • Is ultimately concerned with personal competence and performance in alignment with values.	**Supports:** • Autonomy and self-direction in goal setting and professional practice. • Leadership roles. • Recognition of competence and expertise.

WAY OF KNOWING	ORIENTING CONCERNS	SUPPORTS AND STRETCHES FOR GROWTH
Self-Authoring (Continued) *"Am I demonstrating my competence to the best of my ability?"*	• Can take perspective on relationships. • Views conflict as a natural part of life, work, and leadership.	• Opportunities to offer feedback and ideas. **Stretches:** • Considering and finding value in ideas and viewpoints that feel diametrically opposing to one's own. • Critically examining one's own carefully curated values, beliefs, and philosophies about teaching, leadership, and the world. • Sharing leadership or authority with others.
Self-Transforming *"How can we learn from each other and grow together?"* *"How can I develop more parts of myself— and help others do the same— through mutual collaboration?"*	• Orients to inter-individuality, mutuality, and interconnection. • Can take perspective on own value system. • Recognizes the need for plurality and the continual renegotiation of beliefs and actions. • Wants to grow, improve, and better understand different aspects of self. • Is able to understand and manage tremendous complexity and ambiguity.	**Supports:** • Mutual, collaborative conversations. • Open-ended opportunities for connection and reflection. • Time to listen to and discuss multiple viewpoints and ideas. • Exploring paradoxes, internal and systemic inconsistencies, and different alternatives. **Stretches:** • Managing the loneliness of making meaning in a way that is often different than colleagues. • Balancing the desire for interconnection with the fast pace of education and traditional understandings of leadership. • Turning back toward action amid competing possibilities. • Carving out sustainable spaces for growth and community.

SOURCE: Adapted from Drago-Severson (2009, pp. 40–41, 45, 46, 48, 51) and Drago-Severson and Blum-DeStefano (2018, pp. 35–36).

CLOSING REFLECTION AND TAKEAWAYS
Development and Butterflies

On a closing note, we'd like to acknowledge that, as much as we may sometimes wish to rush development in ourselves or others—especially when so much is at stake—growing one's constructions and perspectives takes hard work, investment, and time. Like a butterfly who needs to use *all* its might to break free from its protective chrysalis, it is often the struggle itself that builds the capacity for what's to come. Sometimes, we can see another person's wings before they do, but the best we can do is create the conditions that invite them to fly—we can't break the chrysalis on their behalf. And sometimes, we need others to help us recognize, remember, or reinvest in our *own* wings, especially when things get hard.

As justice-centering leaders, we are all butterflies and growers of butterflies— caring across so many different phases, heights, and flights. Though it would be wonderful, in some ways, to wave a wand that could help everyone become who they most want to be in a moment, there's wonder, too, in loving people as they learn, in witnessing transformation unfold, and in building connections that allow us to pay forward the holding—and love—we've benefited from in our own lives. In our experience, this kind of love is some of the best fuel for growth, and it doesn't require letting go of urgency. The urgency is a part of it, as love can be a radical act. May the ideas featured in this chapter and book help you on your journey to care for and guide others, and may it help us ever more effectively nurture one another as we step forward together in the struggle for a better future.

In Figure 2.9, we offer an image that brings together the developmental gyre with the domains of leadership we are about to explore in Chapters 3

FIGURE 2.9   THE RANGE OF CAPACITIES DEMONSTRATED BY LEADERS IN OUR STUDY, ATOP THE DOMAINS OF JUSTICE-CENTERING LEADERSHIP

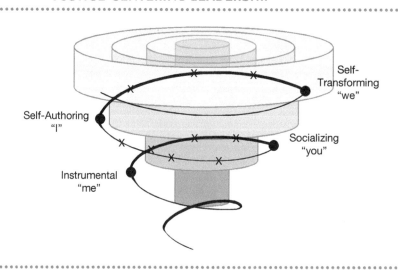

through 6. In Figure 2.10, we offer a series of summative takeaways to help spotlight key ideas from this chapter. We close with a reflective invitation that serves, once again, as an opportunity to connect ideas from the chapter with your own experiences and to tune into or revisit any ideas, questions, or implications that emerged for you as you read.

FIGURE 2.10 CHAPTER TAKEAWAYS

Love recognizes no barriers. It jumps hurdles, leaps fences, penetrates walls to arrive at its destination full of hope.

—Maya Angelou

- Understanding constructive-developmental theory provides language to name things we see in ourselves and others and to connect external behaviors to the meaning making underneath.

- Differentiation is key. It helps us to meet each other where we are.

- Appreciating and understanding our ways of knowing also helps us to appreciate and understand a less-visible kind of diversity—developmental diversity—which is important to recognize, acknowledge, and care for, just as are other forms of diversity.

- In reviewing different lenses and theoretical perspectives, we found that constructive-developmental theory offers a clear language for naming—and bringing together—important concepts that run across different theories of and approaches to social justice. For example, although expressed in different terminology, both *constructivism* and *developmentalism*—as well as the vital role of *perspective taking* (on self, others, history, the educational system, and society)—are prevalent concepts in the literatures about equity, inclusion, and justice. A developmental lens helps bring these ideas together in new ways.

- Understanding constructive-developmental theory can help us to appreciate that adults make sense of the world in qualitatively different ways—and that our ways of knowing influence how we think about and exercise our justice-centering leadership.

- We can grow throughout our lives provided that we can benefit from different kinds of supports and stretching when needed.

- It is important to differentiate the kinds of supports and stretches—or developmental challenges—that we offer to those in our care.

- Developmental diversity will likely exist in any team, school, organization, and system. Therefore, developing an understanding of how to differentiate our supports and stretches can help us to build internal capacity in ourselves, others, and organizations.

- When we grow from one way of knowing to the next, we are able to take a perspective on, understand, and manage more aspects of ourselves, others, the relationship between ourselves and others, and society.

- Development is not a linear process; instead, it is iterative and cyclical. As we grow, we revisit different tensions—between self and other, thinking and feeling, learning and unlearning, knowing and doing—again and again and with new eyes and new internal capacities.

- Each way of knowing has both strengths and growing edges. Adults will move to and through these stages and transitional spaces—please remember the Xs on the gyre—at different paces and rates.

- Being physically and psychologically *present* and *open* to educators as they offer questions, insights, and ideas enables leaders to create contexts in which adults are and feel cared for, respected, listened to, and heard.

- It is important to consider the underlying structural and organizational conditions that could make the education sector even more supportive of interconnection and mutuality.

What is most personal is most general. . . . [W]hat is most personal and unique in each one of us is probably the very element which would, if it were shared or expressed, speak most deeply to others.

—Carl R. Rogers (1961, p. 26)

Before journeying forward, we invite you to reflect on the following prompts as opportunities to pause and consider your own experiences, thoughts, and feelings and any connections you are making at this time. We also invite you to jot down questions you're holding and anything else that feels helpful to you. You might find it meaningful to consider these questions privately and then with colleagues and partners.

1. Why is the work you are leading important to you? Who are the people you rely on for support?

2. After reading this chapter, what feels like it's on the front burner for you? What questions are you holding?

3. What stands out for you in this chapter? What do you find yourself curious about? Wondering about?

4. How, if at all, has the discussion about ways of knowing helped you to understand yourself and/or others in new ways?

5. What—at this time—do you see as your biggest strengths as a leader, teacher, and/or a partner and collaborator? What do you see as your growing edge at this time? After reading this chapter, where do you see yourself on the developmental continuum?

6. What conditions enable you to actively engage in justice conversations? What makes it hard or challenging for you?

7. In your work context—or one of them—how do you and others make spaces to listen to each other? When and where do you have time and space—and create time and space—for educators to engage in private reflection and dialogue about justice-centering leadership? Supports for building capacity? Areas for growth—at the individual and organizational levels?

8. What are the interpersonal, structural, and organizational conditions that exist currently in your team? Organization? System? What else would help you and your colleagues engage more effectively and be more supportive of interconnection and mutuality?

9. What do you see as the critical components that need to be infused when creating conditions for justice-centering conversations with educators—whether in a team, a faculty meeting, or any kind of learning conversations?

10. What, if anything, do you think you will you share with colleagues about ways of knowing and/or other ideas presented in this chapter to build a shared language and/or to grow your practice, teams, and/or organization?

11. What are one or two ways you might be able to build your practices to help those in your care more intentionally come together and scaffold justice work? What different entry points, supports, and contexts for ongoing learning already exist in your work for you and for others? How, if at all, might some of the ideas in this chapter inform and/or influence how you are thinking about them now?

INTERLUDE I

CARRYING CARE FORWARD

Sankofa *is an African word from the Akan tribe in Ghana. The literal translation of the word and the symbol is, "It is not taboo to fetch what is at risk of being left behind."*

—Carter G. Woodson Center, Berea College (n.d.)

Before venturing forward into the next chapters of the book—which feature leaders' stories of advocating for justice across roles, geographies, identities, and the developmental continuum—we are moved to honor the history and resonance of Sankofa. Depicted, as in the symbol that opens this interlude, as a bird heading firmly in one direction but turning back, purposefully, to cradle and carry forward a precious seed or egg, the Sankofa epitomizes valuing the learning and wisdom that came before us and taking hold of that as we go forward (Milton & Brooks Lawrence, 2022). It's about drawing strength and guidance from the past, from ancestors, and from loved ones and cherished guides as a fortifying practice for ourselves, and in honor of those who helped, as Fred "Mr. Rogers" Rogers (1997) explained in a different way, "love us into being," both directly and indirectly.

For the leaders in our study, this practice of looking back—with gratitude and grace—proved an important and ongoing motivation and a deeply personal entry point for their justice-centering work. In addition to carrying the strength, courage, and inspiration others had shared with them in heart, many of the leaders in our study looked back with love to honor family members, teachers, and guides of all kinds—or "catalyst individuals," as one leader dubbed them—who'd impacted their lives in treasured and enduring ways. We share some of their impactful recollections here, as one small way of honoring their forebears' important contributions.

First, we celebrate Thea's reflections about her mother. Thea—a district-level leader focused on teacher leadership development, who identified as a married Black woman, with ten years in education—described how she sees much of her work as a tribute to her mother's support and way of being in the world. As she explained,

> [My mother] helped me see parts of myself that I didn't understand or I denied at a very young age. She always motivated me to know that I was brilliant, that I could do anything that I put my mind to. In times of my life when I was very insecure and did not see that for myself, she motivated me that way. . . . I'm a part of her legacy and I don't ever want to lose that part of me. . . . It's just important for me to keep her alive through what I do and how I live and how I treat people, because she was a very kind, giving person, and I too want to emulate that kindness and giving spirit that she had. So it's important for me to continue that legacy and keep that voice.

We also feel humbled to share Lisa's special connection with her grandmother. Lisa—an early childhood director who recently opened her own center, and who identified as a thirty-seven-year-old Black female of Haitian descent, with seventeen years in education—spoke lovingly of her grandmother's influence and modeling:

> When I look back on it now, I feel like it's in my DNA because, like I said, my grandmother had that nurturing child care, like that

teaching way about her, even though she was not a teacher. But I feel like if she was given the opportunities, she would have been a teacher because my grandmother, she had to drop out of literally elementary school to help raise her three younger sisters when her father died. So you know, she didn't have the luxury of going to school, but I feel like if she did, I think she would have been an educator, so I feel like that's something that she kind of passed on to me. . . . Growing up, my house was always filled with children because she was the person that the neighborhood would trust with their children. . . . She kind of like planted that seed in me . . . and that's why I named the business after her. So I did that as something to remember her by, but also to . . . continue her legacy because this is something that I'm sure if she had the proper channels, if she had the opportunities, she would have done it as well. I mean, she was an immigrant, you know? And I was the first child she ever watched because she emigrated to the United States because I was being born. . . . She did not only impact my life, but she impacted so many people.

This kind of profound gratitude and admiration was similarly expressed by Kristina—an educational consultant who identified as a faith-driven, married Black woman, and a native of a Southern city well-known for its civil rights history—as she spoke of her grandparents and other advocates who stood up to injustice:

I've known a deep sense of appreciation and respect for generations of people that have come before me. . . . So my grandparents . . . participated in the civil rights activities, and part of it is growing up and knowing that my grandmother got hit in the head with a billy club because of trying to vote, and there's just so many things. I've always known about people sacrificing their literal lives and physical safety for a cause that they believed so deeply in. . . . It just gives me a lot of courage to know the courage that they had. . . . They've always kind of lifted me in that way, if that makes sense. And made sacrifices for me.

Others connected their gratitude specifically to teachers and their reasons for being in education. Amaia, for example—a teacher leader and coach who identified as a Mexican American female with eleven years in education—said,

I'm a teacher because, literally, when people talk about education changing their life, I've lived it, and I continue to live it with my students. So I am teaching because I'm experiencing daily the effects of what it can do for you.

Jack—an assistant principal who identified as fifty-four years old, Eastern European/Slavic, and an immigrant—similarly recalled the importance of affirmations from academic mentors during his own journey as a student. "After years of thinking I was a bad student," he explained, he had the opportunity to work with a group of archaeologists on an excavation project. The professors there saw something in him and helped him imagine new possibilities for his future:

> I remember being there and people telling me, "You're really
> smart." I'm, like, "What? Naw, my friend is smart." They said, "No,
> no, no, you're really smart, we know you're smart. The way you
> talk." And I was, like, "Really, 'cause I have shitty grades, so I don't
> know where you're getting this from." And they said, "No, I think
> you should go to college." And I was, like, "What is college?" . . .
> So they inspired me, so I went back and, a few years in a row, kind
> of caught up [on] all the studying that I hadn't done.

Eventually, Jack was accepted into a prestigious program, and carries with him the memory of that accomplishment. As he said, "Up until this day . . . it's just like the best, the biggest achievement in my entire life."

As one last example, we share the gratitude Shokry—an educational consultant who identified as a person of color with Dominican and Egyptian heritage—expressed for the teachers who helped him chart new paths. Recognizing that "we are [all] the recipients of models of inspiration," he offered the following:

> I'm a first-generation college student of two people who
> immigrated to the United States. . . . I'm the recipient now of three
> master's degrees and then finishing a doctorate and that feels
> completely like the result of the kindness of others to me. I think
> about the effects it's had upon my family. My younger brother
> attended college shortly after my attending graduate school because
> it felt like a possibility. It felt like an opportunity. And I mean we
> think about how wide this has gotten now, right? And it began
> with someone saying something as simple as, "You can do it." And
> being present to hear my frustrations or my fears. If I can do that
> for someone else, that to me feels like—I mean it sounds cliché but
> that feels like our purpose in the world, right? To champion others.
> The way that people have championed us. So that everyone can
> seek the opportunities they dream of.

As these stories help illustrate, for many of the leaders in our research, engaging in justice-centering educational leadership, broadly and inclusively defined, meant opening vistas of possibility with and for others, and in honor of those who'd helped them grow into the biggest versions of themselves. We feel similarly fortunate to share and pay forward participants' stories and wisdom with *you*, and we also celebrate the significant people in your lives who've helped you lead with love.

Before turning to the leaders' different strengths, insights, accomplishments, and challenges in the next four chapters, we invite you to pause and take a moment to honor the people, traditions, histories, and experiences that bring *you* to justice work. If you'd like, please take a moment to consider the questions that follow. You may find it helpful to consider them on your own and/or share experiences with a partner or small group.

A REFLECTIVE INVITATION

1. Who do you honor with the work that you do?

2. What legacies are you carrying forward with love?

3. Who inspired you in your life? Helped "love you into being"?

4. What are a few of the experiences you've lived and grown through that inspire your justice journey today? What else informs your "why"?

5. What are you hoping to learn from the chapters that follow?

CHAPTER 3

....

STARTING WITH THE CONCRETE

Leading for Social Justice with Instrumental Capacities

The time is always right to do what is right.

—Martin Luther King, Jr. (1965)

In this chapter, we begin, as they say, at the beginning. As we will explore, for the leaders in our study making meaning with elements of an instrumental way of knowing—and for others looking back at the "spark" that first fixed justice for them as a strong value—the desire to *do good and right* emerged as a powerful way into justice-centering educational leadership. And the best news is that, developmentally speaking, this impulse can serve as a ground-floor entry point into the concrete domain of practice open to anyone eager to engage.

Toward this end, in this chapter, we zoom in on leaders' experiences within the concrete domain of our developmental model for justice-centering leadership, including

- the internal sensemaking informing their work (especially in relation to instrumental capacities),

- examples of promising practices,

- the developmental supports that helped them grow, and

- what it felt like to recognize the need for another layer of focus and practice (i.e., to be in transition, developmentally, between the instrumental and socializing ways of knowing).

By way of reminder, the concrete domain involves a focus on tangible action steps, often in response to specific and immediate needs. A preoccupying question here, for example, might be something like, "What do I need to do to make this right, *right now*?" As illustrated in Figure 3.1, this chapter teases out the concrete domain as the *central cylinder* of our developmental model—a cylinder that runs throughout and remains at the core of the layers that follow.

FIGURE 3.1   INSTRUMENTAL CAPACITIES AS ENTRY POINT INTO THE CONCRETE DOMAIN OF JUSTICE-CENTERING EDUCATIONAL LEADERSHIP PRACTICE

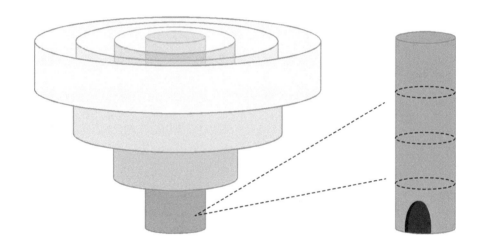

Also, as represented by the open doorway in Figure 3.1, we explore how successful entry into—and engagement with—the concrete domain is connected to leaders' ability to bring *at least* some instrumental capacities to their practice. Although, as you know, leaders with any way of knowing can focus on concrete actions and leadership moves (they remain, as we just mentioned, at the core of all that follows), the capacities that come along with growing into an instrumental way of knowing are of particular importance for leaders foregrounding individual acts or concrete demonstrations of care in their immediate practice.

As we shared in Chapter 2, educators with an instrumental way of knowing can orient strongly to justice as the "right" thing to do, but they have not yet grown the internal capacity to more fully see things through others' eyes— or to see their actions as part of a wider constellation of needed efforts. They are also still working—on the inside—to see beyond the perimeters of their own lived experiences and inherited right/wrong understandings of how the world "works," meaning that they may unintentionally intuit and apply their worldviews as applicable to everyone, regardless of circumstance. (You might remember, from Chapter 2, the hypothetical educator who, with noble intentions, tries to teach their students in the same "right" ways they experienced growing up.) Despite these growing edges, instrumental knowers (and leaders just starting out in their efforts to more explicitly center justice) *can* bring many strengths and commitments to their work, especially in the concrete domain. As the Reverend Doctor Martin Luther King, Jr. expressed in this chapter's epigraph, it's always a good time "to do what is right"—because "right" is so needed, again and again, in both the smallest and largest of things.

To help paint a portrait of some of the foundational leadership moves participants foregrounded in the concrete domain—as well as their connections to instrumental capacities and growing edges—we next share leaders' reflections and recollections about leading for justice in concrete, tangible ways. Though some of the leaders featured in this chapter were making meaning with some elements of an instrumental way of knowing at the time of our interviews, others were looking back at this time in their meaning making— or reflecting on their work with others for whom the instrumental way of knowing felt prominent.

In this and every chapter, we focus on ways leaders foregrounded particular internal capacities, but we do not link individuals with specific developmental "scores." Also, because the fifty leaders who participated in our study were diverse in terms of identity, role, and experience, when we "introduce" a leader for the first time in the chapter, we include the personal identifiers *they* named as most important to them when we interviewed them for this research. Because we know these aspects of a person's self serve as important context for their sharings, we also include, upon any subsequent mentions of that same leader, a parenthetical reminder about the key identifiers they shared as a kind of shorthand that, we hope, honors the importance of identity without essentializing any specific parts of it.

Because, as we mentioned, the concrete domain runs through the core of our model and is open to all leaders with at least some instrumental capacities, we are excited to share that the next sections feature stories from a great many leaders in our study, as they reflected on this particular dimension of their work.

We begin, next, with what many leaders framed as an underlying "call to do right" that can serve as a foundation for justice-centering leadership.

THE CALL TO DO RIGHT

For many of the leaders in our study, regardless of way of knowing, leading on behalf of social justice began with an ingrained call, as many put it, to "do right." As Rana—an independent school head who identified as Egyptian American and Muslim—reflected, "I think I've always been drawn to service and serving others. . . . The idea of doing good in the world and trying to leave a positive impact was something modeled for me and seeded from a very young age." Likewise, D.—a teacher leader in his forties who described himself as a first-generation Latino American—told us that, for him, this call was a fundamental element of his identity and upbringing: "I am a community-oriented person. I grew up in a household where my parents volunteered and they taught me to volunteer."

Indeed, this idea of service—of rightness and goodness—grounded the practice of so many of the leaders in our study and finds echo in some of their most foundational understandings of and motivations toward social justice. As Bernard—a teacher educator and former principal and superintendent who identified as a fifty-seven-year-old African American father—put it, "I'm thinking about values. I'm thinking about a sense of morality. I've tried to model being right, just doing the right thing, and I try to exemplify that in my leadership, in my behavior as a teacher." A related idea was expressed by Yaacov—a teacher leader and middle school coordinator who identified as a thirty-two-year-old Orthodox Jewish father and husband—when he asked, "What's the point of this whole big rock floating through space if not to have a positive impact on your kids' lives and other peoples' lives?"

As these examples suggest, the underlying impulse to make the world a better place proved an important entry point for many leaders' justice-oriented goals and efforts—and one that connected, often, to their upbringings and fundamental understandings of morality and of being a good person in the world. Perhaps, looking forward, tapping into this impulse to do good and right might also help leaders bring more people on board with equity efforts in their schools and educational organizations?

One of the leaders in our study, Joyce—an educational consultant who identified as a Caribbean African American woman in her early thirties, and also the daughter of Jamaican immigrants—described taking this approach as a way into her equity-centered coaching and consulting. When confronted with resistance from teachers or leaders, for instance, or when working with educators who were open to equity learning but not sure where to begin, Joyce tries "to tap into their pedagogy and their reason for being in education." In her experience, teachers often enter the profession with a real care for children and youth, but this care can be fragile, eroded by burnout and hardship, or bounded by fear of change and/or unconscious biases and assumptions. To meet colleagues where they are, Joyce asks herself,

> How can I help them to identify who they are in education? Get them to be on board with this pedagogy of moving education? How can I support leaders in a way where they're still aligned to the reason why they got into education, and then they're being strategic about the moves they're making?

In this way, Joyce explains, she can honor others' potential *and* make inroads toward growth and change. With Joyce's grounding questions as framing, we detail in the next sections some of the concrete, individualized actions leaders took as starting steps in their social justice leadership and as expressions of instrumental capacities. We hope that these examples help add developmental, up-close nuance to the insight offered by educational anthropologist Mica Pollock and colleagues (2010) about how people often enter into diversity learning by first asking, "What can I *do*?"—with an emphasis on concrete steps and behaviors (p. 211).

Before reading on, we invite you to pause and consider the concrete actions and practices most important to *your* work and leadership:

REFLECTIVE INVITATION

1. What is top of mind for you right now?

2. What have been some of the important influences on your understanding of the "right thing"? Who or what has helped shape this for you?

3. What are some concrete things you do in your practice that help make a difference?

4. What do you think others notice you doing?

5. What local or immediate steps might be important to consider for your context?

LEADERS' CONCRETE ORIENTATIONS AND APPROACHES TO CENTERING JUSTICE

> *What you are will show, ultimately. Start now, every day, becoming, in your actions, your regular actions, what you would like to become in the bigger scheme of things.*
>
> Anna Deavere Smith, *Letters to a Young Artist* (2006)

For leaders in our study who were making meaning with some elements of an instrumental way of knowing—and for those looking for places to begin their social justice advocacy—translating the call to do right into action often began with concrete, localized moves, including

- taking tangible action steps, and
- focusing on the measurable and technical.

To begin to address the more intractable, complex, adaptive challenges of education, finding something tangible to *do* or *count* provided important starting places for leaders. Yet, these foundational practices can also grow and develop over time. In other words, although it takes some instrumental capacity to first enter effectively into this domain of practice, leaders from across the developmental continuum can (and must) continue to intentionally *do* things, big and small, as part of their justice-centering efforts.

Capturing this idea, and emphasizing how small things could have big impact, Irene—an independent school director of admissions and enrollment who identified as a white, fifty-six-year-old Jewish mother, whose own mother left Vienna in 1939—explained of her understanding of social justice, "I think the answer—sometimes it's really huge and sometimes it's really small in my mind. . . . I mean, it can be in some ways as little as teaching kids how to be supportive and collaborative in a group, right?" Similarly, Lisa—an early childhood director who identified as a thirty-seven-year-old Black woman of Haitian decent, with seventeen years in education—explained that teaching and leading on behalf of any kind of justice "is like literally peeling an onion. There are so many layers to it that we just have to begin somewhere. We may not get to the end where everything is okay, but we have to start and we have to try at least."

For many of the leaders we learned from in our study, there was indeed wisdom in beginning where one could have the most influence (i.e., within one's immediate locus of control) as a way into challenges that could otherwise feel too big to tackle. As Rana—the head of school introduced earlier in the chapter (Egyptian American/Muslim)—explained, "it's really overwhelming when you look at it [the social justice challenges at hand] all at once, but we can take a moment to focus on our immediate context." Teacher leader D. (introduced earlier, first-generation Latino) likewise begins by asking, "What can I control in my classroom that's making this a place where kids want to be, kids want to learn?" Although these individualized steps may not solve the problem as a whole, it was important, he explained, to "work with what we've got."

As mentioned, for many of the leaders in our study, an emerging sense of agency—and locus of control—began with concrete, local, and immediate actions and foci. Although it is, of course, essential to understand these efforts as part of a larger arc and continuum of social justice leadership and advocacy, we spotlight them here as powerful starting points and essential, granular aspects of a more encompassing, intersectional approach.

Capturing this idea, Jean-Claude—a district-level coordinator of curriculum and teacher leadership who identified as an Asian American male in his forties strongly influenced by the progressive values of his West Coast city—described how taking small steps as an individual helps him better manage the stresses and urgencies of climate change and environmental injustice. "One way of coping with it," he explained, is by "learning more about it and taking some small action within my own life that could somehow help the situation. That's one piece or one way of coping with it." Although Jean-Claude had the internal, developmental capacity needed to have a bigger-picture understanding of the vast complexity of climate change, he simultaneously recognized how engaging in smaller, concrete acts—in concert with other acts and the efforts of others—could add up to significant change over time.

As a core aspect of justice-centering leadership with the potential to carry through *all* layers of our model, then, we next celebrate and explore the promise of leaders' concrete actions, both in schools and out.

TAKING TANGIBLE ACTION STEPS

To help illustrate what it looked and felt like for leaders to engage, as a first step, in the concrete domain, we first share the reflections of Yaacov, the teacher leader and middle school coordinator we introduced earlier (Orthodox Jewish father). Recalling how he tries to operationalize the call to right in concrete but significant ways, he explained, "Try to do a little bit of good every day. That would be my world view, I guess." Further illustrating his stance, he recounted a few examples of moments that stood out to him from his work with students:

> I had this one kid I'd always eat lunch with. I'd bring him peanut butter sandwiches. Like I'd try to do other things, like I don't know, I brought a kid a pair of glasses once 'cause she didn't have glasses. . . . So those are just kind of individual things. Like I'm not changing the world. I'm just buying this one kid glasses 'cause she doesn't have glasses.

As Yaacov explained, working "on a small level" to develop "a connection with a kid"—by providing companionship, sandwiches, and/or glasses—might not make him a "superhero," as he put it, but it *can* make a real difference for the individuals impacted. These connections—made through tangible actions and behaviors—can also, as they did for Yaacov, provide fuel and energy for the hard work ahead. "I guess that's what kind of keeps me coming back as a teacher," he reflected.

In a similarly meaningful story, James—a teacher leader and middle school department chair who identified as a mixed-race/Hispanic male and a born-again Christian—recounted a teaching practice he felt provided students access to more high-level learning *and* built community connections. "My students' elementary education doesn't have a whole lot of science involved in it," he explained. "So when they come to me, I'm a real science teacher. We do experiments, we use microscopes, we do a lot of stuff with plants and dissections." In addition to addressing issues of access, James sees his work as a way of incorporating and paying forward his love of gardening and learning—with and for students. As he shared with us, this love translated into a learning tradition that addressed a particular need in his school *and* connected hundreds of students and families:

> I have a plant that I got in my graduate studies. It's a papyrus plant. So the papyrus plant is used to make paper, right? In ancient Egypt they would make paper out of papyrus. It's an aquatic plant so it grows in water. So they're really easy to keep alive, they submerge, you can just submerge them in water and they'll just grow like crazy. So what I do is I kind of made like . . . four or five lessons at different grade levels where we take the papyrus plants, we cut one of the stems off, and we just put it upside down in water. And from there, it will grow roots, and the roots will fill the container, and it will grow a new plant. . . . So we call it Poppy the Papyrus. That's the name of the plant. And for many years on the last day of school, I would give away like fifty or sixty of these plants and wrap them up in a big sheet of paper that's kind of like when you go to the florist and you get plants. And [the students] would go home on the bus with them, and I have their siblings and their siblings would remember—some of them still have it. . . . It was just like a way to connect to different grades and to kind of have a schoolwide thing going. . . . Hundreds and hundreds of plants we made over a decade.

Hundreds of plants made, shared, and nurtured over a decade! Although James explained that some students called him "the plant guy or the nutty professor or something" because of his lab coats and enthusiasm, he humbly admitted, "Yeah, I think they like it. It's been positive." Reflecting on the literal and figurative beauty of James' papyrus plants sprouting across his community—and sprouting community—over time, we can think of no better symbol for the connective power of concrete actions offered with intention, care, and heart.

In addition, a few participants in our study—like Sylvia, a thirty-eight-year-old district-level leader who identified as Puerto Rican, Christian, and a mother—described the importance of working *outside* of school to be of good service and advance equity. These concrete "extracurricular" efforts were especially important to leaders working in contexts that were less welcoming or even hostile to social justice advocacy, and for leaders who had not yet figured out how to blend their personal commitments to justice with their professional roles. As Sylvia explained, recounting some of the service experiences most important to her,

> I do a food pantry that I organize once a month, and in the community I do a toy drive every year that I organize, a turkey drive for the community. So I'm very active in the community aspect outside of work or what I do, and I think that helps fulfill that part of me.

Evan, too—a district-level curriculum leader who identified as a thirty-six-year-old, white, cisgender male with thirteen years in education—explained that, outside of work, he is very "involved in activism" and political causes, even spearheading and participating in demonstrations. Yet, the "norms and decorum of being an administrator" in his organization made it more difficult to bring these expressions of his commitments explicitly to the foreground, professionally. As he shared,

> It's hard to believe that it's possible to be a special educator or a history educator without translating this into the work in a more specific way. So I'm trying, I guess, to find how to connect the dots in that regard. And it's challenging.

Both in school and out, then, the tangible nature of *doing something* to make the world a better place emerged as an important starting place and focus for leaders. Although, as we mentioned, engaging in immediate, tangible actions can become part of larger, more encompassing approaches as leaders gain more perspective and internal capacity, we find it important to celebrate the call to right as an entry point with an open door for anyone seeking a way into justice-centering leadership.

In the next section, we turn to another important aspect of leading in the concrete domain foregrounded by the leaders in our study: focusing on logistics and the technical, measurable dimensions of practice.

FOCUSING ON THE MEASURABLE AND TECHNICAL

Just as leaders who were making meaning with some element of an instrumental way of knowing (and those seeking to gain a first foothold in the work of justice-centering leadership) tended to begin with a focus on their own, concrete actions, a number of leaders in our study described the importance of attending to the *technical* dimensions of representation and inclusion—in classrooms, curricula, and communications. Although equity certainly cannot be achieved only by attending to the quantitative dimensions of access and representation (i.e., who and what is included in learning spaces and lessons), participants recognized the fundamental importance of interrogating what can be counted in schools by looking both without and within to examine their systems and themselves.

As Angela—a thirty-one-year-old district-level teacher development leader who identified as African American with West Indian heritage, as well as a heterosexual Christian woman with nine years in education—explained,

> One of the ways that I look for equity in the work that I'm doing is I look to see how many students are in the classroom. . . . I'll look to see who gets responded to, who doesn't? Who gets called on? I'll look to see how behaviors are dealt with, you know?

I think looking at teacher interactions with students shows what teachers value and what teachers think students can do or can't do—that's the lens of equity as well. I mean there are so many different things that you never think about until you see it in action. I look to see who sits with who, who doesn't sit with who. I look to see behavior practices 'cause these are all equity, right? Those are the things that I'm kind of getting leaders to shift and look at when they look into classrooms.

In her sharing, Angela explains how she focuses on what can be measured, observed, and adjusted as one key lens for taking stock of the work ahead with the teachers in her care. These important and grounded foci, she also explained, can serve as readily accessible action items for colleagues to notice and attend to.

For some participants, this kind of purposeful noticing and accounting took a more inward turn and coincided with their growing understanding that thinking more critically about their *own* actions, understandings, and positionality was another important responsibility of and expectation for justice-centering leaders. As May—an academic dean in a charter middle school who identified as a white woman in her thirteenth year in education—recounted,

I send out a family memo every week, and it occurred to me as I was putting a picture—I always put one picture a week of either a group of kids or one student, and I was going to put a picture of Matthew, who is blond and white. And I thought, "Let's look back and see who you've had in the past." And I thought, "No, I have representations of too many white kids in here." And I thought, "Wow, I can't believe that I was not even aware of that." That bothered me. So I changed the picture.

Although a welcome and important shift in its own right, May's realization that she had been overrepresenting white students in her school's communications—and her subsequent decision to change her practice in this instance—can feel limited in scope and impact if not incorporated into a larger constellation of efforts. Here, again, we can see how attending to the measurable and technical dimensions of leadership requires *at least* some instrumental capacity—but it can also continue to grow and evolve as leaders gain new internal capacities, perspective, and experience.

Indeed, without additional, coordinated efforts, focusing only on the immediate, tangible, and countable can leave educators struggling to effect the change they really wish to see, even when they approach their work with passionate engagement. For example, D. (teacher leader, first-generation Latino) described how important it was for him to bring issues of equity—and diverse topics and voices—into his curricula, as a matter of principle and conviction. By paying attention to what was—and was not—covered in his classes, he was able to develop more representative and accurate lesson plans for his students. As D. confided, however, his curricular restructuring nonetheless left him feeling isolated within the broader culture of the school, which in his mind still felt unchanged and unchallenged. As he explained,

> The school doesn't celebrate women's history, Latino history, Black history—none of that shit. I'm in the classroom by myself talking about suffrage, suffragettes that history forgot. We're talking about Sojourner Truth, Ida B. Wells. I'm not a U.S. history teacher. I'm a global history teacher . . . but I *have* to weave that in.

Zooming in on and honoring D.'s relatable feeling of frustration, in the next section, we dive more deeply into leaders' feelings of being "stuck" on a growing edge—or, in this case, what it was like for them to lead on the boundary of the concrete domain with what felt like a limited locus of control. We turn also to the supports leaders named as *key developmental stretches* for leadership and internal capacity building through this transition.

DEVELOPMENTAL GROWING EDGES AND KEY SUPPORTS FOR GROWTH: BUILDING ON INSTRUMENTAL CAPACITIES

Lamenting how hard it was to impact the kind of change they wished to see at the time, some of the leaders in our study who were making meaning with elements of an instrumental way of knowing—and those who had not yet grown to expand their practice much beyond the concrete domain—confided feelings of professional frustration and limitation. As Serena—a thirty-one-year-old, central office special education leader who identified as a cisgender, Caribbean American woman—explained, "In terms of my current role, it's very limited. I'm not able to really work for social justice in the way that I want." Confined by what she perceived to be the rules and boundaries of her work, Serena felt stuck between what she was "allowed" to do and what she thought would be best for students and families. Similarly, Jack—a fifty-four-year-old assistant principal who identified as Eastern European/Slavic and an immigrant—described his own feelings of disempowerment, connecting them to the bounded nature of his position. "I would like to impact the profession a lot more," he confided, "[but] I don't have an outlet." Reflecting further, he shared, "I'm trying to attempt change from the wrong position in the organization. I need to become a principal so people value my opinion." For Jack, assuming the principalship would mean amplifying his influence in a hierarchical system, allowing his "voice to be able to reach people." Without that formalized authority, he felt, he wasn't authorized to do the things he'd "love to do but can't." "Nobody listens to me right now," he confided.

Although some participants, like Jack and Serena, attributed their perceived lack of power to their professional role and position in the hierarchy, others described feeling overwhelmed by the sheer magnitude of the world's inequities. As Yaacov put it,

> We have a society that's constructed and . . . some people have been screwed over worse than others. But like what should I do about that, you know? . . . I totally buy into that we're all affected by the decisions of people from hundreds of years ago or thousands of years ago—or the luck of the draw of where you were born and who you were born to. I totally agree with that. I just don't know what I'm supposed to make of that.

Although starting with concrete actions, behaviors, and adjustments is certainly *one* entry point into the complex imperatives of teaching and leading today, a number of leaders shared with us their experiences of realizing they wanted to do and try even more.

Accordingly, we next spotlight two key experiences that leaders named as foundational to stretching their practice and agency:

- explicit learning about issues of equity, identity, history, education, and their intersections (i.e., through reading and purposeful study); and

- making connections and building relationships across lines of difference to expand one's worldview and understandings.

In the next sections, we synthesize insights from leaders across our study who—despite making meaning with different ways of knowing at the time of our interviews—were able to look back on these two shared, foundational learning experiences as key to growing beyond some of their earliest, taken-for-granted, and previously unquestioned understandings of the world, as well as developing the capacity to more fully stand with others in good company. Reminiscent of the insights shared by authors and activists Winona Guo and Priya Vulchi (2019)—who traversed the United States after graduating high school to invite Americans to share their stories and experiences of race and racism—the leaders' reflections we share next illustrate the importance of coupling *informational* learning with the *interpersonal* dimensions of lived experience. In this way, as we will describe, participants were able to begin to heed the call of professor, scholar, and current president of the American Educational Research Association, H. Richard Milner, IV (2020), to *Start Where You Are, But Don't Stay There*—as he titled his impactful book about preparing educators for racially diverse schools and classrooms.

EXPLICIT EQUITY LEARNING FOR GREATER PERSPECTIVE TAKING AND UNDERSTANDING

As May's earlier example (of changing the picture of the white student on her memo to families) makes clear, ongoing learning about oneself, others, and the world is critical for teachers, leaders, and anyone seeking to contribute to greater justice and equity. In fact, for the leaders in our study who, at the time of our interviews, were primarily foregrounding (or remembering) concrete actions and instrumental capacities in their justice-centering leadership, *learning*—through intentional study, self-reflection, and ongoing exposure to diversity and difference—emerged as one of the most important supports for greater perspective taking and capacity building. Developmentally speaking, this kind of targeted learning helped participants enlarge their inner and outer worlds, as they were able to understand more of the "what" and the "why" of equity and justice and better place themselves in historical, professional, and personal perspective. Importantly, explicit learning and study proved to be a support without bounds; participants across the developmental continuum continued to find it of value no matter their level of experience and expertise. Given the vast array of ideas, lenses, theories, and histories to uncover, there's always something new to learn. Yet, for leaders earlier in their journeys—and those looking to stretch their internal capacities beyond the concrete domain—tapping into the literature about social justice proved foundational. As the saying goes, you can't know what you don't know until you know you don't know it.

Perhaps most seminal of all supports, then, explicit and ongoing learning about race, racism, identity, history, and injustice (in school and out) was key for the leaders in our study, and especially for those who were making meaning with some elements of an instrumental way of knowing and/or relying largely on concrete practices earlier in their leadership. Learning more about the world, leaders explained, helped them see beyond the bounds of their individual lived experiences and begin to see more deeply into others'. Toward this same end, and as we will spotlight next, many leaders who identified as white and many leaders of color named explicit learning as *essential* for their development and initiation as justice-centering leaders, although for different reasons.

Seeing the World More Fully as a White Leader

Many of the leaders in our study who identified as white made special mention of the different level of responsibility they felt to engage in learning about race, racism, and history, as it had *not* automatically been a part of their schooling, training, or lived experience growing up white in the United States. Reflecting on the most helpful supports she'd been provided by her school system, for example, May (the academic dean we introduced earlier, white) explained, "We did a lot of professional development around being aware of what you look like and what you bring to the table and what your biases are. So that really added so much depth to my understanding." Like May, many other white leaders in our study named this kind of learning as key to shifting their understandings—of themselves, their unconscious biases, and the lived realities of Black, Indigenous, and other people of color.

Henrietta, for example—a co-founder of an educational nonprofit who identified as a white married female—described the learning and exposure that helped her understand more about the world and herself after growing up on a farm in a rural white community. As she explained, when going to college,

> It started to sort of hit me, you know, wow, there is this whole other world out there. And I will tell you, my first sort of emotional feeling . . . was I was really scared because I didn't want to say something or do something that is stupid and insensitive because I realize how ignorant I am of anything outside of my little small town. So, my first experience at the university was actually one of fear, not because I was afraid of other people, but because I was afraid of myself.

Reading and learning about the connections between education and racism—and injustice more broadly—was likewise essential for Kathy, a teacher leader who also identified as a white woman. As she shared, "if I wasn't exposed to all those texts, I wouldn't know any of what I've been learning about because nobody ever talked to me about this, you know, growing up." Cheryl—a district-level school improvement leader who identified as a white woman, and a wife and mother with eighteen years in education—also recounted the deeper understanding and shift in self-concept that accompanied some of her foundational equity learning. As she explained,

> I think when I first started this, I just couldn't believe that anybody would assume that I would hold racist beliefs or implicit biases. I couldn't believe that 'cause I was like, "Whoa! Then you just don't know me, you know?" So then I did my own education about myself, and like everybody holds racist beliefs because we live in the United States and this is how we're indoctrinated—it's just a fact. And so challenging myself and putting myself out there—that's definitely another key. The leader has to do the work and do it publicly.

Uncovering Hidden Histories as a Leader of Color

Many of our participants of color likewise named the importance of intentional learning—to better understand themselves and others and to deepen understandings of the rich history and contributions of people of color in the United States and across the world. By developing what professor and author Gholdy Muhammad (2020) describes as "historically responsive literacy," students and educators of color—and all people—can situate themselves in fuller and more accurate stories than those typically represented in school curricula. As Janae—a leader in a national philanthropic organization with an educational focus who identified as a Black woman and mother—explained,

> It's no surprise to me that people feel the way they do because of what they're taught in school. You could go to school—my children's school, included, which is why I pulled them out. You can go through school and think and state that no Black person,

no Native American, no Latino person, or no Chinese American or anybody from [groups] other than white did anything important. It could happen.

Relatedly, Luz—a principal who identified as a cisgender, Black Afro-Latina woman with twenty years in education—described her own experiences with unlearning and relearning history to accurately reflect her own cultural power and legacy, as sparked by an awakening in college:

> As a Latina woman of color who grew up not knowing very much about my history and where my people came from, and not discovering that Puerto Ricans had written anything or had been successful in any way up until I made it into college, it was a moment where I felt really robbed of something that I needed to know about myself and my people. It was a really, really painful experience for me when I first realized that I had been robbed of that part of me through my education. It was as heartbreaking and damaging as it was empowering because it led me on this journey to really learn Puerto Rican history and then really figure out the ways in which, when I came into a classroom to teach, that I would never allow young people to exist through a whole high school experience, through a whole school experience not knowing anything about themselves.

Sadly, the whitewashing and deliberate obfuscation described by Janae and Luz remains the norm rather than the exception in many school curricula. And this is despite abundant evidence that learning about race, racism, and the accomplishments and contributions of diverse groups of people throughout one's education can actually *help* children from all backgrounds deepen empathy, reduce bias, and enhance positive cross-racial esteem and solidarity (Lewis, 2022; Mosley & Heiphetz, 2021; Perry, Skinner-Dorkenoo, Wages, & Abaied, 2021). These research findings—and our learnings from leaders' sharings—offer a clear rebuke to attacks on equity learning and bans on theoretical orientations like Critical Race Theory. To center human dignity and potential in schools and in the world, it is essential—in history just as in one's personal psychology—to make conscious the roots and legacies of racism (and isms of all kinds) that have been purposefully constructed and concealed, and thus made more insidious by illusions of inevitability. Unearthing the hidden things that "run" us in the psychological sense—individually and as a society—is one key way to diminish the influence of harmful systems, patterns, and untruths and yield greater empowerment.

Centering Equity Learning in Educator Preparation and Professional Learning

Not only did participants share with us that they often lacked explicit learning about equity, race, and history in their early lives and formal schooling, but—all too often—their training to become a teacher or school leader did not involve explicit learning about equity, identity, cultural literacy, and/or advocacy, especially for educators who had been in the field for many years. As Jean-Claude—the district-level coordinator of curriculum and teacher leadership we introduced earlier (Asian American)—explained,

> A lot of us went into teaching not necessarily knowing how to think about social justice. Or we weren't social scientists necessarily, right? . . . So I think there's a whole lot of learning that we need to engage in. Certainly as educators, but as citizens in general. So whatever opportunities we can create for educators to learn to do this [i.e., support greater equity] and not make the assumptions that they somehow already know how to do this, I think is so crucial. . . . Somehow [we] find ourselves in this position because many of us feel the need and calling to do this work, and want to do it and have a passion to do it, [but it] does not necessarily mean that we have learned how to do it, right?

The importance of continuous learning for educators was echoed by Cheryl, the district-level school improvement leader we introduced earlier (white), when she said of herself and her team, "Just because we're all learning and just because we all have a passion, it doesn't mean we all have the tools."

On the contrary, Yaacov (teacher leader, Orthodox Jewish father) described how learning alongside classmates in his graduate leadership program helped him to lean into the need for learning as universal and as something to be embraced as essential and ongoing:

> I also feel like I gained a lot of . . . confidence [because] all the people in my cohort who have gone on to be principals or APs or whatever, they're also just kind of figuring it out. I feel like that was also very important to learn, that it's not like when you become an AP you magically know everything.

As these leaders' reflections help illustrate, even though teacher and leader preparation programs are increasingly shifting to more explicitly address race and equity in preservice coursework, there remains a palpable need in the field for justice-centering professional learning and training.

CONNECTING ACROSS LINES OF DIFFERENCE: EMBRACING DIVERSITY FOR A LARGER, MORE INCLUSIVE WORLD

In addition to direct learning, leaders from across our study also named *experiencing* diversity—including relationships with people from different backgrounds and exposure to diverse cultures and communities—as another early and ongoing support that helped them first expand their practices and understandings, especially when they were working to see beyond the confines of taken-for-granted worldviews and right/wrong orientations. Whether through travel, day-to-day experiences, or the act of teaching itself, sustained exposure to diversity proved a real gift for participants seeking to grow as advocates for justice—and a kind of developmental springboard for more inclusive, cosmopolitan sensitivities and emerging capacities for empathy and perspective taking.

Travel as a Window Into Diversity

For example, Serena, a central office special education leader (Caribbean American), explained that some of the most important learning for students *and adults* involves developing "an understanding that your reality isn't everybody else's reality, right? Like your political views, your religious views, just your views in general don't have to be everybody else's." Teaching and leading is not, she had come to see, "using political tools to get people to be a certain way or to think the way you do." Rather, it "encompasses empathy."

Reflecting on what enabled this important, developmental shift toward more socializing capacities, Serena told us that travel had been central to her realization. An avid traveler who aspired to visit all of the continents "besides Antarctica" by her thirty-third birthday, Serena felt that travel had endowed her with a deeper understanding of the different realities of people's lives. As she explained, "I think that I wouldn't have the viewpoints that I have if I didn't travel. I think that it's easy to be in a bubble and to have limited viewpoints if you haven't experienced life outside."

Making a similar point, Sylvia, a district-level leader (Puerto Rican/Christian), recounted the transformational impact travel had had on her life *and* her marriage:

> I was probably twenty-one when I did my first overseas trip, twenty-one, twenty-two, and then at twenty-four, I led my first team to an orphanage in Mexico to love on the kids, really support the staff because they're there full time. And so just to really serve them. And they became like my extended family, and for five years, we went straight every summer. I would go to the orphanage. I would bring a team and that was, that was actually [laughs]—that was the deciding factor with my husband, actually. I told him, "Listen, I know that my life and my calling is to do this kind of work, to travel and serve and help kids in need, orphanages, communities, like just helping them. Whether it's to build a school or build a home, this is what I want to do. And if you want to marry me, you have to come with me to one of these trips." So he said, "Okay, sure, why not?". . . . His life was totally transformed. He went from being this guy who had never traveled, never had a passport. His bubble was all he knew. . . . Like how does your life not get transformed?

Although, as you know, travel—like learning—can continue to infuse and inform leaders' understandings as advocates and human beings over the course of a lifetime and regardless of one's way of knowing, it may be an especially impactful and eye-opening experience for leaders foregrounding more instrumental capacities and/or just beginning to expand their under-standings of diversity. As we will discuss next, connecting across lines of difference—within one's professional work just as in travel—emerged as another key experience for leaders working to stretch their capacities and understandings.

Connecting Across Lines of Difference as an Educator

Margot—an assistant superintendent who described herself as white-presenting but multiracial, with Jewish and Native American heritage—recognized how essential it is to grow empathy and cultural capacity as a leader, and how engaging authentically with diversity as an educator can really impact one's worldview and capacity for connection over time. It's a practice, in other words, that we can practice! As Margot explained, linking her learning and current capacity not to travel but to the act of teaching and leading itself,

> You know, [in my work] I encounter many, many, many people and so I just have more experience being in other people's shoes, or trying to be, and so then that of course broadens your overall perspective and it adds to your experiences, and then once you experience that, it's like somehow your brain just grows. Your brain's an amazing thing.

This recollection of teaching and leading as fuel for learning—and (brain) development—was similarly voiced by Donald, a retired teacher leader and higher educator who identified as seventy-five years old, white, and Jewish. As he reflected, "I think the experience of [teaching] makes me [more] aware because I've had the opportunity of really getting to know so many wonderful kids—for decades, so many great kids." Yaacov (teacher leader, Orthodox Jewish father) likewise expressed gratitude for the ways teaching has enriched his life and broadened his perspectives, "just [by] being exposed to like a hundred fifty kids a year from all different walks of life."

Naming the Detrimental Effects of Segregation and Separation

Working across lines of difference can be an enriching experience for all people—regardless of way of knowing or identity—but we were struck by the responsibility felt by many of the leaders in our study, and especially those who identified as white, to acknowledge and take a greater perspec-tive on the lack of diverse experiences and relationships they tended to have growing up. Given the enduring legacy of segregation in this country, and the racist lie perpetuated by white supremacy that, as whiteness scholar Robin

DiAngelo (2021) characterized it, white people "lose nothing of value by living in segregation" (p. 9), this shared realization is perhaps not much of a surprise—even as it remained a powerful call to action.

For example, Norma—a dean and ESL coordinator who identified as a thirty-two-year-old, cisgender white woman who grew up in a low-SES household in the Midwestern United States and who also lived abroad in South Africa—underscored how important diversity had been in her life and ongoing learning. "I know that I've been enriched because I've had the opportunity to learn from a lot of different people," she explained. Yet, when reflecting on her upbringing, she couldn't help but feel a divide separating her from family who'd never had experiences or relationships across lines of difference. As she explained,

> I think it's important for others to connect to people who are different from them so that they are learning new things. When I think about my grandparents, both of them, I love them dearly. But they've lived lives that are very much with people who are similar to them. That leads them to have a very narrow worldview. It's made it hard for us to connect on some level because they don't understand the work I do.

Unlike people of color, who, for the very purpose of *surviving* in a racist society, need to be able to read, understand, and interpret the unspoken norms of the cultural majority, many white adults—like Norma's grandparents—can live much of their lives without needing to engage meaningfully with people from different cultures, backgrounds, races, religions, or political orientations. Even when these adults have developed more sophisticated internal capacities in other domains—like tuning into the feelings and emotional states of loved ones, or advocating for, say, equal pay or good working conditions—they often find that, when it comes to understanding race, diversity, and inequity, there are parts of their self-systems that remain underdeveloped or even unacknowledged by virtue of their life experiences. Although different, in some ways, than the shift instrumental knowers must make when growing beyond their right/wrong orientations and inherited understandings of the world, adults in this position can follow learning pathways parallel to the ones described just above as they work to bring these parts of themselves into more conscious awareness. The truth is, we all have lesser-seen parts of ourselves that we can grow, explore, and fill up as developing human beings.

For educators who, we argue, are tasked by their very profession to teach about and model fundamental human dignity and potential, this kind of intentional learning and growth is especially essential to mitigate the steep learning curves some educators enter with in relation to identity and equity. As Angela, a district-level teacher development leader (African American/West Indian/Christian) explained, schools have to "make sure that students are not suffering at the hands of adults because adults don't know." Donald, too, (the retired teacher leader/higher educator we introduced earlier, white/Jewish) recognized this kind of learning and empathy as a *responsibility* for justice-centering leaders. As he put it, "We live [and work] in a diverse community, and so therefore there's a certain responsibility to understand what other people are like and to see their perspective." As these leaders' sharings suggest, connecting across lines of difference can be a powerful support for many leaders' growth—but growing beyond the concrete domain of justice-centering leadership means coming also to recognize and embrace the beauty of diversity for its own sake and not just as a learning opportunity for some.

In the next and final section of this chapter, we share leaders' close-up reflections about living and learning their way *beyond* the concrete domain of practice—and accompanying others as they integrated their instrumental capacities and concrete orientations into larger, more encompassing approaches to centering justice.

LEADERSHIP IN TRANSITION: GROWING BEYOND THE CONCRETE DOMAIN

Throughout this chapter, we shared examples of what it looked like, sounded like, and felt like when leaders foregrounded instrumental, concrete approaches to centering justice—often as initial or early steps into leading on behalf of equity and justice. Even though leaders across the developmental continuum can—and should—continue to act in ways that include tangible demonstrations of care as part of a larger constellation of efforts and initiatives (remember: the core cylinder representing the concrete domain runs throughout the *entirety* of our model), our focus so far has largely been on leaders' bounded experiences *within* the concrete domain, up and down the "cylinder." But what was it like for leaders to grow their locus of control and agency upward and out toward the next domain—the interpersonal? What internal shifts, new understandings, and capacities accompanied this transition? What helped leaders recognize concrete actions not as their *only* response, but as an important *part* of a multiplicity of responses, their own and others'?

In this section, and as illustrated in Figure 3.2, we focus on the transition *between* domains and how growing toward a more socializing way of knowing provided leaders with an entry point into a new and qualitatively distinct area of focus: the interpersonal.

Specifically, we share leaders' experiences with two important developmental shifts that informed their practice as growing leaders:

- an emerging capacity to see beyond "right" and "wrong," as defined by one's inherited worldview, and

- a willingness to look beyond technical, concrete solutions.

We hope that these leaders' stories help bring to even greater life the on-the-ground experience of developing as advocates and leaders for justice.

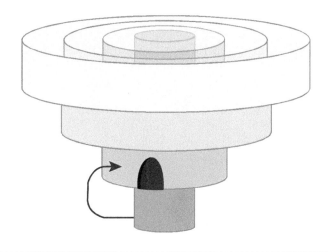

GROWING BEYOND RIGHT AND WRONG

From a developmental perspective, the capacity to look beyond one's immediate circumstances and understandings of what is "right" or "wrong" is
indeed a key advance on the constructive-developmental gyre (i.e., moving
from an instrumental to a more socializing way of knowing). It is also a shift
that leaders in our study offered much insight into.

Looking back on a deeply personal time of growth and upheaval, for instance,
Brent—an assistant principal who identified as a white, gay, married male in
his mid-thirties—reflected on what it was like to move through this kind of
transition, or as he put it, to be "kicked out of all the black and white lines"
as he worked to understand and accept his sexuality. As he shared,

> I thought I wanted to be a teacher from a pretty young age. You
> know, I'd play school with stuffed animals and teach them and
> draft my brother and sister into it as well. It was either that or
> [religious service], but I think that both in my mind were very
> related. Both were a form of education to try and make a difference
> in the world. And so those two lines were very connected and then
> I decided to go to a Christian college and pursue a more devoted
> life to the church. I continued to wrestle with that and with my
> sexual orientation, and after college, I majored in writing and
> theology. And, after college I decided to move and join what I
> would identify now as a cult, and was involved with that, doing
> reparative therapy to try to not be gay for about three years. And
> while there, I attended seminary with the idea in mind that I would

become either a religious studies professor or a minister. And about three years into the experience there, and the reparative therapy, I just said I can't do this anymore, I can't, I think that I am gay and that's a part of my identity that's not, that I'm not able to shift. So that was a real crisis of who I was and of faith because it seemed to conflict with everything I believed about the universe.

Although incredibly painful, Brent shared how his journey helped him to see beyond an ingrained belief that "there's a right way to be a human being." "Real learning is all gray," he concluded, because the black and white lines "can't work for everyone." And, "if they can't work for everyone, they can't work for democracy."

Paralleling the importance of disentangling *oneself* from taken-for-granted and imprinted worldviews, Ella—a director of culture and language learning who identified as a thirty-four-year-old African American woman—reflected on how the internal, developmental shift toward more socializing capacities can help educators avoid teaching or leading from an assumptive stance about who others are or should be. As she explained,

> I think a lot of it has to do with people's own cultural backgrounds and how they were raised and them kind of wanting children to have the same experience. . . . I don't think that's equality. I think that that's just like—I would say elitism. It's this idea that my background is superior, so I'm going to use my background and apply it to this context. And I think that that's been a lot that's happened. People kind of bring their, you know, "This is what my experience was. I think it was great. I'm doing well, so I want them to have the same experience."

Further illustrating what it was like to shift from a *me*-focus to a *you*-focus as an educator (i.e., leading with questions like, "What's important to you?" and "How are you experiencing what's happening?" instead of, "How does this affect me?" or "How might my understandings apply?"), Ella recounted an important transformation in her own development as a teacher— specifically as a new teacher working with emergent multilingual students:

> My first year of teaching, I saw a lot of how my judgment of my students played out in how I was teaching them. And how some of them were not really receiving the lessons because they weren't connected to the idea of the student I was teaching. What I mean is, I was a bilingual education teacher. I had students who were considered long-term English language learners. When I came into this school, they were accustomed to taking ESL in Spanish. Which seems counterintuitive, right? So, I came in, I said, "No, you're not going to be learning English in Spanish. You're going to be learning English in English, 'cause that's how you learn." For a

thirteen-year-old, an eighth grader? They were just beyond upset. They were like, "You don't know how to teach, you don't know what you're doing." A part of me was just like, "Really though?" Because I was thinking, "This is obvious. . . . Like, how are you missing this?" So part of my bias came in as this: these are just kids that really need a lot of help, 'cause they just don't know. And the reality is that they had a lot to offer. And that I had created this space where *I* was the knower, and they needed to realize that I knew. When in reality, I was the *teacher*, and within that definition of teacher to me, it means that you're also a student. And so, there has to be this space for a teacher to model what it means to be a student. And being a student is not one that thinks they know everything. You can't fill a cup that's already filled. In shifting my perspective, I shifted my approach.

As we share next, this internal transition described by Ella—from applying one's own understandings and beliefs to really seeing the inherent value, beauty, dignity, and potentialities of others—was also a key developmental shift for leaders working to expand and reframe concrete leadership strategies and understandings.

SEEING BEYOND CONCRETE, TECHNICAL SOLUTIONS

As mentioned in Chapter 2, when a person grows from an instrumental way of knowing to a more socializing way of knowing, their preoccupying concerns change as well. Whereas leaders who were primarily foregrounding instrumental capacities at the time of our study tended to prioritize and attend to more concrete, demonstrable elements of justice-centering practices in their work, other leaders were able to reflect on what it felt like when emerging socializing capacities helped them see more deeply into the internal, affective, and interpersonal dimensions of practice.

For example, Sylvia (district leader, Puerto Rican/Christian) recounted how important the relational side of her service work felt to her, both abroad and at home. Beyond the impulse to do good *for* others, she learned to stand *with* people and to appreciate the gifts she received as part of sharing herself. As she explained,

> Charity is an interesting thing. I think [in] our country, people do it so they can feel good and that's not the reason why I do it. I don't do it to feel good. I don't do it so my kids can feel good. It's really building relationships, empowering people, really supporting people. . . . When we do service, we [tend to] think of how much we're offering them, and it's really what they're doing for us. Like when I go to the orphanage—my first year I went I said, "Oh my God, I'm going to do such great things. I'm going to impact them." Heck no. They changed me.

Developing this socializing capacity to embrace the broader, connective power of concrete actions as part of a larger tapestry of change and healing can also help leaders move beyond what scholar, advocate, and author Gloria Ladson-Billings (2014) described as "very limited and superficial notions" of culturally relevant or socially just pedagogy (p. 77), or "the idea that adding some books about people of color, having a classroom Kwanzaa celebration, or posting 'diverse' images makes one 'culturally relevant'" (p. 82).

Indeed, when offered as one-off practices or in isolation from broader cultural shifts, lone diversity initiatives—although well-intended—can exacerbate feelings of harm and exclusion, a frustration shared by Ella (director of culture and language, African American) after a multicultural day at her diverse school:

> We had a multicultural day but I am not happy about it . . . but it was a good data point because the feedback we got was that a lot of parents didn't understand the purpose of a multicultural day because if you're your culture every day, why are we having one day to celebrate it? Like my child attends this school on an everyday basis.

Although we have experienced and learned about many school cultural celebrations that had a much different effect, especially when approached as part of an integrative suite of efforts, Ella's sharing foregrounds the stark limitation of only attending to culture and identity *sometimes*—or as a yes/no item to be checked off on a "to do" list of best practices.

Connecting this challenge explicitly to development and the growing edges of instrumental knowers who may see such concrete practices as meeting the "rules" and "requirements" for advancing equity, Thea—a district-level leader focused on teacher leadership who identified as a Black, married woman with ten years in education—offered the following:

> I think sometimes folks just want to be told what to do. When you think about that first part of the ways of knowing [instrumental], that's very challenging, I find, when you're doing this racial equity work because I can give you some ideas, but what it turns into— schools, they're looking for something concrete, right? Like give me the rubric or the checklist that shows me that I'm being racially literate. . . . They're looking for something very concrete, which I understand . . . but folks need to really think about it by looking at themselves first as a part of it, and practice developing these things together.

Irene, the independent school director of admissions introduced earlier in the chapter (white, Jewish), recounted a similar challenge in her context: "The issue was what the faculty wanted was [answers to questions like] 'How do we fix this?' You know, 'What do we *do*?' 'Give us the answers,' right?"

Taking an even wider view on why focusing primarily on the concrete in schools can be both a challenge and a lure, Shokry—an educational consultant who identified as a thirty-four-year-old person of color with mixed Dominican and Egyptian heritage—referenced the systemic push toward action and certainty confronting many school and political leaders. As he explained, "I think what I see in our media, [and] even from our government, is that they often seek to Band-Aid the symptoms of what are social justice issues with technical solutions." The same holds true in schools, he argued:

> Thinking about a lot of the problems that we look to resolve in schools and our classrooms, a lot of them tend to be challenges that can be resolved by a purchase. You know when it's a very direct issue and it's a matter of providing a resource, it allows us to feel like we accomplished something. But it very often doesn't get to the root of the more complex problems. I think helping people to understand that solving those complex problems isn't a matter of identifying them and throwing a solution at them, it's about gathering the stakeholders necessary to then . . . unearth the root of these problems.

To do this, Shokry explained, people need to be "engaged in the work" of examining "their bias, their errors, their misunderstandings—and often uncovering their fears." "That," he offered, "feels to me like much more progress than when I first began this work and [was] looking at technical solutions." Making this shift, as you know, also requires new, more complex internal capacities that leaders can grow and develop.

Although schools and society will always need concrete actions, policies, and laws to combat injustice and step toward change—especially in our current climate, in which many, many battles old and new are being fought on legal fronts—growing the capacity to take a wider perspective on the concrete, and to see more deeply into the affective, less tangible dimensions of lived experience and relationships emerged as an important developmental transition for leaders seeking to grow toward the interpersonal domain of practice. As we will explore in the next chapter, layering socializing capacities overtop instrumental ones provided leaders with a new entry point into justice-centering leadership, allowing them to expand both their focus and locus of control.

CHAPTER SYNOPSIS AND KEY TAKEAWAYS

How lovely to think that no one need wait a moment; we can start now, start slowly changing the world!

—Anne Frank (1959)

In this chapter, we focused on the leaders' experiences, practices, and sense-making within the central, concrete domain of justice-centering leadership—a domain that runs through and infuses each consecutive layer of our developmental model. We also recognized how leaders' instrumental capacities can serve as an entry point into this domain, even as leaders with more complex ways of making meaning can—and should—continue to take concrete steps toward "right" and "good" as part of their more encompassing, expansive approaches to centering justice. Toward this end, we heard from leaders about what it *felt like* to begin to stretch beyond the concrete by developing socializing capacities that, as we will explore in Chapter 4, provided a pathway toward the next domain in our model, the interpersonal.

To help synthesize and summarize some of the biggest ideas from this chapter, we present, in Figure 3.3, a list of takeaways. We also, in Table 3.1, provide an overview of leaders' featured practices in the concrete domain, as well as the stretches leaders named as most helpful for expanding their internal capacities and range of practice.

FIGURE 3.3 CHAPTER 3 TAKEAWAYS

- The desire to do good and right can serve as a powerful, ground-floor entry point into justice-centering educational leadership for adults with any way of knowing.

- To engage in the concrete domain of justice-centering practice, adults need at least some instrumental capacities, although they can continue to focus on the concrete and tangible as parts of a greater constellation of approaches as they grow.

- Many leaders who make meaning with an instrumental way of knowing—or those just starting out as justice-centering leaders—often find it helpful to begin with a focus on the concrete, tangible, observable, or measurable.

- Stretching beyond the concrete domain requires new, internal capacities (i.e., at least some element of a socializing way of knowing) that can be nurtured through explicit learning about equity, history, race and racism, education, and the intersections of all of these.

- Engaging authentically across lines of difference—through travel, teaching, and day-to-day life—can also be a powerful stretch for leaders' growth.

- Growing beyond the concrete domain of practice often means stretching beyond instrumental capacities—with a new perspective on one's inherited worldview and a sense that one's strictly right/wrong understandings of the world are incomplete.

- Although ways of knowing provide one important lens for considering leaders' experiences, they are interactive with and cannot be fully separated from other aspects of identity like race, culture, gender identity, sexual orientation, and more.

- All of these aspects of self influence the selves we bring to justice-centering leadership.

TABLE 3.1 OVERVIEW OF LEADERS' PRACTICE—AND GROWTH—IN THE CONCRETE DOMAIN

DOMAIN OF JUSTICE-CENTERING LEADERSHIP PRACTICE	PRIMARY FOCUS	PREREQUISITE INTERNAL CAPACITIES	FOREGROUNDED PRACTICES AND APPROACHES	EXPERIENCES THAT SUPPORT DEVELOPMENTAL STRETCHING AND GROWTH	REPRESENTATIVE QUOTES
Concrete	The local and immediate What can be done, seen, or measured	Instrumental	Recognizing and committing to social justice as a value Taking concrete, tangible, individual action steps Attending to the measurable and technical	Explicit learning about issues of equity, identity, history, education, and their intersections Making connections and building relationships across lines of difference to expand one's worldview and understandings	"What do I need to do to make this right, right now?" "I had this one kid I'd always eat lunch with. I'd bring him peanut butter sandwiches.... So those are just kind of individual things." "The idea of doing good in the world and trying to leave a positive impact was something modeled for me and seeded from a very young age."

Before turning to the next chapter, we invite you to consider the following questions. You might want to reflect on them privately first and then perhaps engage in discussion with a partner and/or team.

1. After reading this chapter, what is top of mind and top or bottom of heart for you?

2. How, if at all, do you feel any of the stories, ideas, and discussions connect with your own experience and wisdom? Your own justice-centering leadership?

3. What are two or three of the larger insights you've had as you read this chapter? Who, if anyone, are you thinking about?

4. How, if at all, might you share some of the stories, ideas, and/or practices featured in this chapter?

5. After reading this chapter and considering leaders' stories about the concrete domain of the model, what, if anything, might you like to practice and/or do differently in general? In your justice-centering leadership?

6. Early in the chapter, Bernard said, "I've tried to model being right, just doing the right thing, and I try to exemplify that in my leadership, in my behavior as a teacher." What are some ways you try to model "doing the right thing"? Where do you think your understanding of "right" has come from?

7. Yaacov summed up his worldview as "Try to do a little bit of good every day." What are some concrete, tangible steps you currently take—and/or some others that you'd like to take—to make a positive contribution?

8. Serena reflected about how "it's easy to be in a bubble and to have limited viewpoints if you haven't experienced life outside." Who or what has helped you see the world through others' eyes? What experiences and/or learning opportunities have felt most formative to you in this way? What was it about those that felt helpful? Meaningful? Important?

9. After reading this chapter, what is something you'd like to think more deeply about? Do differently? Learn more about?

10. What, if anything, would you like to think more about before turning to Chapter 4?

CHAPTER 4

....

RELATING AND CONNECTING IN COMMUNITY

Leading for Social Justice With Socializing Capacities

There is one skill at the center of any healthy family, company, classroom, community, university, or nation: the ability to see someone else deeply, to know another person profoundly, to make them feel heard and understood.

—David Brooks (2020)

In this chapter, we turn to the second domain in our developmental model for justice-centering leadership: the interpersonal. But what do we mean by "interpersonal"? As we define it, the interpersonal domain involves a focus on the emotional, relational work essential for strengthening bonds, belonging, and inclusion between people and groups. It is, in other words, about caring for people's inner, emotional states and the learning and transformation that can happen through relationships. A preoccupying question in this domain, for example, might be something like, "How do I make sure others are feeling cared for and seen?" As illustrated in Figure 4.1, this chapter teases out the interpersonal domain as the second cylindrical layer of our developmental model—that runs through the layers above *and* still incorporates elements of the concrete domain that came before (in the diagram, you can see the concrete domain inside).

FIGURE 4.1 SOCIALIZING CAPACITIES AS ENTRY POINT INTO THE INTERPERSONAL DOMAIN OF JUSTICE-CENTERING EDUCATIONAL LEADERSHIP

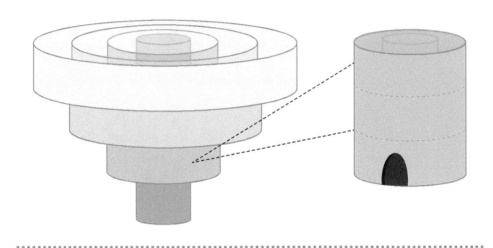

Once again, the open door in the diagram is a reminder that entering the interpersonal domain of practice requires specific internal capacities—in this case, at least some elements of a socializing way of knowing and a centering concern for others—although leaders can, of course, still engage very effectively in the interpersonal domain as self-authoring and self-transforming knowers (hence the stacked height of the cylinder).

As we began to explore in Chapter 3, moving beyond the concrete domain of practice involves recognizing that one's inherited, right/wrong views of the world don't necessarily apply universally—and involves the emergence of a greater capacity for perspective taking and empathy. Although leaders making meaning largely with instrumental ways of knowing can, of course, have and value relationships—and can be very generous and caring—they have not yet grown the capacity to more fully stand in another's shoes. A hallmark of the socializing way of knowing, this new capacity—to really tune into others' needs, feelings, and experiences—can help leaders incorporate concrete practices into an even wider field of action and agency that now includes highly effective *interpersonal* practices. In other words, it's not about letting go of concrete actions, but rather about working hard toward justice *while caring deeply for and attending to people's inner worlds*. In this new domain of practice, the two go hand in hand. As Jean-Claude—a district-level coordinator of curriculum and teacher leadership who identified as an Asian American male in his forties—put it, capturing this big idea, "Social justice is about changing things bit by bit, brick by brick . . . [but] it also means . . . getting at people's emotions as well, because I think there's a whole affective piece that's involved."

With these affective elements in mind, in this chapter we focus on some of the foundational leadership moves leaders made when foregrounding interpersonal approaches—and highlight their connections to socializing capacities and growing edges. Just as in the last chapter, we share stories from leaders across our sample—some who were making meaning with elements of a socializing way of knowing at the time of our interviews, and some who were looking back at that time in their development. To further illustrate the promise and range of the practices in the interpersonal domain, we also, at times, draw from the stories of leaders engaging more toward the "top" of the cylinder, but who were foregrounding more relational practices as part of their overall approach to leadership. As a reminder, in order to keep the focus here on the practices—and their connections to internal capacities that can live in multiple meaning making systems—we do not link individual leaders with particular developmental scores. In all cases, the stories we share in this chapter help bring to life to the imperative highlighted by David Brooks in this chapter's epigraph: that it can be incredibly transformative, humanizing, and liberatory "to see someone else deeply, to know another person profoundly, to make them feel heard and understood."

In the next sections, with a focus on participants' experiences of engaging in the interpersonal domain, we explore leaders'

- internal sensemaking (particularly as connected to socializing capacities as an entry point),

- interpersonal practices and approaches for centering justice in classrooms, schools, districts, and educational organizations,

- key supports and stretches for growth, and

- experiences growing toward the next domain of practice (i.e., leaders' reflections on being in transition, developmentally, between the socializing and self-authoring ways of knowing).

Once again, when introducing leaders for the first time in the chapter, we include the personal identifiers *they* shared with us in interviews—and then, upon subsequent appearances, include parenthetical reminders about key identifiers as important but non-essentializing context for their sharing. We begin, next, by exploring what felt most front-of-mind for leaders engaging in this domain: namely, honoring others through care, relationships, and empathy.

FOREGROUNDING EMPATHY AND CARE

Although many of the leaders in our study—as we explored in the prior chapter—first began their work as justice-centering leaders by answering a deeply ingrained call to *do* right, when leading from within the interpersonal domain, many leaders came to foreground, as well, the urgency of caring for others and their emotional experiences. As Kathy—a teacher leader who identified as a white woman—representatively described this impulse, "Making other people feel good and helping other people is the best feeling in the world." Similarly, Dana—an elementary school teacher leader who identified as an African American male and father—situated much of his current "why" in the desire to express genuine care. As he explained, "I have found great fulfillment in trying to embrace the life of others. It gives me a sense of purpose and it makes me feel like I'm valued—and [it's] the thing that I will always just hold dear to my heart."

Educators can, of course, demonstrate care in many different ways and from many different vantage points along the developmental continuum, but the kind of caring we're spotlighting here involves bringing at least some level of socializing capacity to one's work. When leaders bring elements of a socializing way of knowing to their practice, they bring with them a greater capacity to lead with others' experiences and fundamental value at the fore—and a greater capacity for empathy, which can feel deeply embedded in one's psyche and sense of self.

Reflecting, for instance, on how empathy now infuses and defines her work, Hazel—a college persistence counselor who identified as Filipino American, married, and the daughter of Filipino immigrants—shared,

> It's just something about the way that I see the world. I think, empathy-wise, I'm very aware of how people could be feeling or I try to be more aware of how people could be feeling or if they're going through something. I do this with everything. I do this even to a fault, I think now.

Similarly, Rana—a head of school who identified as an Egyptian American Muslim woman—explained, "I think that one of my strengths as a person is my empathy, my ability to really, truly care deeply about the experiences of others." This idea was echoed by others, too, like Sylvia—a thirty-eight-year-old district-level teacher support administrator who identified as a Puerto Rican woman and Christian mother—who expressed that "empathy toward the other person" is "something at the core" of who she is. Likewise, Ladan Jahani—a social worker in a transfer high school who identified as Iranian American, straight, female, partnered, bilingual, and thirty-nine years old—shared, "I'm a very emotional person. I feel my empath level is kind of high." Kathy (teacher leader, white) similarly explained that her empathy "just came naturally." "I feel like I have this natural connection with children," she shared.

Throughout this chapter, we will continue to explore how this desire to really tune into and care for others—first fueled by socializing capacities—provided many leaders with another important entry point into and driver for justice-centering leadership.

1. What is top of mind for you right now?

2. What are some interpersonal, relational approaches you engage with in your justice-centering leadership?

3. How do you show others you care?

4. How do you think others would describe the way they feel in your care?

5. Who has helped you feel most nurtured and cared for as a justice-centering leader? Why do you think that is?

6. In what additional ways, if any, might you want to foreground empathy and relationships in your work?

LEADERS' INTERPERSONAL ORIENTATIONS AND APPROACHES TO CENTERING JUSTICE

> *Caregiving often calls us to lean into love we didn't know possible.*
>
> —Tia Walker, *The Inspired Caregiver*

For many of the leaders in our study, justice-centering teaching and leadership were deeply personal, relational endeavors. Grounded in commitments to dignity, care, and collaborative work, participants describing their work in the interpersonal domain emphasized key stances and strengths of practice, including

- embracing fundamental value and holism,

- honoring diverse cultural capital and funds of knowledge,

- disrupting and mitigating harm,

- listening with the intent to hear, and

- nurturing professional relationships and collaborations.

Embracing Fundamental Value and Holism

Honoring the fundamental dignity, value, and full selfhood of all members of a school community was one of the greatest priorities for educators leading in the interpersonal domain. As Ladan Jahani (social worker, Iranian

American) representatively explained, for her, the *most important* element of successful teaching and leading

> is just seeing a person as a whole person, whoever they are. I think that's really important for me. That relationship piece is a driver certainly in leadership, but also in anything. . . . That becomes the wind in the sails.

Ladan told us that when working with students and colleagues, she strives to convey to others, with all her words and actions, that she appreciates "who you are in the big, big world that you live in," and that "your idea has value to me, your presence here is worthy to me." Evan—a district-level curriculum leader who identified as a thirty-six-year-old, white, cisgender male—too, expressed that, at its core, justice-centering leadership for him is "about ensuring the essential humanity and dignity of every person."

Underscoring this kind of authentic recognition and respect as prerequisites for successful participation in a learning community, D.—a teacher leader who identified as a first-generation Latino American man in his forties—argued that "we need to make sure that young people are feeling secure, that they feel welcome, that they feel all of those things, because nothing's going to happen without that." Further describing his stance as a teacher leader, D. elaborated:

> Do I tell the young people that I love them? Yes, I do. All the time. Do they get shocked? They're like, "What? He just said he loves me?" I'm like, "Yeah, bro, I love you. You're my guy." And they're like, "What?" And I'm like, "It's okay for a man to say that he loves you, okay? Because I do, I care about you." I hope to have people feel that way, I really do. I hope that my eleven-, twelve-, and thirteen-year-old young people feel like, "Yeah, D. had my back. He really saw me for who I am, you know?" And that's what's really important to me, is to empower these young people to . . . leave with who you are.

Dana (elementary teacher leader, African American father), too, explained that when working with students his stance is, "You are a gift to me and because you *are* a gift, I'm going to treat you as such, and treat everyone else as such."

A common thread linking many leaders' foundational thinking in this domain, the emphasis on fundamental value and holism, we argue, requires at least some socializing capacity to most effectively activate (although leaders may carry this powerful stance forward as part of evolving, growing value systems and ways of making meaning). Moreover, when coupled with critical and cultural knowledge, the imperative to really see and honor individuals can serve as a springboard for more culturally responsive and sustaining practices (Ladson-Billings, 1995a, 1995b, 2014; Gay, 2010, 2013;

Paris, 2012; Paris & Alim, 2017; Yosso, 2005) with and for children, families, and colleagues, as we discuss next.

Honoring Diverse Cultural Capital and Funds of Knowledge

Although many leaders foregrounding work in the interpersonal domain recognized, as did Ella—a director of culture and language learning who identified as a thirty-four-year-old African American woman—that "everybody has immense value that they bring to every single space," others also emphasized the specific importance of love as a radical, political act in a world mired by racism, anti-Blackness, sexism, misogynoir, homophobia, transphobia, xenophobia, ableism, linguistic and religious discrimination, and injustice writ large. As Ella explained, "I think as human beings, we all want to connect and we all want to feel like we're valued, but our society has this really subtle and not-so-subtle message that you're not of value if you're not quote-unquote standard." As she further explained,

> When I'm holding space for kids, it's keeping the space open to see all of who they could be in that moment, and not making the assumption or having the bias that they're going to be something that another would perceive as negative, or bothersome. It's just where they are right now. . . . Part of my work over the years has been getting people to see the value of understanding—understanding and holding value to the cultural and linguistic diversity of the students in their classroom.

Thea—a district-level leader focused on teacher leadership development, who identified as a married Black woman with ten years in education—similarly reflected,

> I do think a part of the school's role in social justice is to really begin to look at students and families and communities as assets coming with a wealth of knowledge and culture, coming with a brilliance, coming with a race history. How can we support communities in recognizing that value? Because what I find is that, often, when your schools are in high poverty, high traumatic environments, sometimes, not always, the perception about that community is deficit-based. So we already think of the students coming, "Oh, they're poor children, you know, they're already coming with [trauma]." And while there's truth that . . . a lot of our children are in shelters and do experience some trauma at early ages, those students still come with a wealth of knowledge. They come with a culture—they're not empty receptacles. So I think the school's role is to really find a way to serve the community by learning more about the community and being able to think about how we're creating curriculum that is reflective of the students that we serve.

This priority was likewise highlighted by Elena—a forty-five-year-old elementary school assistant principal specializing in support for English Language Learners, who identified as Latin American, born and raised in her early years in the Dominican Republic. As she explained,

> The more welcome the students feel, the bigger the possibility for us to make an impact on their lives. . . . If the students feel that we really care about them, and then they see that we also care about their loved ones, I think that will increase the possibilities to make the difference in a child's life.

Yet, as Micki—an assistant principal/dean of students in an alternative high school who identified as a Black woman in her fifties—explained, this kind of authentic, culturally responsive seeing and caring unfortunately cannot be taken for granted. "It's bad when you've heard in your own district from administrators—and that's another reason I left one of the traditional high schools—to hear an administrator call a kid of piece of shit. That floored me," she offered. Leading on behalf of justice, she explained, means combating and shifting these egregious ways of thinking and acting: "I know that every kid can learn. I know that every kid is valuable—and we need to change the mindset."

As we hope these examples help illustrate, leaders effectively foregrounding cultural responsiveness in the interpersonal domain bring sophisticated capacities and passions for seeing, honoring, and valuing all students, families, and community members—and especially those who have been minoritized, excluded, pushed aside, mis-seen, or undermined. Although we see this as a lifelong commitment and process that can carry through and even come to define leaders' value systems and stances as they grow, we also recognize how—though not a guarantee of this critically loving orientation—developing at least some socializing capacities can provide leaders with a greater *readiness* for engaging and leading in these ways, especially when accompanied by purposeful study, practice, and self-reflection.

Adults Too!

In our work with practicing and aspiring leaders across roles and geographies, one of the most profound leadership shifts we strive to support as faculty committed to adult development involves expanding the circle of love—that for educators tends to more easily encompass children—to include the adults in a school community as well. Teachers, parents, family members, and community stakeholders all bring value, stories, and selves worthy of deep care and respect. This turn toward loving and valuing "grownups" was something leaders in our study described as well—in general but especially in relation to equity efforts and initiatives.

As D. (teacher leader, first-generation Latino American) explained, "We're trying to do equity work for kids, but we can't get equity for kids if there's not equity for teachers—if teachers feel like their voices aren't heard or they are not empowered." Ladan Jahani (social worker, Iranian American) likewise lamented the disconnect that can sometimes occur between a school's espoused commitment to holism and care and the way that adults are treated: "If a teacher is not seen, or somebody who's on staff, is not seen as a whole person—if all you see of them is like a title or this one-dimensional thing—we miss out and we don't give all that we can into that person." May—an academic dean in a charter middle school who identified as a white woman in her thirteenth year in education—relatedly reflected that teachers need to feel "like they are safe, and connected, and cared for." As she put it, "It makes people feel good about coming to work when they know that they can be human."

Similarly recognizing her work supporting teacher development as a kind of parallel practice to teachers' work with young people, Thea (district-level leader, Black woman) offered the following:

> When I work with teachers, [it's] like what we do with students. We want them to recognize their brilliance. Some of them don't see it, or they've been told a narrative, or been labeled that they're not smart, that they can't learn, or that there's something deficient inside of them because of where they come from or the color of their skin. But helping them recognize their brilliance, their intrinsic gifts and talents that are stored up inside of them [is part of my work]. And when they begin to unlearn the false narratives that we have been perpetuating, or the stereotypes, we deconstruct those [untruths] and we're able to help children see that they can [deconstruct them, too].

Leading in ways, then, that acknowledge the complex fullness of adults—their pain and potential, their "blind spots" and brilliance—was another interpersonal approach leaders named as key to supporting all in an educational space to take risks, contribute, learn, grow, and bring their best and fullest selves.

As Ella (director of culture and language learning, African American woman) put it, summing up the importance of treating adults with all due respect and care,

> I actually think that's a huge part of social justice, right? To speak to people in ways that are nourishing and affirming, honest, and truthful. And being able to in every communication have that capacity—whether it's like email, whether it's in person or leaving a message—there's always this energy of, "I'm your biggest fan." And that's beautiful. Like to me, I really honestly see that as actual social justice, too, because what if we lived in a world where everyone spoke to each other and saw each other [through the lens of] "I'm learning so much from you and I'm your biggest fan"?

Disrupting and Mitigating Harm

For many of the leaders in our study—especially BIPOC leaders and those who'd experienced other kinds of marginalization (i.e., around sexual orientation or learning variations)—seeing the fullness of others through loving eyes was also a way to intentionally disrupt cycles of harm, particularly racialized harm, and transfigure wounds still carried from their own (mis)educational experiences. We include this deeply personal motivation as an expression of leaders' commitment in the interpersonal domain, as it connects profoundly with their own lived experiences and those of the people in their care. It is all about, in other words, prioritizing how people *feel*—or are made to feel—on their educational journeys.

For example, when describing his reason for getting into teaching, D. (teacher leader, Latino) explained, "I want young people to not have to suffer like I did." Looking back on his years in the public education system, he explained, "I can't think of any teacher who really made me empowered. Everybody from coaches in baseball always belittled me, always tried to chop me down in some sense."

Margot—an assistant superintendent who identified as multiracial, with Jewish and Native American heritage—also described the fire she now gets from the mislabeling and mistreatment she endured as a young child:

> I knew at a young age that [my experience] was not what public school was supposed to be about. . . . I knew I was smart, but that the people in that school didn't believe I was smart. So that really stuck with me. . . . And so that experience, as awful as it was, I'm thankful because it really was motivation for me. . . . So my life's work is really making sure that doesn't happen to any other child.

Similarly, Bernard—a teacher educator and former principal/superintendent who identified as a fifty-seven-year-old African American father—recalled the pain of his own early studenthood:

> When I became a student in the school system, that's when I felt probably most vulnerable, being a child, upon reflection. 'Cause I didn't feel like I was understood. Yeah, I definitely wasn't understood, and I didn't understand things. I didn't understand the whole school piece, the way the school was. . . . I can always be in touch with that inner child in me. The kid who was labeled.

Nat—a STEAM educational technologist/teacher leader who identified as a cisgender Puerto Rican woman—too, reflected on the irony of her current work in and passion for education, given the negative associations formal schooling had for her as a young person:

> It's really remarkable to me because I've always been involved with children since I was little, but I didn't like school. The experience of

school for me was so anxiety inducing. From the second grade, I would cry every single day. I didn't want to go to school. . . . I truly experienced what it was like to be in classes with teachers who didn't like their students. . . . There was also that element of being exposed to racial problems without having any tools as a kid to protect yourself or even communicate to your mother like, "This is what's bothering me." All I knew was like my teacher yelled at me, you know? And so I always said I would never go back to school because I just didn't like the buildings. I didn't like anything about school, but I loved to learn.

Providing another example, Rana (head of school, Egyptian American, Muslim) linked her own success with more "challenging" students to her personal experience with difference and judgment as a student:

I ended up being a teacher that all the challenging kids got because I was able to connect with them and work with them. And that was probably borne out of the fact that, growing up, I was in a really homogeneous community where I didn't look anything like the people that I went to school with, and so I oftentimes got in trouble for things that [I did not do]. I was often overlooked by teachers to the point where I actually ended up kind of turning and being a little bit of a rebel in school because I was like, "Well, here I'm trying to do everything right and do what I'm supposed to do, and you're always still accusing me of something." So I just kind of became a rabble rouser because I was like, "Well, I guess if that's what you think of me." . . . And so for me, I think part of the reason I was so successful working with kids who really struggled in school was because I saw them and I was able to support them and who they were in the context of my classroom.

We were also moved by Luz—the principal of a high school dedicated to human rights, who identified as a Black Afro-Latina, cisgender woman with twenty years in education—who recounted how the outright and unjust dismissal of her college application prospects by a high school counselor fueled her passion for educational justice:

That moment for me made me feel like, "No, I want to teach, and I actually want to teach kids just like me." And so I feel like I've had the opportunity. I've been blessed to not only teach kids who are somewhat like me—I feel like there are pieces of me in all of their stories in terms of being Latino, the young people—but more importantly, I feel like I have the honor and privilege to lead a school that I wish I would have been a part of as a teenager and I didn't have.

Given the insidious ways that anti-Blackness and sexism continue to permeate—and intersect—in society and educational spaces, it is perhaps no surprise but nonetheless essential to recount how many of the leaders in our study who identified as Black women described their experiences navigating multiple and intersectional marginalizations as students, teachers, and leaders. Powerfully, they also described working to translate these painful wounds into fuel for advocacy and authentic care for self and others.

For example, Loile—a district-level leader and former principal who identified as a thirty-four-year-old African American/Black cisgender female of Caribbean/Jamaican descent—shared the following about the effects of attending a private boarding school as a young woman of color:

> For me, I'm a grown woman and I still carry some of those conversations because, developmentally, when you're in the middle of looking for approval, well, how was I going to get approval from a system that didn't see me, you know? I'm Ralph Ellison's invisible man. . . . So in all of that, I recognize that there's a whole sort of psychic demand that comes with learning how to—the term used to be code switch—for environments and cultures and norms that nobody taught you, and that's a lot of stress. It's a lot of stress, and from my perspective, while I can say and demonstrate that I got a quality education, that quality education came at a personal cost. You know, my notions of self-worth are rooted in norms that are distinct from my physical being, my home exposure, and my desires. I'm still sort of integrating my understanding of who I am because it's heavily informed by a world that didn't value me. That's just plain and simple. It didn't value me.

Joyce—an educational consultant who identified as a Caribbean African American woman—also connected her current passion for educational equity with a need to interrupt the racism she experienced as a student growing up:

> I think my high school years, I experienced a lot of microaggressive racism without knowing I experienced it, but I learned how to navigate it. It wasn't 'til I was a grown-up that I could sit here and tell you, "Oh, I know what that was, I know what that was." . . . I can write a book on the things that are said to me, but I have realized that I don't want our next generation to have to navigate that. I shouldn't have had to navigate that, but I did.

The inequitable weight carried by Black women in schools and society was specifically called out by Lisa—an early childhood director who recently opened her own center, and who identified as a thirty-seven-year-old Black female of Haitian descent, with seventeen years in education—when she confided,

> [As] not just a woman of color, but a Black woman, I feel like it is particularly—you spend your entire life trying to be seen, just to say, "Hey, I exist, I'm not the stereotype of the person with the attitude that always has a chip on their shoulder." . . . As Black

women, we're always trying to prove ourselves. And even in the proving ourselves, people don't understand us because they feel like we're trying too hard. So it's like if we don't try, we're damned. If we do try, you're trying too hard to gain the affections of everybody else, when we're just trying to be a human being.

As one final example, Kristina—an educational consultant who identified as a married, faith-driven Black woman from a Southern city well-known for its civil rights history—explained, "In every place that I've been in, I've been in a position of being looked at as less than or not as good as other folks around me." For Kristina, the ongoing hurt and harm she's experienced reinforces the urgency of her leadership and underscores the power of representation—a related topic we will explore next. As she explained,

> Whether it's being African American or whether it's being a woman, there are just so many parts of my identity [through] which I understand the struggles—I've been counted out or discriminated [against]—and so that fuels me, though, because I know that—well, I know a couple of things. I know that it's important that I have a seat at different tables because having a seat at different tables is not about me, but it's about so many people that I also represent, and those people who also deserve to be in that space as well. And so that keeps me going, you know?

The Power—and Beautiful Feeling—of Representation

Indeed, as another expression of an interpersonal focus, many of the leaders in our study emphasized the relational, psychological, and healing benefits of representation—for children, adults, and *themselves*. Layered atop the moral and quantitative imperative of a teaching force that is reflective of the community it serves, many of the BIPOC leaders who participated in our study, in particular, understood their presence in educational spaces as another kind of opposition to and disruption of the harms described above—and spoke powerfully of what it *felt like* to *look like* the students and adults in their care. Kristina, for example—who, in the section just above expressed how important it was for her, as a Black woman, to have "a seat at different tables"—reflected on her choice to serve in communities similar to her own:

> I don't wanna say by coincidence because it was a definite, intentional choice. The children in schools that I've led and worked in are my exact same everything, so these are children coming from poverty. These are children that are African American and in the South. Like, I could go to some of their homes and feel like I was with my little cousin or siblings, you know? And so part of it is growing up in similar environments and kind of thinking through, like, "What did my mom want for me, and what do I want? What would I [have needed], what was I lacking, you know, as a Black child in school or a child coming from poverty?"

Sylvia (district-level leader, Puerto Rican, Christian), too, reflected on how her own experiences helped her connect more deeply with—and hopefully inspire—students who'd traveled similar paths. As she said,

> I want to empower students who are coming from a similar background like me, as my mom was a single mom. For a little while, we were on welfare, and she went back to school when I was nine. And so just this thing of like, well, if I could make it, like how much more powerful it would be if kids from similar backgrounds saw me and said, "Wow, I can do that. I can achieve that."

A similar sentiment was shared by Hazel (college persistence counselor, Filipino American) when she offered the following:

> I could really relate with the students in the program [because] a lot of them were coming from Asian countries like Malaysia and Burma, and I looked like them too—and that was a big thing for me. They felt open to talking to me and asking me questions and were so curious about what it was like to grow up and to be born in the States. . . . I could see that that really made an impact on them and also me.

A related idea was echoed by Angela—a thirty-one-year-old district-level teacher development leader who identified as African American with West Indian heritage, as well as a heterosexual Christian woman with nine years in education—in her heartfelt sharing about the students in her classrooms, schools, and districts:

> I wanted them to see that, yeah, I look like you. I'm from the neighborhood you're from. You can experience love from me and you can do this when you get to this age. . . . You can do it.

And also by Loile (district-level leader, African American woman):

> The one thing I'm clear about is that [if] there's someplace where a little brown girl doesn't know if she fits [pauses] she can see me. Or [if] a little brown boy doesn't know if he fits, he'll see, "She looks like my mother." And so, like, it's that.

Amaia—a teacher leader and coach who identified as a Mexican American female in her eleventh year of education—likewise underscored the healing importance of representation, especially in light of the absence of such role models in her own school experience:

> I think it's important to have kids read and listen to people who look like them and sound like them to kind of make them feel like they matter, they exist, they're represented because there's nothing worse than—I mean my experience growing up was, I told them,

I had never ever read anything about Mexican Americans or Mexicans in general until I was in college, I think. And that's hard because that makes you feel like you don't belong.

Just as participants powerfully articulated the benefits of serving as reciprocal mirrors for students who looked like them, others also emphasized the wider imperatives of representation and diversity for all in a democratic society. Reflecting on the impact of his relationships with students across lines of racial difference, for instance, Dana (elementary teacher leader, African American man) explained, "It was just as important for my white students, my non-minority students, to have contact with me as it was for the African American and Hispanic students to see me." Kristina (district-level leader, African American woman) likewise saw a parallel between her work supporting BIPOC teachers and leaders and her capacity to effectively coach and support white colleagues seeking to grow as equity contributors:

> I have tons of experiences in which I in some ways felt othered, you know? And so in being able to advise, consult, design, and lead professional development and coaching and everything, I'm primarily working with—I'm working with a lot of Black and Brown leaders and teachers, and really supporting the work that they're doing to understand where they're coming from, and really being transparent about some of the experiences that they've had that I can directly relate to, while at the same time supporting leaders and teachers who are not Black or Brown as well, but are very much socially conscious [and] on this continuum of always increasing their effectiveness of the work they do.

Bringing the fullness of her intersecting identities, experiences, and expertise to the fore in all of these relationships allowed Kristina to more effectively tap into the fullness of others—no matter their age or positionality.

Listening With the Intent to Hear

When describing some of their most impactful work in the interpersonal domain with young people and adults, the leaders in our study named *listening*—really listening, with the intent to actually hear—as key to operationalizing the care, sensitivity, and cultural responsiveness driving their work. All too often, participants explained, leaders (broadly defined) are expected to know the answer or provide a solution. Yet, as Ladan Jahani (social worker, Iranian American) reflected,

> I think one big thing is to listen, to not talk. To create space for people to be heard. I think that's always a thousand times more valuable than interjecting your thoughts, particularly at first. I mean, it's holding people's stories, giving a space for people to be able to decompress, to feel like somebody cares.

To engage in this kind of authentic listening, May (academic dean, white) explained, it is imperative that leaders "not listen through peepholes" or interject their own opinions upfront. On the contrary, as Hazel (college persistence counselor, Filipino American) explained, real listening means "just being more aware of what it is that someone needs in that moment." This, as you know, is a developmental shift that requires *at least* some socializing capacity. Describing how she was able to make this shift in her own sense-making and practice, Hazel confided,

> Before it was so much about, "I'm gonna get them to really hear me." And that's just not what it is for me anymore. Like that's not the most important thing. The most important thing is I'm going to get [people] to recognize that they can talk to me and that I'm going to listen. And they can define for me what it is they need.

Although we'd argue that listening is a very important leadership skill that can be deepened and enhanced with time and practice (and development), coming to recognize the importance of *really* listening—as an interpersonal support and approach to centering justice—emerged for many leaders as another core emphasis in this domain. As Donald—a retired teacher leader and higher educator who identified as seventy-five years old, white, and Jewish—put it, listening is ultimately a way "to be human, to reach out to others and to better yourself through more understanding." Similarly, Linda—an educational consultant and former principal who identified as a Black woman—recognized listening as the only way, really, to make sure people feel heard. "I find that that's usually the thing that people want from you," she explained. "They just want to be heard, you know?"

For other leaders, listening was also a first and ongoing step into another key dimension of their justice-centering leadership: namely, building and nurturing positive professional relationships and collaborations.

Nurturing Professional Relationships and Collaborations

As Elena (assistant principal, Latin American) explained, she'd come to see that "it takes a village" to make change as a leader. Whenever embarking on new initiatives, she felt, leaders need to always ask, "How many people can be a part of this so that we can support each other?" Jean-Claude (coordinator of curriculum and teacher leadership, Asian American) likewise underscored the importance of building connections—not just with students but also with and among adults—when teaching and leading for equity. As he explained,

> I think teachers, including myself, didn't really go into teaching necessarily to work with other adults. There's a sort of assumption that, you know, we get to work with kids all day long, right? But then for us to be effective, we really have to work with adults to learn from each other as well. So I think that's a whole set of skills this kind of work calls for.

In the interpersonal domain, engaging effectively in these important collaborations, leaders shared, involved building the necessary relationships, conditions, and connections to come together in service of greater justice. For many of the leaders in our study—especially those making meaning with some elements of a socializing way of knowing—this meant seeing the good and potential in others and carrying forward their care for adults' feelings and experiences, as described earlier in this chapter.

As Charlotte—a district-level leader who identified as a white woman with thirty-three years in education—put it, sometimes "you have to figure out people's capacity to be good." For Charlotte, as a team leader, this meant "talking to [the people on the team], interacting with them, getting to know them, talking to them about what's important to them, what they like about their work and what they don't like about their work, and what they wished we'd do." This relational investment helped Charlotte orient to her teamwork as an opportunity to do something important, collectively. As she explained, "I love that feeling of possibilities. So at the beginning of a planning process together or the beginning of a team, you're thinking about ways to bring people together so that you can make something wonderful together."

May (academic dean, white woman) also explained how important it is to embrace and acknowledge positives—even and especially amid the challenges and urgencies of each school day. As she recounted, "I do a lot of affirmation. I go out of the way to tell people, 'You did this really well and I appreciated this,' and all these nice things. The reality is just I'm very, very busy, and that takes time . . . but I know it goes a really, really long way when you make people feel valued." Importantly, May explained, positivity only works when it's authentic. As she emphasized, "It's not that I'm not being genuine—I really do feel that way."

The importance of *genuine* positivity was likewise emphasized by Sylvia (district-level leader, Puerto Rican, Christian) who reflected on the challenge of balancing positivity with authenticity. As she explained it,

> Like that balance of being nice, but being honest and kind—I think our society does separate the two, right? They say like, "Well, if you're such a nice person, you won't [complain]." But that's not genuine niceness. . . . Or they think like you're weak and people step all over you because you're too nice and, and it's like, "No, you can actually be nice and be kind *and* still be honest."

Leaders shared that although it is certainly time-consuming and complex work, building relationships through genuine positivity and care—and what we'd call the *kind frankness* emphasized by Sylvia—can provide "a stepping stone to more authentic connections that may invite everybody to really feel like we're all on the same team," as Ella (director of culture and language learning, African American) put it.

Keeping an eye on—and working toward—positive outcomes and experiences was also something Thea (district-level leader, Black) was working to do in her equity facilitation, as a support for others and herself. As she explained,

> When you're doing equity work, you often approach it like, "Oh, it is a heavy topic and it comes with a lot of weight." But there's also joy in it, and that's something I'm actually learning more now in my development—that there's joy in helping us see each other as human beings, approaching each other with love, and there's joy in unlearning negativity and developing a positive disposition about the world in which we live. So there's joy about being able to impact your own biases and deconstruct them and say, "Okay, tomorrow's lesson, I'm going to do better," or "I'm going to really engage my students in their culture in a different way." So I think that there is a burden and there is a weight, but there's also a joy in what comes out of really sharing, you know, your experiences with people and learning.

Summing up this idea, and bringing together the powerful potentialities of so many of the practices and dispositions described in this chapter, we close this section with another quote from Thea, which, we think, captures the essence of an interpersonal approach to justice-centering leadership: "I put a lot of love into what I do 'cause I believe when you lead with love, you bring out the best in people because you've created that space for them to be themselves."

DEVELOPMENTAL GROWING EDGES AND KEY SUPPORTS FOR GROWTH: BUILDING ON SOCIALIZING CAPACITIES

While the leaders in our study foregrounded powerful, interpersonal leadership approaches and priorities sparked by socializing capacities—such as authentic positivity, kindness, care, and deep respect for diverse cultures and identities—a developmental lens helps pull back the curtain on a growing edge that can emerge for many leaders in the interpersonal domain, especially when they have not yet grown *beyond* the socializing way of knowing. We're talking here about conflict.

As we discussed in Chapter 2, because socializing knowers have not yet grown the capacity to take a perspective on the opinions, assessments, and judgments of valued others (i.e., they are still "run" by their relationships in the psychological sense, and cannot yet hold them out as "object" to reflect on them), it can be incredibly difficult for leaders making meaning in this way to engage authentically in difficult conversations, to share unpopular opinions, or to advocate for changes they feel may be controversial or unpopular. When their relationships are out of balance, socializing knowers tend to feel torn apart on the inside. Yet, as shared by many of the leaders in our study who were making meaning in this way (or remembering back to a time when they were), caring deeply about others and justice and *not* speaking up can create a different kind of inner turmoil and distress—and an impetus for growth.

In the next sections, we explore, with gratitude, leaders' reflections about

- coming to recognize necessary conflict as a developmental growing edge, and

- the importance of external support from valued others when stepping forward, courageously.

FEELING CONFLICTED ABOUT CONFLICT: RECOGNIZING THE NEED FOR NEW CAPACITIES

Naming conflict directly as something that's been challenging in his leadership, Carter—a high school principal who identified as a thirty-one-year-old, white, cisgender male—described his ongoing struggle to step outside of what he called his "people-pleasing tendencies." "I just don't like confrontation," he earnestly shared. As he continued,

> I love to feel [like] that positive model of how good and selfless a person can be to someone. By contrast, I don't love being the person that drew the hard line, or anything like that. Simply put, I would say I need to be liked. That's the most basic way.

For Carter, the personal sting of difficult conversations sometimes even left him wondering about his effectiveness and how people saw him after delivering uncomfortable news. As he explained,

> Sometimes, I'll literally imagine what they're saying about me. You know what I'm saying? After they've left, what they'd be talking to their partner or friend about . . . I'll think of those moments and just be upset that in someone's eyes I am not a good memory, or not a good character for them. Because—for so long in my life—I worked very hard to be a neutral, at the minimum, but also a positive presence in the people's lives around me.

Similarly, Celine—a regional leader of a national educational nonprofit who identified as a multiracial, physically abled, partnered mother, and the daughter of a Chinese immigrant—shared how much of her leadership was defined by care for others. As she explained,

> I think [what worries me is] the possibility of letting people down or disappointing people. The possibility of people feeling like I didn't do what I said I was going to do—I think that's what it is.

Because it's my identity. Like that's who I identify as. . . . I don't like saying no to people, that's one. And I like to be needed.

D. (teacher leader, Latino) recounted the sometimes agonizing experience of working up to hard conversations or confrontations in a way that communicates and doesn't cancel out his authentic care:

I'm the type of person who—I really think about how conversations might go. . . . I get anxiety over, I get like stressed in my back, in my shoulders. I don't sleep maybe. I really consider what's the best approach, or how do I not—how do I let this person know I'm coming to hear your voice? I'm coming to really be an ally.

This stress was similarly experienced by Amaia (teacher leader/coach, Mexican American), especially when working to support "teachers who still struggle with forming relationships with really challenging kids." As she explained, "My reason for going into education is so intensely personal that I take it personally when I can sense that someone doesn't approach it with the same passion or intensity." Yet, what to *do* with this discomfort was at times less clear for Amaia, who worried about hurting others with her judgment. "I think if I really told them how I felt," she shared, "I think they would probably feel terrible about themselves. I mean, it's uncomfortable when someone tells you, 'Look, you're being this way.'" Capturing a sentiment common to many of our participants, Amaia shared, "It's so hard working with adults. It's so hard. It's really hard not to take things personally."

Dana (teacher leader, African American), similarly described his challenging relationship with conflict:

Even though I'm working on it, I don't always do well with conflict. My goal is to avoid it, and I often hear myself trying to understand, at least if I can, the alternate opinion, position, whatever it might be—you know, the opposite side of the issue. And so, as a result, I'm not always outspoken about the things that really trouble me if I do think that there's any kind of indiscretion [or] impropriety—or if I feel like there's been something that's an intrusion into social justice. . . . I mean, I'm definitely not a middle-of-the-roader, but I'm just also not necessarily the person who's a frontline type of person. And that bothers my wife sometimes [laughs] because she's a little more like that.

As these leaders' sharings help illustrate, balancing an interpersonal orientation with the need to, as Sylvia (district-level leader, Puerto Rican) put it, "still hold people accountable with compassion," is essential for educational leaders. Without the capacity to speak up and out, the "culture of nice" that permeates most schools (MacDonald, 2011)—and the norms of silence that reinforce white supremacy culture (Jones & Okun, 2001)—will continue to perpetuate inequity.

Reflecting on the internal tension that can arise when working to balance love and accountability, Adam—an assistant superintendent who identified as forty-four-year-old, white, cisgender father—explained, "I gravitate toward that positive, idealistic energy of educators, right? . . . I have deep-rooted respect and love for educators, but simultaneously I'm continuously frustrated by them and some of the archetypes they perpetuate." Indeed, taking a perspective on—and action within—this delicate balance requires ongoing support, practice, and developmental capacity. As Kathy (teacher leader, white) confided,

> I still struggle with it. I'm like, "We all have to be on the same page, we all have to be positive"—and that's not a reality. I have to be—I'm learning how to be okay with that, that it's okay.

The Price of False or Superficial "Kindness"

Although real "niceness"—in its most honest, authentic form, and as described by participants in earlier sections of this chapter—can serve as a healing balm and disruptor of dehumanizing practices, superficial niceness as a default frequency only masks ongoing harm, allowing it to fester, grow, and reproduce (Castagno, 2019). Describing what this artificially "nice" culture felt like in his school, for instance, amid the increasingly distressing and traumatic news cycles of the past years, Dana (teacher leader, African American) offered the following:

> I wouldn't want to mis-paint the picture, like everything is, as my grandmother would say, all gravy. I mean, there definitely are days where I maybe am frustrated by things that are going on nationally, in the country, and I feel alone in my school where I can't talk about it with the students. It's [also] a little bit of taboo to talk about it with your colleagues because sometimes, I feel like they know that I probably wear anything that's really trouble to me on my face, and I feel like most of them, except for my closest, closest colleagues, wouldn't feel comfortable enough to pat me on the shoulder and say, "Hey, you know, hang in there, you know, keep your head up," or even just anything positive or encouraging.

Even amid the "abnormally large amount of recorded police shootings of unarmed Black males," Dana shared, it was disappointingly silent for him—a Black man—at work. "It was really kind of crickets in my school building. When I say crickets, I mean like *quiet.*"

Although people have different and complex reasons for avoiding topics like race and racism at work and also in general—and we acknowledge here, too, the *much* higher risk faced by BIPOC, LGBTQIA+, and multiply marginalized educators when voicing warranted dissent, in schools and out—we have found a developmental lens to be a helpful complement to sociocultural understandings when working with educators from all backgrounds striving to lean further into necessary conflict. Positivity is all well and good, but real positivity and loving leadership, participants shared, means honoring others enough to share one's truth, not just keep the peace. As Luz (principal, Black/Afro-Latina) put it, "accountability plus love equals liberation."

Perhaps ironically, growing to understand conflict and hard conversations as essential elements of leadership can be fueled, for socializing knowers, by their strong value for connection and relationships. As Celine explained (regional nonprofit director, multiracial),

> True connection with people means that you have to be willing to take the risk of some vulnerability. You have to be willing to accept that there's dependence, per se, or there's a trust there. . . . Those are both necessary, in my opinion, preconditions to having those kinds of relationships with people.

Courage, too, can come from caring greatly for others, as it did for Ladan Jahani, a social worker who identified as Iranian American. "I've always been a much better advocate for other people than I have been for myself," she explained. Coming to see this pattern, she reflected, helped her bring into even more conscious awareness her readiness to "speak what's needed" *as needed*—and to work on the feelings of "crippling humility" that occasionally reemerged as a "carryover from the past that sometimes presents itself in the now."

EXTERNAL SUPPORT FROM VALUED OTHERS

Just as the leaders in our study who were foregrounding interpersonal strategies and approaches shared their gifts with others through authentic seeing, respect, and care, those who were making meaning primarily with a socializing way of knowing (or remembering back to when they were) named *support from valued others*—like close colleagues, trusted supervisors, and advisors—as *the* most powerful push for their growth and development. In addition to making more conscious some of their growing edges regarding conflict, external support helped many participants *feel* the affirming, scaffolding care they sought to provide for others. Capturing the idea of receiving loving care as an important counterpoint to giving it, Hazel (college persistence counselor, Filipino American) explained,

> I want to be able to live a life where I know that I have people who will always love me and support me unconditionally. . . . So it's a reciprocity thing. They're my most fulfilling relationships. If I make a mistake, there's going to be no judgment, no lack of forgiveness. I am who I am for them and I don't need to, you know, provide any explanations, and it's the same way for them.

For Hazel, positive relationships with mentors, confidants, and trusted others were essential—as their support helped her, in ways that felt quite literal, to be who she wanted to be. As she described it, "I think they're just my lifeline.

They're just the people that I go to at the end of the day and they're my go-to people, for different things. But I feel like I can't exist without them."

Capturing the double-edged gift of making meaning with a socializing way of knowing, Dana (elementary teacher leader, African American) likewise explained,

> I feel like I make my own self-worth from others' progress, growth, development, and how they think of me. So to be held in the kind of high regard that my students hold me, and my colleagues, it fuels me and inspires me and keeps me going.

As we explained in Chapter 2, for socializing knowers, one's sense of self is psychologically co-constructed, so receiving external validation can be positively reinforcing and transformative. Reflecting on the people in his life who helped him better see and truly accept his own self-worth, for example, D. (teacher leader, Latino) emotionally explained, "I never felt worthy. . . . I always struggled with my place in society, how people view me." Yet, with the help of some professional colleagues, cohort-mates, and professors in his leadership preparation program, and especially his wife over time (who D. described as his "personal champion of change"), D. felt more like "that little green [bud] that popped out of the seed, out of the fertile soil." As he powerfully shared, "All of a sudden, I started to feel like, 'Yo, my worth is important.' . . . That happened because of people helping me, honestly. Telling me that I was worthy, you know?"

In a parallel example, Gabriel—a former principal and current CEO of a reading-focused institute, who identified as a thirty-seven-year-old, African American father—explained how his self-confidence in leadership was, at least at first, a gift given by others. As he explained,

> I think I had others that saw certain gifts in me and really encouraged me to engage in opportunities to lead. I was really fortunate to have folks kind of cultivate and give me opportunities to lead at the grade level, or lead certain projects, and the supports to be able to do that, to have a more profound impact on kids.

Angela (district-level leader/coach, African American) shared with us how valued others helped her see *herself* as a leader—and maintain the courage to do the work she most cares about. As she explained,

> Most of the experiences that I would deem successful have all been off the strength of relationships with people who have seen something in me that I couldn't name for myself but I projected. Which is very encouraging. It's also validating. It's a validation, and it gives me the confidence that I need to do the hard work that I try to do every day. So the relationships definitely have been the foundation to my success as an educator.

Angela also movingly reflected on how interpersonal support from others felt even more lifting to her as a young, Black, female leader engaged in the risk-taking of equity work. As she shared,

> Oh my goodness, it's hard to be a courageous educator. It's hard to be a courageous young educator, and it's hard to be a courageous young leader. And then, when you add the race to it, and then the gender to it, it's hard to break away from old systems. It's hard to bring who you are to a place when you know it's right. I think it's due to the relationships that I have with educators in the system and just really being in awesome company. I really feel like the validation of like, "No, you're right, you got it," and the different conversations that I have in different spaces. . . . [This has] definitely given me the confidence to continue to try, and I say try because every day is a conscious decision, to show up as myself.

Like Angela, leaders who participated in our research—who were making meaning with some elements of a socializing way of knowing—emphasized how important it was to *feel* supported and encouraged, especially when engaging in equity work—or to have, as Amaia (teacher leader/coach, Mexican American) put it, "people to believe in me . . . and [put] the wind in my sails." "If I am going to take that risk [of standing up], I need to feel supported," Amaia explained. "I need to have everyone rallying behind me saying, 'You got this. We've got you.'" Sylvia (district-level leader, Puerto Rican, Christian) likewise confirmed how steadying external support can feel when taking an advocacy stance: "When you hear it from someone else, it's like, 'Okay, that affirms it. That's good—I'm on the right track.'"

In an example we think helps really illustrate the potentially transformational, developmental power of support from valued others, we close this section with a story from Rana (head of school, Egyptian American, Muslim), who recounted how an encouraging nudge from two important colleagues helped her, as she explained, "lean into my leadership and embrace it and not second-guess myself a thousand times." As she began,

> I'm sort of used to my voice being silenced or ignored or just not heard. . . . So there's always this part of me that worries about having to kind of justify, explain, or kind of make sure that everyone understands why I'm making whatever decision I'm making, or what I'm doing. I've been working really hard over the past year to say, "You know what? I am working really, really hard and I am coming from a place of integrity and I do love this work and I've done an exceptional job." And I don't have to kind of explain myself.

Underscoring, too, the intersections of meaning making with culture, gender, and positionality more broadly, Rana continued,

> So, I'm obviously a woman, a woman of color. I also, you know, wear the hijab, so then I'm openly presenting as a Muslim woman. So there are any number of identities that I juggle and it was really eye-opening when . . . two teachers came to me. One was a white teacher who I really love, and then another was a Black teacher, again another one of my teachers who I really love. And, in different contexts and at different times in the last few months, they both essentially said the same thing, which is, "You can stop explaining yourself and you can stop explaining every decision." And it was really jarring. They didn't say it as directly as that, but that was essentially the subtext of what they were trying to tell me, which is, "You don't have to explain every decision, nor do you have to have someone cosign on that decision. Like, you don't have to present us with a research article or this or that, you know? It's enough for you to just say it." And I know that the reason I was doing that is because there is a level of critique and criticism that as a person of color, and perhaps also because I'm Muslim, that I experience that my white counterparts do not or have not. . . . I mean it was eye-opening, and I thanked them both. I was so grateful to them because the feeling I had initially was almost embarrassment. Like—oh my God—I'm really kind of showing myself [laughs] you know, my insecurities. But, I was also just super grateful to them because they had the courage to come tell me and that was awesome. And also, I needed to hear it and stop doing it—or at least work to stop doing it.

Having a greater perspective on this pattern of behavior and the encouragement to embrace change was freeing for Rana, as it was for many of the leaders in our study growing through and beyond a socializing way of knowing. As Rana expressed—of further freeing herself from the weight of others' expectations and judgments—"It's just not as exhausting, right?" Right indeed! Even though growing to take a broader perspective on socializing orientations can take great time and investment—and can also be quite emotional and even painful—one thing we especially like to highlight when teaching educators about this developmental shift is that expanding one's internal capacities in this way doesn't mean giving up one's care for others. On the contrary, one can still care deeply for and about others *and* not be run in the psychological sense by external approval. In the next and final section of this chapter, we dive more deeply into this empowering transition and highlight participants' accounts of growing further into voice, agency, and the self-authoring capacities that serve as entry points into the next domain of practice in our model: the system-focused.

LEADERSHIP IN TRANSITION: GROWING BEYOND THE INTERPERSONAL DOMAIN

Throughout this chapter, we shared up-close and on-the-ground reflections from leaders foregrounding the interpersonal domain of justice-centering leadership, with a focus on how socializing capacities can serve as an entry point into—and fuel for—effective engagement in this layer of practice. As we have begun to explore, growing up and out toward the next domain in our model—the system-focused domain—requires additional developmental stretching toward self-authoring capacities. Accordingly, in this next section, and as illustrated in Figure 4.2, we focus on the transition *between* the interpersonal and system-focused domains and share leaders' reflections on coming to greater and fuller voice.

FIGURE 4.2   DEVELOPING SELF-AUTHORING CAPACITIES AS AN ENTRY POINT INTO THE SYSTEM-FOCUSED DOMAIN OF PRACTICE

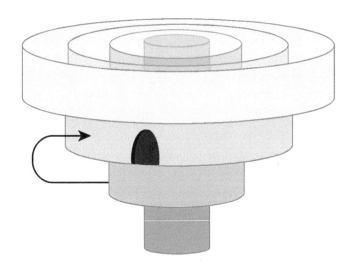

More specifically, we next share, with deep and humble gratitude, leaders' intimate and empowering recollections about the experience of coming to

● more fully embrace one's own voice, agency, and philosophies.

These stories, we think, provide a rare glimpse into the internal experience of leading—and advocating—in the transition between the socializing and self-authoring way of knowing.

Coming to Fuller Voice

Leaders who participated in our study who were making—or reflecting on—the shift from a socializing to a more self-authoring way of making meaning described, in powerful detail, the experience of coming to fuller voice. By taking a greater perspective on their feelings about conflict, often with the support of valued others, participants were able to more actively and effectively advocate for children, families, colleagues, and themselves. Acknowledging and centering, again and always, how leaders with different identities and positionalities face starkly different risks and responses when using their voices for change, we pay forward these stories in celebration of participants who felt newly ready to speak *when they chose and decided to*. We thank them for their courage, both in their work and in their sharing with us.

To begin, we pay forward Elena's (assistant principal, Latin American) growing "understanding that [her] voice can be heard." For Elena, speaking up as a leader was both an affirmation of her own expertise and an expression of her love for others. As she explained, "In breaking silence and advocating for yourself, you don't only advocate for yourself. You also advocate for others and then you also support others in advocating for themselves."

Luz (principal, Black/Afro-Latina) likewise recounted her journey toward embracing her voice and calling as a leader. As she explained, "I found later on in life that the leader I had been searching for had been in me all along." Reflecting further, Luz shared,

> A couple of years ago, I was much quieter and shyer and sort of seeking more permission to speak, and now I'm feeling it's my duty and my obligation and my calling to speak, so that I can share the gift that I've been sort of blessed with . . . because we need it right now. We've always needed it, and so I feel like I'm honoring my calling as a leader.

Janae—a leader in a national philanthropic organization who identified as a Black woman—similarly recalled the importance of her internal and external shift toward greater voice and agency. In the past, she explained, "I was going out of my way all the time to make people comfortable." Over time, however, Janae came to see that her "beliefs around serving and giving" were "actually imprisoning"—and forcing "choices that weren't the best" for her or others. Describing her emerging certainty and power, Janae explained,

> So instead of being silent, [I] call it out. I never did before. I would just take it. I would get really upset about it because I didn't have any allies to even affirm that it was true at times, being the only person [of color]. . . . [But] I don't have to coach that way, I don't have to consult that way, I don't have to do that. And so [it's]

giving me permission to be more authentic about my life and not always be focused on others so much. . . . And I'm learning how to stand in my own power and in my own voice.

Embracing one's voice and fullness was similarly transformative for Cheryl—a district-level school improvement leader who identified as a white woman—who told us, "I just feel like a more whole person" after growing and learning in her role. As she explained, "I think four years ago—if my whole self is an apple, I think I was only like a slice four years ago." After some "new and different and unique experiences," as well as "trials and learning from other folks," Cheryl describes feeling more "rounded out." As she put it, "I can be a leader who's human and a woman and have faults, and I can also be really strong."

Finally, we close with Kristina's (consultant, Black woman) account of this empowering—and often developmental—shift.

> I think when you have the orientation to please other people, you wouldn't dare do anything that would make other people shun something that you've done. And you want them to be proud of you. And, what I had to realize is that my happiness is also important, you know? . . . I definitely can say that it's an artifact of the past. But it's a recent past. This is a recent place that I have grown into over the past, I would say, four years. I think what shifted it for me was school leadership. . . . I recognized that it was impossible for me to please everybody, and, you know, I wanted to, but I just felt such internal conflict because to please certain teachers meant that I would lie and not tell them the truth about where they were, about what their gaps were, or not have the difficult conversations that needed to be had. So I think I just had to really make a decision and say, "You know what? I have to do what's right because if I don't, I'm actually going to be in some ways holding kids back, *and* holding the school back from meeting our goals and outcomes." So all that sacrifice for that person liking me. . . . I think for the first time in my life I am like fully walking in the high version of who I am, being able to bring every layer of my identity into my work, so it shows up a lot in how I lead authentically. And I haven't before now felt as free.

We felt so honored to listen to and receive participants' stories of growth and becoming and feel so excited now to share them with you. We hope they foreground, as prequel to turning to the system-focused domain of practice in the next chapter, the ways that development can be a pathway toward greater freedom, inside and out.

CHAPTER SYNOPSIS AND KEY TAKEAWAYS

Love takes off the masks that we fear we cannot live without and know we cannot live within.

—James Baldwin, *The Fire Next Time*

In this chapter, we focused on the practices and priorities leaders foregrounded in the interpersonal domain of justice-centering leadership—and connected successful engagement in this domain to having *at least* some socializing capacities (although relationships and care can remain central as leaders continue to grow and develop). We ended with powerful and intimate stories from leaders about what it felt like to grow toward greater self-authorship. As we will explore in Chapter 5, these new, emerging capacities to stand in one's power and voice can open a door into the next domain of practice: the system-focused.

To help bring together some of the biggest ideas from this chapter, we present, in Figure 4.3, a list of key takeaways. We have also created, in Table 4.1, a summative overview of leaders' practices in the interpersonal domain and the experiences that most helped them stretch and grow.

FIGURE 4.3 CHAPTER TAKEAWAYS

- The deeply felt responsibility to care for, honor, respect, and celebrate others—in all of their fullness, holism, and rich, intersectional diversity—can serve as another powerful way into justice-centering leadership.

- To more fully see and stand with others in the interpersonal domain, leaders need to have at least some socializing capacity, although relationships can remain at the center of even more encompassing approaches as leaders' ways of making meaning continue to grow more complex.

- Leading in the interpersonal domain can be deeply personal—rooted, often, in the desire to care for others' feelings and lived experiences, especially those who have been marginalized or minoritized.

- Leaders with socializing capacities can foreground empathy, listening, affirmation, and collaboration in the interpersonal domain—but may struggle with engaging in necessary conflict.

- Growing beyond the interpersonal domain requires developmental stretching toward greater self-authorship and voice.

- Leaders making meaning with elements of a socializing way of knowing often benefit from the support and encouragement of valued others, who can stand with them as they are growing and trying out new capacities for justice-centering leadership.

TABLE 4.1 OVERVIEW OF LEADERS' PRACTICE—AND GROWTH—IN THE INTERPERSONAL DOMAIN

DOMAIN OF JUSTICE-CENTERING LEADERSHIP PRACTICE	PRIMARY FOCUS	PREREQUISITE INTERNAL CAPACITIES	FOREGROUNDED PRACTICES AND APPROACHES	EXPERIENCES THAT SUPPORT DEVELOPMENTAL STRETCHING AND GROWTH	REPRESENTATIVE QUOTES
Interpersonal	Emotional states of others and self Professional and personal relationships Classroom and school communities	Socializing	Making and sustaining deep connections Embracing fundamental value/holism Honoring diverse cultural capital and funds of knowledge Disrupting and mitigating harm Listening with the intent to hear Nurturing professional relationships and collaborations	Feeling affirmed and validated in progress Receiving encouragement and support from valued others Support in looking internally for self-assessment of actions rather than externally	"How do I make sure *others* are feeling cared for and seen?" "We need to make sure that young people are feeling secure, that they feel welcome, that they feel all of those things, because nothing's going to happen without that."

REFLECTIVE INVITATION

Before moving to the next chapter and turn in the developmental gyre, we invite you to consider the following reflective questions. You might want to reflect privately first and then engage with a partner and/or team, to help you continue a generative dialogue.

1. After reading this chapter, what is top of mind and top or bottom of heart for you?

2. How, if at all, do the stories, ideas, and discussions in this chapter connect with your own experience and wisdom? Your own justice-centering leadership?

3. What are some of the larger insights you've had as you read this chapter? Who, if anyone, are you thinking about? What else are you thinking about? How are you feeling?

4. How, if at all, might you share some of the stories, ideas, and/or practices from this chapter? With whom? When? What's your next step?

5. After reading this chapter and considering these leaders' stories about the interpersonal domain of the model, what, if anything, might you like to practice and/or do differently in general? For your justice-centering leadership?

6. Early in the chapter, Evan shared how he grounds his practice in "the essential dignity and humanity of every person." Similarly, Dana described how he approaches interactions with others with the mindset of, "You are a gift to me." What are some of the ways you honor the fullness of those in your care, both children and adults?

7. Linda shared that feeling heard is "usually the thing people want from you." What is one practice you engage in on a regular basis, by yourself or with colleagues, that supports authentic listening? How is it working?

8. Hazel talked with us about how much she treasured her "go-to people" as a "lifeline" of support and encouragement. Who do you turn to for advice and encouragement? Who's helped you to find your voice? When and with whom do you feel most comfortable sharing your truth now? Your inner voice?

9. Elena shared her powerful realization that, "In breaking silence for yourself . . . you also support others." Who or what gives you strength as an advocate? Gives you courage to break silence?

10. After reading this chapter, what is something you'd like to think more deeply about? Do differently? Get better at? Learn more about?

11. What, if anything, would you like to think more about before turning to Chapter 5?

CHAPTER 5

∙∙∙∙∙∙∙∙∙∙∙∙∙∙∙∙∙∙∙∙∙∙∙∙∙∙∙∙∙∙

ADVOCATING AS SYSTEMS AGENTS

Leading for Social Justice With Self-Authoring Capacities

We all have a sphere of influence. Each of us needs to find our own sources of courage so that we can begin to speak. There are many problems to address, and we cannot avoid them indefinitely. We cannot continue to be silent.

—Beverly Daniel Tatum (2017)

In this chapter, we dive deeply into the third domain of our developmental model for justice-centering leadership: the system-focused. As you may recall, the system-focused domain involves a leader's *purposeful alignment* of efforts and initiatives within a school or educational organization, in keeping with their personally generated (i.e., self-authored) vision and guiding values. Put another way, it's a domain that draws heavily from leaders' internal capacity to decide, for themselves, what is most important and urgent when centering justice—and to use that benchmark of judgment to guide their agency and advocacy throughout an expanding sphere of influence (i.e., their school, district, team, and/or organization). Guiding questions for leaders in this domain could be things like, "How do the different initiatives I'm spearheading across my organization move things closer to my vision for justice?" or "Does this person, effort, or initiative align with what I know to be most important for meeting my goals for justice and equity?"

As illustrated in Figure 5.1, this chapter pulls out the system-focused domain as the third cylindrical layer of our developmental model—that incorporates and builds upon the capacities and approaches that came before *and* continues to run through and inform the domain that follows next.

FIGURE 5.1 **SELF-AUTHORING CAPACITIES AS ENTRY POINT INTO THE SYSTEM-FOCUSED DOMAIN OF JUSTICE-CENTERING EDUCATIONAL LEADERSHIP**

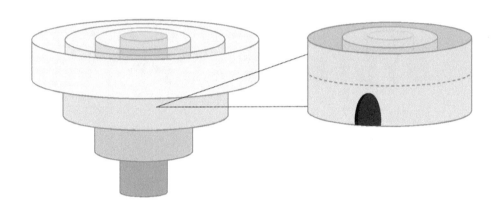

Once again, the open door in the diagram is a reminder that entering most successfully into the system-focused domain requires *at least* some self-authoring capacity—although the agentive approach foregrounded in this domain can continue to flow through and inform leaders' practice even as self-transforming knowers.

By way of reminder, growing toward a self-authoring way of knowing involves developing new capacities to take a greater perspective on one's relationships and the opinions of valued others. Although self-authoring knowers can still hold a strong value for relationships, kindness, and care, they are no longer "run"—in the psychological sense—by a need for external approval, and they have come to author, for themselves, a set of values, principles, and beliefs that constitute a guiding philosophy. As such, when it comes to justice-centering leadership, self-authoring knowers are better equipped to bring a strong vision for justice and how to achieve it to their work, as well as a greater readiness to take strong stands for what they believe in and engage in difficult conversations. In other words, they have readied the courage—as author, psychologist, and scholar Beverly Daniel Tatum put it in the chapter epigraph—to speak up and claim authority within their spheres of influence. Nevertheless, as we shared in Chapter 2, a growing edge for self-authoring knowers can be letting others more organically *into* their visions and sensemaking, and recognizing that no matter how powerful, impactful, or urgent their current advocacy, there are always parts of justice and injustice still to uncover.

Also, as you know, making meaning with a self-authoring way of knowing does not *guarantee* a leader's commitment to justice or equity. In fact, self-authoring knowers can—and do—hold all kinds of values and philosophies, as a way of knowing is epistemologically neutral. That said, our focus in this chapter is on the stories of leaders demonstrating self-authoring capacities as expressions of their explicit commitments to justice in the educational sector. We hope their deeply personal reflections will help bring to life both the strengths and growing edges of leading with self-authoring capacities at the fore.

In the next sections, with a focus on participants' leadership in the system-focused domain, we explore leaders'

- internal sensemaking (particularly as connected to self-authoring capacities as an entry point),
- system-focused practices and approaches for centering justice as advocates and allies,
- key supports and stretches for growth, and
- experiences growing toward the next domain of practice (i.e., leaders' reflections on being in transition, developmentally, between the self-authoring and self-transforming ways of knowing).

By way of reminder, when we introduce leaders for the first time in the chapter, we will include a list of the personal identifiers they shared with us in interviews. If a leader reappears later in the chapter, we will then use a parenthetical reminder of key identifiers to provide context for their sharing—without essentializing these dimensions of identity. We begin, next, by exploring what felt most front of mind for leaders engaging in this domain: actively engaging throughout the parts of the educational system in their purview, with carefully honed purpose and deep conviction.

CARING FOR THE SYSTEM WITH PURPOSE AND CONVICTION

Layered atop the powerful, interpersonal approaches outlined in the prior chapter, many of the leaders in our study recognized the importance of growing to include a more system-level, agentive focus in their justice-centering leadership. Their interest, in other words, was expanding the scope of their influence so as to better advocate for—and advance—their vision for justice. Although, as we just mentioned, leaders foregrounding self-authoring capacities could still hold a strong value for relationships, they came to see that—on their own—interpersonal approaches were not enough. They needed to be able to do, see, hold, care for, and design *more* to really effect change as they wished.

As Shokry—an educational consultant with Dominican/Egyptian heritage—explained, looking back on his own evolving practice, "I went from looking at advocacy as being a championing of people [and] supporting them in their endeavors to also becoming a designer or re-designer of our systems." Like

Shokry, who underscored the importance of the additive nature of this shift (i.e., he used the world "also" rather than "instead"), Lee—a national-level leader of an educational nonprofit who identified as a forty-year-old, white, cisgender, gay, Jewish, partnered male—similarly spoke of how critical it was not to "stop" at love. As he explained,

> On the one hand, you might have a leader who's all about concern and love and . . . making people feel a sense of real connection with one another. And that's beautiful and that would certainly help in building a community. And yet, if that is all you did in building your community, then you might not actually achieve any results. . . .
> I think there's probably a spectrum of activities that one can pursue that are closer and closer to getting to the root issues, but to me, social justice is about constantly asking the question, "Well, why is this situation the way it is?"

A system-level, organizational focus as an extension of relational approaches was similarly emphasized by Ian—an elementary teacher leader who identified as a thirty-one-year-old, white, cisgender male. As he offered,

> It's really important that schools look at themselves on an institutional level and how they reinforce societal racism, right? So, like, wage gaps and disparities in terms of privilege. . . . Schools need to be willing to take a serious look at themselves and be willing then to make changes so that we don't reinforce structural racism through institutional racism. Getting good at interpersonal interactions is important, but if you don't always have that institutional level lens, it's likely that you have processes in place which are just reinforcing racism—and will undermine any one-on-one, person-to-person work that you're trying to do.

Like each of the entry points described in this book, leading in a more system-focused way calls for the internal capacity—or, as we've explained in this case, the self-authoring capacity—to see multiple parts and layers of a system simultaneously, and to balance one's care for individuals with an understanding of the bigger picture. As Ladan Jahani—a social worker in a transfer high school who identified as Iranian American—captured this internal skill and negotiation, "I see things and operate on a more macro level, but I still do see kids individually."

As we will explore next, the leaders in our study foregrounding strong self-authoring capacities described two main drivers of their efforts to engage more systemically:

- their strong identification, psychologically, with their sense of values and purpose, and

- their decisions to pursue educational leadership as an opportunity to have greater impact and expand their locus of control.

PURPOSE AS DRIVER AND IDENTITY

In addition to emphasizing the importance of taking a more systems-level view, many of the leaders in our study who made meaning with at least some form of a self-authoring way of knowing identified so strongly with the values and commitments they'd developed that those beliefs, values, and commitments seemed, in the psychological sense, a core part of *who they were* as people and educators. Moreover, these deeply held convictions served as forceful, nonnegotiable drivers for their leadership and advocacy.

As Margot—an assistant superintendent who identified as white-presenting but multiracial, with Jewish and Native American heritage—explained, "The only way I can describe it [is] as a relentless pursuit for equality in education. . . . All my systems work, all of my business process redesign, everything—it really just comes down to that." Joyce—an educational consultant who identified as Caribbean African American—made a similar point when she explained, "My whole moral compass is on uplifting."

This idea finds echo in the sharing of Dr. B—a teacher educator and former principal who identified as a forty-one-year-old African American mother—who explained, "I tell people, this is not what I do. This is who I am. And it's my ministry." Loile—a district-level leader who identified as an African American woman of Caribbean/Jamaican descent—likewise emphasized her *purpose* as something central and fueling: "My purpose is what governs me," she explained. "Not my resume, not how it looks, not just the other dumb things, right?" In fact, for leaders who felt this way, like Nat—a STEAM educational technologist who identified as a cisgender Puerto Rican woman—"walking in one's purpose" was imperative and also a clear expression of the self-authored values driving their advocacy.

CHOOSING SCHOOL LEADERSHIP

As systems-thinkers driven by their own internal value systems and strong senses of purpose, many leaders in our study with elements of a self-authoring way of knowing intentionally chose educational leadership as a lever for change *and* greater agency. Reflecting on the role schools could potentially play in societal transformation, for instance, and why that was personally important, Carter—a high school principal who identified as a white, cisgender male—said, "I wouldn't be an educator if I didn't think it was a site for the pursuit of social justice." Joyce, too (consultant, Caribbean African American), agreed strongly with the idea that "change starts from the schools." Teaching and leading, she explained, is about preparing children and adults "for a world that hasn't really been created yet." Ian (teacher leader, white) offered a similar point when he reflected, "Education, I think, is our best opportunity to create a more equitable society in the future. It's having kids be in a school that is a better version of the society around us." Relatedly, Kristina—an educational consultant who identified as a Southern,

Black, faith-driven woman—shared why investing in education made sense for her as an advocate:

> I see a lot of possibility and opportunity within schools because I think our profession is really sacred, you know? It's the one thing that's at the forefront of everything else. We literally educate the next generation of human beings every single day.

Choosing educational leadership, then, was an opportunity for these participants and others who demonstrated self-authoring capacities to take a more active, agentive role in the educational system—and to continue the work, as Kristina put it, "in a more macro way."

In addition to seeing schools as potential sites for change, leaders with strong self-authoring capacities described their eagerness to bring their *own* values more to the fore—to expand, in other words, their personal reach and impact. From a developmental perspective, as we will explore throughout this chapter, assuming leadership roles through this agentive entry point involved a certain level of confidence and assurance—in oneself and the fitness of one's voice and vision.

Brent, for example—an assistant principal who identified as a white, married, gay male—linked his decision to move into an administrative role with his frustration with inequitable policies and structures and an eagerness to work toward solutions. "[Moving] into more formal leadership," he explained, "was really a choice that I made in order to try to have more influence—for my work to be able to shift and shape policies." Margot (assistant superintendent, multiracial) likewise sought out leadership as a way of expanding her reach:

> As a teacher, I wanted what was happening in my class to happen in the classroom next door to me and it wasn't. And when I became a principal—that's why I became a principal—then I could make that happen in my school. And then when I was a principal, I wanted the same thing to happen in the school next to me and it wasn't, right? So then I wanted to kind of keep going up and up and have just a wider scope of influence over what classroom instruction would look like and the kinds of teachers we would have in the classroom. . . . So it all kind of comes back to that same place of, like, this is an equity agenda. It is absolutely an equity agenda. It's not a job. You know, I don't think of it as a job. It's just how do I do my part to make our schools great for all kids.

Celine—a regional leader of an educational nonprofit, who identified as multiracial and the daughter of a Chinese immigrant—described a similar trajectory of leadership roles, which led her from teaching, to the principalship, and then on to district-level and nonprofit work:

When I was a teacher, I thought it was very, very frustrating to make a year or more of growth with my students and then pass them on to the next teacher, who either was or was not committed to the same thing. And so that was one of the reasons I decided to become a principal. And when I was a principal, I got very frustrated with all the focus on absolute metrics and not on progress metrics. And really just our inability to think strategically and systemically about solving problems for students who were really not served by the system.

In parallel example, Angela—a district-level teacher development and evaluation coach, who identified as an African American woman with West Indian heritage—likewise explained how leadership was an opportunity to expand her sphere of influence, initially in relation to her work supporting language learning practices:

What I really wanted was to have more autonomy and just more voice around how ENL students were learning. . . . [I]f you go into leadership, you have more opportunities to reach more students and . . . [you can] reach more professionals, getting them to change their mindset.

Ultimately, as these examples help illustrate, assuming formal leadership roles provided many of the more self-authoring leaders with the means to *enact* and *impart* their deeply held values. Although in some ways the self-authoring way of knowing is similar, at least on the surface, to a more instrumental/concrete approach to "doing the right thing" (and seeking more authority), we mark here the important developmental distinction between leading with a universalized understanding of "the one right way" on the one hand, and leading with a personally curated vision or system of values on the other. As we discussed in Chapter 2, the self-authoring way of knowing lives on the same "side" of the developmental gyre as the instrumental way of knowing (and can sometimes look similar from the outside—especially if we are observing behaviors or listening to words without probing to understand their big "whys"). Moving on the developmental helix toward self-authorship means returning to a more individualistic focus *with a greater capacity for perspective taking*—on self, others, and the world.

As we like to share when teaching about this developmental transition, growing into a self-authoring way of knowing is much like developing one's "I" voice. In other words, it involves understanding that—although people in the world can hold many different viewpoints and values for lots of different and important reasons—taking action according to one's *own* benchmark of judgment feels essential for self-authoring leaders' integrity.

Although self-authoring leaders can absolutely hold strong values for relationships and collaboration (and equity), they rely primarily on *their* vision for and understanding of these values as guideposts for action. As Norma—a dean and ESL coordinator who identified as a white cisgender woman—representatively explained, "I have a vision for what I want." Moreover, for Norma, formal leadership was an intentional way for her to "influence other people to get on board with that vision."

Capturing a similar sentiment, and summing up how a self-authoring approach really brings things "back to agency," Loile (district-level leader, African American) explained that assuming leadership in her institution meant leveraging her position strategically for change. As she explained, "I worked to take jobs with different levels of responsibility with the belief that functioning at different levels . . . would afford me the reach to impact the issues that I am committed to addressing." Put another way, facing deep challenge but buoyed by conviction, Loile approached her leadership knowing, "I can do something about this, and I can get other people to do it with me." Next, we zoom in on the overarching strategies and stances leaders with system-focused, self-authoring capacities enacted in their practice.

REFLECTIVE INVITATION

1. What is top of mind for you right now?

2. What do you see as central to your vision for education? Justice? How might the two connect?

3. What do you see as your core values, beliefs, and commitments? When you think about it, where did your deeply held convictions, commitments, and nonnegotiables originate?

4. What do you see as your sphere(s) of influence? How did this come to be?

5. In what new ways, if any, might you want to foreground agency and/or advocacy in your work?

6. How prepared do you feel to do so? What supports do you have—or might you need—to enhance this part of your leadership?

LEADERS' SYSTEM-FOCUSED, AGENTIVE ORIENTATIONS AND APPROACHES TO CENTERING JUSTICE

Our most important learnings come not simply when we see the world anew, but specifically when we see ourselves—and our role in creating the world—anew.

—Ursula Versteegen (cited in Barnum & Kahane, 2011)

For many of the leaders in our study who were able to bring self-authoring capacities to their work, engaging in justice-centering leadership took the form of system-level agency. Although an agentive approach took different shapes and forms in practice, thematic to and underlying this entry point for these participants were the following:

- a focus on systems alignment—meaning strategic, big-picture thinking guided by a clear set of values,

- a growing commitment to reflection and self-awareness, and

- an enhanced capacity for advocacy, including engaging in necessary conflict, principled disruption, and boundary setting.

We explore and share examples of these orientations, practices, and expressions of internal capacities in the sections that follow.

SYSTEM ALIGNMENT: MAKING STRATEGIC, VALUES-INFORMED DECISIONS

Perhaps most characteristic of what we're describing as a system-focused approach to justice-centering leadership was the purposeful alignment of individual, micro actions under the umbrella of a more encompassing macro purpose. To do this, participants explained, the capacity to take and hold a broader perspective was key. As Evan—a district-level curriculum leader who identified as a white, cisgender male—related it, "You need to understand it on a wide level in order to narrow the focus of your work on any given day." Making a similar point, Harris—the principal of a high school for English language learners, who identified as a forty-eight-year-old, white, gay male—spoke passionately about the need for "systematic changes in schools" that would better support students as emerging multilingual learners, from the ground up and back again. "How do we, as systems leaders, need to be thinking more wisely about our policies and practices?" he wondered. Joyce (consultant, Caribbean African American) likewise shared how growing to see the bigger picture helped her work more strategically and purposefully within the educational system:

> My first two years I felt like I was just putting out flames everywhere I was going, and I kind of felt like a chicken with no head. Just, like, every time something came up, I would just run and fix it, run and fix it, run and fix it, without thinking about the macro. So as a teacher, I was very micro. [As a] literacy coach the first two years, I was very micro as well. I want to say [my leadership program] helped me think about things on a macro level. And once I started thinking about things on a macro level, that kind of gave me the tools for how can I help teachers change.

Adam, too—an assistant superintendent who identified as a forty-four-year-old, white, cisgender father—described himself as a "systems architect" and a "cultural engineer." He explained how developing a wider-angle view helped him work, very deliberately, to "re-engineer the system of education." As he characterized this shift in focus, "I think . . . that my effort in work [now] is much more focused and planful and deliberate and intentional, and not as much by feel." By growing the capacity to more fully take in and understand schools and organizations as *systems*, the leaders in our study who, like Adam, were foregrounding self-authoring capacities used their big-picture thinking as a way to *align* different efforts and initiatives toward greater justice.

For example, Adam used his equity lens to bring together and synergize many distinct aspects of his work, including recruiting and supporting more teachers of color to better reflect the diversity of the district community, advocating for blocks of time in the schedule that would create more opportunities for extended student engagement, and adjusting seemingly "simple" things—like lighting and stairwell gratings—that shifted the feel and experience of physical spaces in his schools. As Adam described when addressing this values-driven alignment, "We do have a North Star, so to speak. . . . And so all of the work we do—we have building goals, the district road maps, and all of the initiatives . . . are aligned to that." Brooke—an interim head of school who identified as a white, cisgender, gay female in her late forties—also described her work, at least in part, as an effort to align community-wide practices with overarching goals: "The school really values global awareness, anti-ethnocentrism, pro-inclusivity and diversity, and things around ethical leadership, and I get to help shepherd things that connect to that."

The intentional alignment of initiatives to values was similarly highlighted by Bernard—a teacher educator and former principal and superintendent who identified as African American—who explained,

> It rings so clear that it's important, first of all, to have a vision that we're all clear about, and then to have strategies to bring about what we say we see as our goal, our mission, etcetera. You can't just espouse certain things. . . . What is your blueprint for leadership? Because you can be strategic in planning how you're going to move forward to leadership and then you gotta bring all these things into being, the values. What are the values?

Aligning actions with values was also noted by Ian (teacher leader, white), who shared, "I work with a starting set of beliefs and values and approaches . . . and then go from there to actually make decisions or plans." Doing this, he explained, allowed him to stand firmly in his convictions and self-authoring capacities: "I will do what I believe in and get it done the way I think it should be done," he continued. A similar orientation was described by Lee (national-level nonprofit leader, white, gay, Jewish), who said, "I have my internal values, I have my beliefs, I'm growing my own understandings of what I think needs to be done and what needs to be true, and that's going to govern my choices." Carter, too (principal, white), recognized it as a leader's responsibility to "build the school around a vision and an idea and actually make sure all the dots get connected." "I love setting vision and direction and mobilizing people around that," he shared. "I love, love, love that."

As justice-centering leaders, this infusion of guiding values was especially essential. As Cheryl—a district-level school improvement leader who identified as a white woman—put it, "As a leader, you want people to know your foundation." Luz—a high school principal who identified as Black/Afro-Latina—relatedly described how themes of social justice are foundational and integrated "into everything" at her high school dedicated to human rights. Through explicit modeling and what her organization calls "Soul Standards"—which center students' holistic well-being, community responsibilities, and transformative potential—teachers and students are encouraged to work toward not just academic goals but social and personal betterment. As Luz continued, "When I ask staff to hand in curriculum maps or lesson plans, they are to be aligned not just with the Common Core." "The most common of our core," she poetically explained, "are Soul Standards and our principles," which are part of "everything that we do."

In a parallel example, Thea—a district-level leader with a teacher leadership focus who identified as a Black woman—emphasized the importance of prioritizing equity as a *central driver* of her work and leadership—rather than an ad hoc addition:

> As they get different initiatives to roll out across the system, I'm being intentional about always having that racial equity, social justice lens in everything we do, and it's not something in isolation. It's not something that we think about one time and we never go back to. But it should always be something continual. It should be something that we observe through everything. It should be something that is constantly leading how we show up and what we do. So I'm trying to . . . bring cohesion and connection to the work with racial equity, social justice, and these ideas. What does it really look like as a teacher to do this or as a teacher leader to do this, as a school leader to do this more explicitly?

DEEPENING SELF-AWARENESS

Central, of course, to enacting a values-driven vision is the capacity and self-awareness to name and define one's own values in the first place—and to take a greater perspective on one's inner workings and positionality in the world. For leaders in our study foregrounding self-authoring leadership capacities and approaches, thoughtful reflection on one's own identity, experiences, and beliefs emerged as both a vital prerequisite and an ongoing commitment. As Joyce (consultant, Caribbean African American) shared, "the common thread is how teachers perceive education," so it is essential for educators at all levels to more consciously understand and explore "their own personal experience with education, and then their instructional practices."

Lee (national-level nonprofit leader, white, gay, Jewish) similarly argued that "one of the most powerful ways you can think about your leadership is by thinking about the specific identity markers that you carry and how you might leverage those to contribute to change." Succinctly capturing this big idea, Linda—an educational consultant and former principal who identified as a Black woman—simply and profoundly said, "You gotta know where you're from. You gotta know your history." Indeed, making explicit the connection between one's internal understandings and leadership efficacy, Thea (district-level leader, Black woman) recognized that, as leaders, "We have to look at ourselves first before we can say what's going on outside of us."

Pulling these points together, Kristina (consultant, Black woman) described the important role her capacity to see and understand *herself* plays in her leadership:

> [I'm] operating with an immense amount of self-awareness, like, really understanding what are my strengths, what are my areas for growth, just as a human being, as a person—to [understanding] how I engage with other people. Like, how am I being cognizant of my tone and my facial expression and my body language? How are these things coming across to other people? You know, how am I being conscious of my own thinking and how . . . my past and my background and things I've been through in my lifetime are influencing this moment or my engagement with this group of people?

Powerfully, for the leaders in our study foregrounding self-authoring capacities, such thoughtful introspection was both something they could bring to practice in real time *and* something they reinvested in, again and again. As Donald—a retired teacher leader/higher educator who identified as white and Jewish—explained, "I'm going to be seventy-five in about a couple of weeks. . . . I think it is interesting that I'm still seeing who I am and still thinking about how I really identify in many, many different planes."

As we will explore next, for many of the leaders in our study who identified as white, the self-authoring capacity to look within—with a critical, reflective stance—was imperative for deepening understandings of white privilege (Collins, 2018; DiAngelo, 2010, 2018; McIntosh, 1989, 2015, 2018; Lensmire, McManimon, Tierney, Lee-Nichols, Casey, Lensmire, & Davis, 2013). Although, as you know, leaders with any way of knowing can have an intellectual understanding of the concept, those with more self-authoring capacities demonstrated a greater internalized readiness to name, explore, and bring into conscious awareness how growing up white influenced their experiences and life chances.

Examining White Privilege

The capacity to look within and really interrogate white privilege emerged as a related subtheme for many of the leaders in our study who demonstrated self-authoring capacities and identified as white. Reflecting on her own experience with this process, for instance, Henrietta—a co-founder of an educational nonprofit who identified as a white woman from a rural community—offered the following:

> People desperately want to say, like, "Oh, you are where you are because you worked so hard." And they mean that in the nicest way possible, but it's just not true; it's just not true. But I am where I am because of all the privileges that have surrounded me because of my whiteness. . . . And I feel like people sometimes that are in positions of privilege have a very difficult time acknowledging that that is the case because they feel like to acknowledge that somehow diminishes their experience.

Reflecting on the complicated implications of his own whiteness as a leader serving a diverse community, Carter (high school principal, cisgender white man) similarly described the critical role a deep, inner dive into identity has played, and continues to play, in his leadership, especially as connected to his admission to a highly competitive college after high school:

> So I had to become aware of my own privilege because I didn't really [pauses]—I mean, I did a lot in high school and I was a good person and I worked really hard, but I didn't really do anything exceptional. . . . And it was interesting because I think when it happened [i.e., getting into college], it felt so merit-based. Like, I wasn't necessarily the smartest in my high school, but I knew that I worked harder than almost everybody, and I tried really hard to do that while being a good, generous person . . . and so I felt both practically and cognitively like I had earned what I got. And then when I got there [to college], I was like, "Oh, what would have happened if I had not gone to [my] high school or had been born somewhere else or even if, like, my mom, after she divorced my dad when I was little, had decided to move somewhere [different]?" You know, like, there were all these questions that kind of came to the fore. . . . I talk about being aware that I'm a white man leading a school that is largely kids of color and the complications of that and the fears that come with it and, like, all these things. And I do it [i.e., talk about it] just to do it, but I also do it because I want everyone to know that this is a space I am okay with us entering, and I actually think that we *need* to enter and can't be afraid to talk about, and I'm willing to take the first plunge.

Engaging in this internal excavation in public ways, Carter felt, was a fundamental way to demonstrate his care and commitment. "It's just a lot of inner work that I have to do," he explained, "but it's where I want to be, and I'm willing to have those dialogues and figure that out."

TURNING TOWARD CONFLICT: COURAGEOUS ADVOCACY

Along with evolving understandings of self, leaders with agentive, self-authoring capacities for justice-centering leadership demonstrated a more ready willingness and capacity to engage—often publicly—in advocacy and/or what they understood as necessary conflict. As Amaia—a teacher leader and coach who identified as Mexican American—explained, courageous, values-aligned leadership means getting comfortable (enough) with discomfort:

> Social justice means having very, very difficult, very uncomfortable conversations about sexuality, about gender, about race, about things that are happening in our country, things that have been happening—not just all these terrible things that have been happening, because these things [didn't] just start happening, right? . . . So yeah, I feel like social justice is not comfortable at all. I don't know that it should be either.

Making a similar point, Thea (district-level leader, Black woman) reflected, "This work is not going to be done without resistance and I don't think there's ever going to be a point where everybody says, 'Yeah, I agree a hundred percent.' But it's an ongoing process." Linda (consultant/former principal, Black woman) similarly understood that justice-centering leadership is really "about having the courage to actually do it"—and to make, as Brent (assistant principal, white, gay) called them, "the hard decisions you need to make to most support students."

Many of the leaders in our study spoke passionately about this self-authoring capacity to speak truth to power when advocating for greater justice and equity. For example, Micki—an assistant principal/dean of students who identified as a Black woman—shared the following with us, recounting her unflinching willingness to speak out:

> I refuse to play the game. It's [not] one of those where, oh, you can get along with everybody if you just be quiet—that's not me. . . . I'm not here for you to like me. I'm here to do a good job. . . . It's a lonely walk, but you know what? I can't be afraid and I'm not going to be afraid and I'm not going to stop being vocal. I'm not going to stop working for kids and parents. And so I am all of that regardless of if they like it or if they don't.

From a developmental perspective, this capacity to step into advocacy—and to balance the push and pull of others' expectations, resistance, judgments, emotions, and responses—marks a qualitative shift of meaning making that can serve as a powerful expansion of the interpersonal, socializing orientations discussed in the previous chapter. Although leaders with a strongly self-authoring style can *still* care deeply about others' feelings and experiences, they are no longer "run" by them in the psychological sense. As

Bernard (teacher educator, formal principal and superintendent, African American) described this capacity, "I can listen to you and I can hear you. And I can disagree with you. And I think that's an important skill set to have." Loile (district-level leader, African American woman) similarly helped put this capacity into words when she explained, "My emotional energy does not shift based on how other people are working around me."

Likewise, Nick—the head of an independent lower school who identified as a forty-one-year-old, white, heterosexual male—explained that although he tries to "lead or be present in a way that is gentle, compassionate, and honest," there are times when leading authentically inevitably "leads to fracture." Even though this can be painful, he sets an intention "to be brave in those situations." As Nick put it, "[I try to] not allow a fracture that could form to deter me from what might feel right in a given situation or true in a given situation." Ultimately, as Joyce (consultant, Caribbean African American) explained, embracing conflict as a necessary part of growth and learning is really part and parcel of a justice-centering leader's role and something to practice and grow into. In her words,

> I learned how to allow people to go through conflict 'cause there's power in that, and believing that they can figure it out, and when I should interject and how I should interject. 'Cause conflict is going to happen regardless. I'm not going to tell myself that my role is to eliminate conflict. That's not my role. My role is to give people the tools to navigate it.

Principled Disruption

In terms of the ways leaders foregrounding self-authorship "wore" and described their out-loud capacities for agency and advocacy, we found a strong theme around principled, determined disruption—by which we mean leaders' eagerness to push for change and interrupt injustice whenever and wherever possible. For example, Rana—a school head who identified as Egyptian American and Muslim—described her role by explaining, "I feel like I've been very much an interrupter." Ella—a director of culture and language who identified as an African American woman—similarly said, "There is a part of me that likes to disrupt and push the envelope. Like, if we're going to have this conversation, the envelope is going to be pushed. I'm going to be disruptive." Likewise, Joyce (consultant, Caribbean African American) shared, "I like to go into schools and shake things up. . . . Not everything has to be beautified. Some things just need to be said."

Reflecting on how this kind of inner strength and persistence has served her well *and* required great determination in the face of resistance, Janae—a national nonprofit leader who identified as a Black woman—expressed the following:

> I'm going to do whatever it takes. It's that mindset of not giving up and changing my behavior. . . . I'm an idea generator and a

designer and I don't see limits and I work really hard to push things forward. And as a result of that, I haven't always been welcomed in the system.

Making a similar point, Bernard (teacher educator, former principal/superintendent, African American) explained, "I can't be corrupted." Elaborating further, he shared how speaking up—even at the risk of great personal consequence—was never a question for him:

> Throughout my leadership, when I saw something that was not right, I felt compelled to do something about it. You know, this was before the slogan, "See Something, Say Something"! [laughs] And I believe, if you see something, do something. . . . If you see it, how can you walk away from it? You know, you can't see that and then just act like you didn't see it. . . . When I look at individuals and leadership, I often say that it does take courage. I think that's—if I had to pick a virtue, it would be courage. . . . And I say to my aspiring school leaders, or actually anyone who I'm mentoring or working with, I say, "You know, you should never put your financial security over the security of children." And I believe that. I mean, I truly believe that. And the decisions that I made to walk away from jobs is evidence that I practice what I preach.

Margot, too (assistant superintendent, multiracial), reflected on how speaking up was something she was known for and something she now saw as integral to her character. As she put it, "I'm pretty vocal and I think my colleagues lean on me to say things that maybe everyone's thinking but nobody really wants to say. I tend to be the person that says it." Ultimately, Margot's advocacy was an expression of her larger purpose and drive. As she said, "I'm not willing to accept no for an answer. . . . If it's something that's important to me, I'm going to find a way."

Despite the risk—and the pushback and disagreement that can come with publicly speaking out—participants employed their self-authoring capacities to demand change, even and in spite of the challenges. As Dr. B (teacher educator/former principal, African American woman) summed it up, "At night I sleep well, knowing I was doing right by children."

Boundary Setting

Last but certainly not least under the umbrella themes of conflict and advocacy, many of the leaders in our study foregrounding self-authoring capacities reflected on the need to set boundaries—at least at times—to protect themselves and others and maintain the integrity of their work. Characteristic of self-authoring knowers, these leaders understood that—although people bring different levels of motivation, commitment, and experience to equity work—they had the right to decide for themselves, as leaders and human beings, if and when it was time to draw a line regarding support for others.

Especially when working with adults who they perceived as having viewpoints diametrically opposed to their own—or ways of teaching and leading fundamentally misaligned with their core values—saying "no" was an essential way of moving forward.

For example, Christopher—a leader in a national philanthropic organization who identified as a forty-one-year-old, Christian, African American father—described the kind of thinking that, for him, was a clear sign that "enough was enough":

> It's just, like, talking to people with privilege about race and the vestiges of slavery and things like that. If I have to argue with them whether or not slavery was real, that it was intentional, that racism is structural, and that the vestiges of those decisions live within society today—if we disagree about the fundamental truth of those facts, if we're so far apart that I don't have enough breath in life to come to a good place with you, I'm not the guy for you for then.

Taylor—a dean and ESL coordinator who identified as a white woman—likewise identified a clear-cut moral line for determining when it was time to say "goodbye" to resistant colleagues. As she explained,

> One thing we do come across here is that people think that . . . especially the students who are undocumented, [that] they shouldn't be here. If that's how you feel, I'm not going to be able to convince you otherwise, and I don't really care to at this point. I'm not going to waste my time on that. You just need to go . . . find somewhere else.

Margot (assistant superintendent, multiracial) described a similarly hard and clear line she held when deciding about whether or not to further engage with challenging colleagues:

> So if it's somebody that I think has their heart is in the right place, they want the same thing ultimately, but they have a different strategy, I'm certainly willing to adjust my thinking. Like that, to me, that's what it's all about—hearing diverse perspectives and trying to make the idea better. But if you have contrary values, like, if you just fundamentally don't believe that all kids should have access to, let's just say, AP coursework because you fundamentally don't believe that all kids are smart enough, there's nothing you can say or do to make me change my mind, right? And I'm just going to stop listening to you because you don't have the same value system that I have. Like, we just fundamentally will never agree. And there are people, and there are things like that in education . . . where people just have very different values and very different views about what children are capable of. And so I happen to work with like-minded people who are really committed

and believe that all children and students can do engaging, college-level work. We believe that. When we encounter people that don't believe that, there's no reasoning with them. And I don't know that we have to. You know? Like, if you just fundamentally are racist, it's not my job to make you not racist.

Linda (consultant/former principal, Black woman) likewise identified a commitment to equity as a core of someone's being—and an immutable prerequisite for serving as an educator:

> It has to be something that really is a part of you. And if you know that you want to do this work, go for it. But if you truly know this is not the place for you and you're only doing this to get to someplace else, then go, 'cause we don't need you in this field. And you know, I think people really have to make that kind of reality check within themselves, and it's okay. It really is okay that this is not for you. But what is not okay is pretense, and if you're pretending to be something that you're not, kids will point that out to you in a heartbeat.

When, as an educational leader, Linda was confronted with this kind of intractability in one particular colleague, she felt at peace about her decision to relieve that teacher of their position. "So I finally got to the point," she explained, "where I said, 'Okay, I'm going to give you a decision. I fire you, or you quit. . . . It just doesn't work for me.'"

Finally, and representative of the thinking and meaning making underlying leaders' self-authoring capacity for boundary setting, we share Kristina's (consultant, Black woman) reflections on navigating the line between support for others and care for self:

> I definitely believe in the continuum of cultural competency. . . . I do think it is possible for all of us to be on the spectrum of continuously learning and getting better. At the same time, I think the power of any of those frameworks is [the] desire to learn and grow. . . . When someone doesn't articulate that desire or they don't have it, I personally don't engage, you know? Like, out of a sense of self-care and preservation, 'cause I feel like it's constantly walking into a brick wall. And I think that's really different than having a different opinion from someone. . . . I just think that when a person [has] . . . almost hatred or closed-mindedness in their heart, I just don't think it's worth the energy, and I think that energy should be devoted to other places where there is hope for change.

Powerfully, Kristina uses this moral compass as a way of focusing her investments—of time, self, and advocacy. As she put it, "I get to choose who

I'm willing to invest in and spend time with." This capacity proved especially helpful in her work as a consultant centering equity and justice:

> If I am engaged in a consultation or a set of experiences and I say and know, like, this doesn't feel good . . . [or] this is a person or organization that I really don't think is willing to work . . . I definitely make choices about what battles I wanna fight, you know? And there are some times where I'm just like, "Yes." [laughs] I know all this *and* I am going to work with this organization or this person because I see the potential and I will be that person for them. And there are other organizations where I'm like, "Absolutely not." I will not and I'm okay with it because someone else may be the person for them. But I make those choices about fit.

As we hope these examples and those in the previous sections make clear, leaders making meaning with elements of a self-authoring way of knowing were able to exercise many essential capacities and approaches in the system-focused domain of justice-centering leadership. In the next section, we explore the aspects of practice and meaning making that leaders foregrounding self-authoring capacities named as *growing edges*—and the developmental experiences and supports that most helped them stretch forward.

DEVELOPMENTAL GROWING EDGES AND KEY SUPPORTS FOR GROWTH: BUILDING ON SELF-AUTHORING CAPACITIES

On the flip side of many participants' capacities to take a strong stand for their values and visions was what Carter (principal, white) described as "a lone warrior phenomenon." As we shared in Chapter 2, self-authoring capacities can help arm leaders with the confidence, capacities, and conviction to fight for what they believe in—like a developmental suit of armor that helps protect and deflect the sting of conflict. Yet, sometimes, developmentally speaking, this suit of armor can inadvertently block others—and their ideas—*out*, like a barrier. Reflecting on and capturing the essence of this challenge, Carter shared the following:

> Something I definitely don't delegate is my vision. [My vision] is very strong and I think that it has really good strength in some ways, and people respond to it and get behind me and feel motivated and inspired by it. [pauses] But I don't necessarily invite many other people into that vision or that envisioning with me. Like, they'll be a part of sketching it out at the smaller scale, but . . . my vision of equity and excellence—or my vision of justice—has really been my own, for as long as I can recall. And so I'm not really having a lot of, like, input or push from the people that are engaged in the work with me, and I think that feels like a growing edge.

Ian, too (teacher leader, white), described how such a solitary orientation has served as both a foundation *and* a limitation of his work:

> I think one of the pitfalls of my experience in general about race and also my career trajectory has been I've tended to be one of the few people who are interested in like, say, social justice or, like, child-centered curriculum or progressive education in the space I'm in. I've always been sort of isolated and a little bit different in my interests and beliefs than other people, so I've had to do it on my own and figure out things my own way and assume that no one else would quite understand, or wouldn't necessarily be on the same page as me, or be able to fully support me or be a partner in the way I'm thinking. So I've gotten used to kind of doing things on my own and being my own compass and being my own, you know, thought partner. I do think that that ultimately is a limitation . . . especially since I believe so strongly in collaboration and I think collaboration is, like, one of the tools for liberation, for justice, for equity, right? It has to be through people working together, and I don't have tons of experience of working together with other people in thinking about how to be a more equitable, thoughtful, social justice–focused teacher or leader. And maybe part of it is that, you know, part of it is definitely there's just not a lot of people who I tend to be on the same page with right away. Maybe I don't give everyone, enough people, the benefit of the doubt. Maybe I could learn from them in this area, as I should, 'cause maybe I'm sort of dismissive of people who have very, very different experiences than me, especially white teachers in particular.

As Carter's and Ian's examples help illustrate, developing a strong "I" voice for leadership can help leaders feel and be more successful—in general and especially as advocates for equity—but teaching and leading primarily from the "I" can also leave leaders holding feelings of great stress, responsibility, and loneliness. For example, looking back on her time as a school principal, Dr. B (teacher educator, African American woman) explained, "I felt like I was carrying the cross of a whole community." Carrying the bulk of this weight on her own for so long, Dr. B explained, didn't come without a cost. "I was moving so fast and so furious, I wasn't really present in any moment," she explained. "I didn't really live life during that time. I was just going, going, going, trying to get through everything, but not really having any meaningful experiences." Coming to see this pattern, she explained, was a critical "change in really wanting to enjoy life, a change as far as my health becoming important for me."

The toll of holding things up largely on one's own was shared by many of the participants in our study who were leading with self-authoring capacities at the fore. Adam (assistant superintendent, white), for example, described what it was like for him—on the inside—to feel the weight of his leadership:

> I carry all of the ills of society on my own back and take responsibility for them, in the sense that there's no better way to address them than proactively in the next generation. . . . So, you know, I carry a tremendous burden with that and a responsibility, but I also recognize the power in that and that's what keeps me up at night and also, you know, gets me right out of bed in the morning to be at work. It's super valuable work and it could be very frustrating. It could be very gratifying all the same. . . . I guess maybe part of where that frustration comes from . . . is that I thought that we would be further along as a society, and all that work that I've put into it, in an overly idealistic way back to my roots in education, [thinking] it would really change the world and change our culture and society. I feel sometimes, like, you know, when I'm rolling that boulder up, up the slippery mountain, [pauses] sometimes that boulder feels like it's rolling right over me.

Cheryl (district-level leader, white) similarly explained, "As a leader I always feel so, so, so responsible, you know? If there's, like, a neon sign that flashes in my head as a leader, it's the word *responsible*." Harris (principal, white) also reflected on the heaviness of his role: "There's a part of me that now realizes that the responsibility falls on me. Everything comes back to me, ultimately, at the end." As these examples help illustrate, standing firmly in one's agency, but alone, can only take a person so far. Recognizing the importance of taking a broader perspective on the self-authoring impulse to "go it alone," Ella (director of culture and language, African American), shared the following:

> I need to regulate myself so I don't go down a path of, "How do I fix this?" It is very easy for me to get caught up in, "Oh my gosh, this is going on, I need to be this person, I need to be the responsible one, I need to be the one that makes sure that everybody's heard" . . . and just overwhelm myself.

Not taking a beat to check this, Ella explained, is an easy leadership trap to fall back into, especially in a world that constructs leadership as a largely individual act. (Most schools, after all, have just one principal.) Ironically, though, such a solitary approach comes with built-in limitations. As she put it, when leaders try too hard to exert influence and authority, "it just seems to me that the very thing you're claiming you're combating is the very thing you embody at the same time."

VALUES-INFORMED SUPPORT

In another demonstration of self-awareness, leaders with strong self-authoring capacities were able to describe the kinds of supports they needed to best grow, stretch, and learn. At the top of that list—and in keeping with their intrinsic identification with their values and beliefs—was a good fit, ideologically, with their colleagues and organizations. As Micki (assistant principal/dean of students, Black woman) put it, "I need to be working with people who really want what I have to offer." Cheryl, too (district-level leader, white), had a strong sense of what was most important to her when assessing professional fit:

> I have needs in terms of my job. I need to feel really connected to the mission of what we're doing in order to stay, and I am. I have a need to feel like I have autonomy and that my skill sets are being used, and I do. I also feel like I need to feel I'm growing and developing, and I do here. . . . I have to feel like I'm growing in order to stay somewhere.

Also incredibly important for the leaders in our study with strong self-authoring capacities was support from trusted others who not only cared about them but also felt *similarly* about the issues and values they cared most about. Describing the importance of such kindred thought partners, Gabriel—the CEO of a reading-focused institute who identified as an African American father—emphasized "the need to network, the need to not be isolated in your role, the need to have other progressive partners to bounce ideas off of." Doing this, he explained, is essential—"just to have other people that you can learn and grow from."

Elaborating further, Ian (teacher leader, white) shared that what would feel most helpful to him would be "having someone who understands me and my perspective and sort of what I care about and believe in and could recognize when it's not showing up in real life." "Having other people to help me grow-slash-hold me accountable," he explained, "would be a big growing edge for me." Looking ahead, especially, to the prospect of taking on a more formal leadership role, Ian expressed how important this kind of values-aligned support and challenge would be:

> Especially if I'm moving into a leadership position, I will really want mentors or collaborators or peers who I respect . . . [and] feel like they're sort of on a similar page in our careers and in our thinking. And that I can learn from and who can push me because I don't always feel pushed in the directions that I care most about at my job, and I kind of have to push myself. And that's hard when I already have so many other pushes and pulls in so many other areas.

Paralleling Ian's sharing, the desire for thought partners who could be trusted to both "get it" *and* hold one accountable to core values emerged as a prevalent theme for leaders with strong self-authoring capacities. To help paint a picture of how different leaders experienced and articulated this need, we next share some representative examples.

Christopher (leader in a national philanthropic organization, African American) explained, "I want allies, but I don't want yes people. . . . Like, sometimes you just need someone to be with you when you're angry and be with you when you're wrong—but *not* to tell you that you're right. When you're wrong, that not actually useful." Similarly, Charlotte—a district-level leader with a teacher leadership focus who identified as a white woman—reflected, "People surround themselves with others who tell them that they have the best ideas, and I don't want to be surrounded by yes-men. I want to be surrounded by people who say, 'I think that's not the best thing for us to do,' and then we hash it all out." Nat (STEAM educational technologist, Puerto Rican woman) likewise described the importance of "folks who can be that kind of mirror for me because I need somebody to point out my blind spots." Sometimes, she explained, "It's like, 'Oops! I didn't realize that I was the problem in that situation,' you know?"

Describing, in some depth, how she was "in the midst of creating a stronger community of support," Ella (director of culture and language, African American) also expressed deep gratitude for the wise people in her life she could turn to for help and support. "They are treasures," she explained. "They're jewels; I collect them." Specifically, she explained, she felt their love and wisdom most clearly when they cared enough about her to share their truths, honestly and with kind frankness. As she put it,

> If they address something that I said that they felt was out of order, that's sign number one, the fact that they spoke up to say, "You know what, reconsider this." I said, "Wait. You cared enough to take your time and energy to say, 'Hey, I really believe in you, and hold you up to this high standard, so I'm going to tell you, this is kind of where you missed the mark.'" That means bunches to me. That means everything. To choose to do that, it means that they really respect me but also respect themselves.

As these examples help illustrate, looking to others for authentic, values-aligned feedback and colleagueship provided important developmental support for participants with strong self-authoring capacities, and helped them, as Margot (assistant superintendent, multiracial) explained, widen the circle of leadership and responsibility:

> It's not just me by myself. Yes, I'm a leader. Yes, the responsibility ultimately lies on my shoulders, but I have people I can count on who are smarter than me, right? I have people . . . who know things I just don't know, it's just not my background, and I want it that way. I want people to know more than me. . . . You can't know everything. You can't.

In the next section of this chapter, we dive more deeply into the important transition—inside and out—that can happen when leaders grow toward greater connectivity and collaboration as they stretch beyond self-authoring capacities. As we will share, doing so also opens a new entry point into the fourth domain of practice in our developmental model: the interconnecting.

LEADERSHIP IN TRANSITION: GROWING BEYOND THE SYSTEM-FOCUSED DOMAIN

In this chapter, we shared the stories and reflections of leaders foregrounding self-authoring capacities—for advocacy, agency, reflection, and systems alignment—in the system-focused domain of justice-centering leadership. As we just mentioned, reaching most effectively beyond self-authorship toward the interconnecting domain of practice requires the development of *at least* some self-transforming capacities, which can serve as an entry point into an even more expansive focus (as illustrated in Figure 5.2).

FIGURE 5.2   DEVELOPING SELF-TRANSFORMING CAPACITIES AS AN ENTRY POINT INTO THE INTERCONNECTING DOMAIN OF PRACTICE

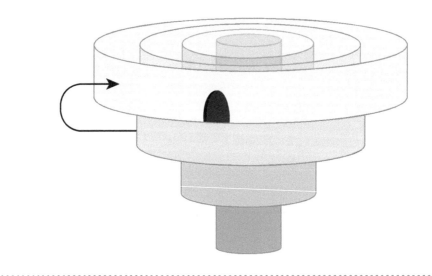

Accordingly, in this next section, we focus on leaders' experiences transitioning *between* the system-focused and interconnecting domains, with an emphasis on the ways they came to reprioritize connection and collaboration as essential for justice. Whereas before, as socializing knowers, leaders often oriented to the feelings, experiences, and approval of others as a way to feel whole and complete, leaders with emerging self-transforming capacities were coming to see that they needed others, not just to feel *more*

complete, but also to see more deeply into their selves and systems, as no one perspective or vision—however powerful or far-reaching—could ever cover the vast expanse and infinite horizons of justice needing excavation and exploration.

With this transition as our focus, we next explore leaders' experiences

- expanding their leadership vision and self-awareness, and
- turning back toward others as essential partners and collaborators.

Reflecting, for example, on how emphases on individualism and certainty can impede leaders' justice-oriented efforts when not coupled with the capacity to take a greater perspective on them psychologically, Ian (teacher leader, white) shared the following story about his own school leaders' perceived self-authorship and the turnover challenge at his school:

> It's been a trend at our school where a lot of teachers have left once they've reached a certain point, where they're interested in doing outside-of-the-classroom teacher leadership work more. It's sort of at this point in teachers' careers when we've had a lot of turnover and . . . I'd say one thing I've definitely noticed and think a lot about with adult development—I think all of our school leaders have a very strong, self-authoring sense. . . . They all have a strong vision of what the school should look like, and what leadership should look like, and how everything should go, and [they're] not very open to more of a transformative division of leadership, or taking in other people's perspectives and incorporating them into their own and coming up with something new and different. So they don't do a lot of asking questions about what other people think. They'll listen but then ultimately— usually—it goes with whatever they were thinking.

Recognizing, like Ian, that meeting the imperatives of justice and liberation requires even more than traditionally self-authoring capacities, many leaders in our study who were bumping up into the borders of the system-focused domain were working to take a continually broader perspective on *their own* value systems, positionalities, and responsibilities, as we explore next.

EXPANDING ONE'S VISION AND SELF-AWARENESS

For many of the leaders we had the honor of learning from in this work, growing to take a perspective on their internally generated values and philosophies meant realizing, over and over again, that their visions and expertise were inherently—and always—incomplete. Although disorienting and sometimes painful, truly recognizing one's fundamental partiality could actually be energizing and empowering, participants shared. As Brooke (head of school, white, gay) explained, "The older I get, the more I realize it's awesome to continue to change." Charlotte (district-level leader, white) also shared that growing in this way made her really stop and consider, "Why is it that competence or efficacy is so important to me?" "Maybe," she offered, "I was just in complete denial about showing people that I'm vulnerable."

Kristina (consultant, Black woman) likewise reflected on how important it was to face, with courage and honesty, the limits of one's own knowing. As she explained,

> It's humbling to recognize that you'll never reach this perfect place of knowing everything there is to know about any and every injustice. . . . There's always work to do to increase our own awareness and to make decisions that really help dismantle and not perpetuate [inequity].

Ian (teacher leader, white) similarly described his iterative process of learning and unlearning as a justice-centering educator. When given the opportunity, for instance, to observe a colleague whose practice in this arena he truly admired, Ian realized,

> Oh, there are so many more levels deeper that I could go, and so many ways I could improve, you know? So I think I've been struck by how little, in retrospect—I thought I was really well-informed on everything about being a social justice teacher when I was twenty-two, and now ten years later, I feel like there's much, much more that I need to know and be able to do and grow in order to be a teacher and leader that cares about social justice.

The experience of letting go of former certainty—and the assurance and comfort that came along with it—was further detailed by Brent (assistant principal, white, gay), who confided,

> I want to learn how to find contentment in un-specialness. I don't know how else to phrase that. But I think that might be a little bit harder to do. And so it costs more. [laughs] So that loss of those feelings of pleasure derived from the exclusivity and specialness of feeling that way, I think has been maybe the most painful.

ORIENTING DIFFERENTLY TO—AND SEEKING OUT—OTHERS

In addition to seeing oneself—and the limitations of one's perspective—more clearly, letting go of the "lone warrior" approach to leadership that many self-authoring leaders described also involved turning and looking back to others for more authentic partnership. Bringing together both sides of this perspective-taking coin, Joyce (consultant, Caribbean African American) recounted the following:

> I've developed a thicker skin. I've developed critical thinking skills. I've developed how to manage my emotions. I've developed how to be thoughtful about people and what they bring to the table. *And* I've developed this theory that I can't do it alone. That in order for me to do something, I need a team, so I have to figure out how I'm going to create that team, and not this idea that I'm doing the work.

Better understanding, like Joyce, that advocacy needs to be a shared endeavor—or like Shokry (consultant, Egyptian/Dominican heritage), who recognized that any individual's work, no matter how powerful, is really just "a pixel in a very large picture"—necessitates a recalibration of one's judgments of and orientations to others. As Shokry shared, reflecting on his evolving approach,

> I think my approach previously was to try to be loud and present in a way in which we would see change rapidly. A lot of those changes, unfortunately, that happened rapidly tended to happen on a very surface level. When we start talking about retooling and or even, in some cases, removing systems to create new ones, those are longer processes, so I see my advocacy as also having a responsibility to educate others about the ways in which *they* can be advocates because . . . I'm cognizant of the ways that the work will outlive me.

Dr. B (teacher educator/former principal, African American woman) likewise described the freeing shifts in thinking that came along with letting go of certainty and judgment. As she explained,

> I have a friend of mine, she's a therapist and she said, "You know, we would be so much better off in relationships if we would leave the three Cs behind us, which are convince, condemn, and convert." And so that's kind of my thing. I can let you be where you are and still love you. We can agree to disagree. You haven't traveled, you haven't gone through this, you didn't experience [what] I experienced. You didn't walk this walk with me. You did not take this journey with me. And so I cannot expect for you to see things through this lens that I see them through. And I, too, have not walked in your shoes. So—I just told my students the other day, "We really don't see things objectively. We see things through our experiences and our beliefs. That's how we see things." And once you become aware of that—that what I see is

based on my experiences and my belief system, and the same is true for you—then it makes it easy for me to let you be where you are because no matter how much we look alike, [it] doesn't matter, you know?

Brent (assistant principal, white, gay) described a similar shift in his approach to resistant colleagues. Pointing out the irony of his previously "exclusionary" approach to promoting inclusion, he explained,

I used to get pretty defensive because—especially as we began shifting the culture of the school and trying to implement this more inclusive learning model—there was a lot of resistance from teachers. . . . I would say, "No, you're wrong," and I would just be angry inside. I wrote so many angry emails that I just really don't ever want to look back at. [laughs] And so initially . . . I would get angry with them. . . . I think that's changed over the past, even just the past year. . . . [Now] I've been trying to practice what I preach, to understand their perspective, not exclude them because I was very exclusionary. I was like, "You're either in with this inclusion movement or you're out." [laughs] So it's now like, "What the hell was I thinking?" [laughs] But I still sometimes tense up a little bit, depending on how strong this feeling is or if it touches a nerve. But now I try instead to listen, to understand, so that I can include them.

In a parallel example, Thea (district-level leader, Black woman) shared,

I've been really on a healing journey, and I realize that when I see my colleagues across the system, even though they may present as resistant, they really need healing as well because we're all a part of the system. So what I'm learning more is to really approach folks with more compassion and curiosity and love, which I think previously I was more like, "You better get this and I don't understand why you're not getting it" and "Why don't you see this urgency that I feel?" But now I'm in a place [where] I feel like I'm a little bit more centered in this work, and realize that folks just really need to be loved on, specifically adults who are cast with so many things as a teacher, as a leader—to lead a school of families, of students. So I've become more humbled in this work, more reflective of who I am as a teacher and a learner and a leader.

In one final, representative story of transition, we share Margot's (assistant superintendent, multiracial) recollections of her internal experience leaning into collaboration as part of an important, districtwide initiative she was spearheading. Although, as Margot shared, she had a strong sense of what *should* happen to move things forward, she slowed things down to more authentically bring others into the visioning and planning. As she explained,

> I was willing to go through this process because this was bigger than me. Like, this has never been about me. This is about our students and our teachers, and I didn't want my own ego to get in the way of that, even though I had this all worked out. I knew what I wanted. I knew what it should look like. I had the architecture in my mind. I could have sat down with my three smartest friends and we could have designed this thing. It wouldn't have stuck.

Doing it with key stakeholders, rather than on her own, she shared, "is the real work and the way you make it stick because it's theirs." Still, it was hard at times for Margot because it meant giving up at least some of the control. "I wanted to move faster!" she confessed. Yet, because she "likes winning" and knew that a collaborative approach was the best one, she worked through her discomfort for the good of all. As she reasoned,

> I like to win, so if this is the process that's going to get the biggest win, this is the process I'm going to use. . . . I still want what I want. But I'm strategic and smart enough to know that process, inclusion, modeling, empathy—all of those things really matter and they actually have a better outcome than just trying to do it your way. I know that. I mean, I've seen it, I've been involved in it, I've watched it. So I've lived it, and yeah. I mean, I'm definitely a better leader now because I've learned these skills and strategies and I've seen it, what it does. I've seen what it does.

In the next chapter, we dive further into the shifts in leadership thinking and practice that can accompany a transition beyond self-authorship into the interconnecting domain. We hope that, like Margot's story, this next chapter helps illustrate, in a close-up way, what a more self-transforming, interconnective approach to centering justice in education can look like, feel like, and accomplish.

CHAPTER SYNOPSIS AND KEY TAKEAWAYS

The more you know yourself, the more patience you have for what you see in others. You don't have to accept what people do, but understand what leads them to do it. The stance this leads to is to forgive even though you still oppose.

—Joan Erikson (cited in Goleman, 1988)

Throughout this chapter, we explored the practices, approaches, and orientations of leaders working—with self-authoring capacities—to center justice in the system-focused domain of practice, as well as their developmental growing edges and experiences stretching toward further growth. As we will explore in Chapter 6, leaders can absolutely still ground their practice in a strong personal vision and a set of internally generated values as they grow toward more self-transforming ways of knowing and leading. However, as leaders grow to take a greater perspective on these parts of their selves and identities, their philosophies and beliefs can become incorporated into even larger self-systems. This will be the focus of our next chapter.

First, though, to bring together some of the most important ideas from Chapter 5, we present, in Figure 5.3, a list of key chapter takeaways. We have also created, in Table 5.1, a summative overview of leaders' practices in the system-focused domain and the experiences that most helped them stretch and grow.

FIGURE 5.3 CHAPTER TAKEAWAYS

- Leaders engaging in the system-focused domain of practice with strong self-authoring capacities often identify, psychologically, with their internally generated values and senses of purpose.

- Formal leadership roles often serve, for leaders making meaning in this way, as opportunities to further enact and expand the reach of their self-authored visions.

- Leading in the system-focused domain involves aligning initiatives across a school, district, team, or organization in keeping with one's guiding values and vision.

- Leaders with elements of a self-authoring way of knowing also demonstrate expanded capacities for reflection and self-awareness—in general and in relation to issues of identity and race.

- Leaders' self-authoring capacities also help them more readily speak out as advocates, as they recognize necessary conflict as part of the work of centering justice in an unjust system and world.

- Because self-authoring leaders in the system-focused domain rely so heavily on their own benchmark of judgment, they run the risk of operating as "lone wolves," or feeling the pressure of solitary responsibility.

- Turning back toward others—and opening up one's self-system to greater critique and collaborative insight—can be supported, often, through the encouragement and thought partnership of like-minded colleagues who can serve as accountability partners.

TABLE 5.1 OVERVIEW OF LEADERS' PRACTICE–AND GROWTH–IN THE SYSTEM-FOCUSED DOMAIN

DOMAIN OF JUSTICE-CENTERING LEADERSHIP PRACTICE	PRIMARY FOCUS	PREREQUISITE INTERNAL CAPACITIES	FOREGROUNDED PRACTICES AND APPROACHES	EXPERIENCES THAT SUPPORT DEVELOPMENTAL STRETCHING AND GROWTH	REPRESENTATIVE QUOTES
System-focused	Leading and living in accordance with internally generated values and standards Expanding locus of control, agency, and advocacy Meta view on schools and districts as organizations	Self-authoring	Strategic, big-picture thinking guided by clear values Aligning practices across an organization in keeping with personal values and vision A growing commitment to reflection and self-awareness Enhanced capacities for advocacy, engaging in necessary conflict, principled disruption, and boundary setting	Encouragement to pause and look beyond one's own actions, sphere of influence, and expertise Working with others toward collective goals Including others in the visioning and leadership work Values-informed support/mentoring	"How do the different initiatives I'm spearheading across my organization move things closer to my vision for justice?" "Does this person, effort, or initiative align with what I know to be most important for meeting my goals for justice and equity?" "I tell people, this is not what I do. This is who I am." "I can listen to you and I can hear you. And I can disagree with you."

Before turning to Chapter 6, we invite you, once again, to consider a series of reflective questions. They are offered as an opportunity to reflect on your own powerful experiences with justice-centering leadership and as a chance to connect what we've shared in this chapter with your own practice. You might want to reflect on these privately first, and then engage with a partner and/or with a team to dive deeper in generative, collective dialogue.

After listening to the leaders featured in this chapter discuss their commitments, growing edges, strengths, pain points, and convictions of heart and mind,

1. What is top of mind and top or bottom of heart for you after reading this chapter?

2. How, if at all, do the stories, ideas, and discussions in this chapter connect with your own experience and wisdom? Your own justice-centering leadership?

3. What are two or three of the larger insights you've had as you read this chapter? Who, if anyone, are you thinking about?

4. How, if at all, might you share some of the stories, ideas, and/or practices from this chapter? With whom? When? What's your next step?

5. After reading this chapter and considering leaders' stories about the system-focused domain of the model, what, if anything, might you like to practice and/or do differently in general? For your justice-centering leadership?

6. Early in the chapter, Harris described the importance of "thinking more wisely about our policies and practices" to make "systematic changes in schools." In what ways do you work systematically to center justice in your school or organization? To align policies and practices for greater equity?

7. Many of the leaders in this chapter, like Janae, described a commitment and capacity "to do whatever it takes," even in the face of resistance. Can you think of a time you've successfully taken a stand for something important to you? How did it go? What else might you want to speak up and out about? What conditions would support this advocacy?

8. Nat talked with us about how important she feels it is to have people in her life who can "be that kind of mirror for me" and point out "blind spots" and inconsistencies. Who in your life do you trust for authentic and honest feedback? Who are your mirrors?

9. Margot talked about the importance of widening "the circle of leadership and responsibility." How, if at all, does this resonate with you? Who do you want to bring into the circle of your leadership and vision? Who can you reach out to?

10. After reading this chapter, what is something you'd like to think more deeply about? Do differently? Get better at? Learn more about?

11. What, if anything, would you like to think more about before turning to Chapter 6?

CHAPTER 6

....

CONNECTING AND GROWING ACROSS SYSTEMS AND SELVES

Leading for Social Justice With Self-Transforming Capacities

We define who we are by what we include.

—Gloria Anzaldúa (2002, p. 3)

In this chapter, we paint a portrait of leaders' practice in the fourth domain of our developmental model for justice-centering leadership: the interconnecting. Though less commonly surfaced in our study, an interconnecting approach is, by way of reminder, distinguished by an emphasis on *interdependence*—of schools and broader social systems, of people across roles and positionalities—and the need for coalition when leading for justice and change. As represented by the doorway in Figure 6.1, the most successful engagement in this domain is also connected, developmentally, to the growth of at least *some* self-transforming capacity.

As we explored in Chapter 2, self-transforming knowers have grown the capacity to take a greater perspective on and critique their personal value systems—value systems which, as self-authoring knowers, they had previously been "run" by and embedded in, psychologically. Yet, as you might suspect, stepping outside of oneself—to uncover and explore the hidden recesses of complexities, paradoxes, and contradictions (in systems internal and external)—cannot be accomplished alone. Self-transforming

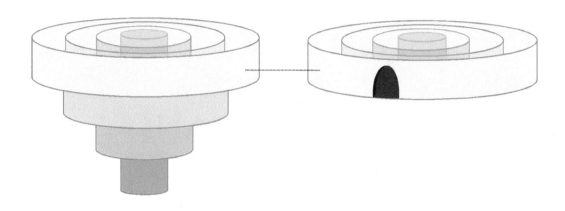

knowers, then, seek out relationships and contexts grounded in mutuality and reciprocity—in order to grow and help others grow. Leading questions for leaders who make meaning in this way, for instance, could be wonderings like, "How can we help each other see more deeply into ourselves and the world around us?" and "What might we help each other recognize and address with more conscious awareness?" or "What parts of this issue, complexity, or imperative do I not yet understand?"

In terms of justice-centering leadership, engaging in the interconnecting domain also means integrating each of the layers that came before. Indeed, if you were to look at the banded diagram of the interconnecting domain in Figure 6.1 *from up above*, you'd see, again, our original mapping of the continuum of practice, as represented by the concentric circles in Figure 6.2.

In other words, when leaders are able to bring elements of a self-transforming way of knowing to the outermost domain of practice, they then also have—in their justice-centering leadership toolboxes—the internal capacities to (a) engage in the interconnecting approaches described in this chapter, (b) take a stand for what they believe in and work in accordance with their personal benchmark of judgment (i.e., in the system-focused domain), (c) tune into and care for others' inner, emotional states (i.e., in the interpersonal domain), *and* (d) take clear and tangible action steps for change (i.e., in the concrete domain). They just engage in these approaches with new perspectives and capacities—and as reinforcing facets and expressions of their commitments to justice.

No one person can do all of these things all of the time, but developing the capacity to engage more effectively in each domain—as appropriate and as needed—allows leaders to pull from a greater range of practices to differentiate their leadership, meet the shifting demands of a moment, and

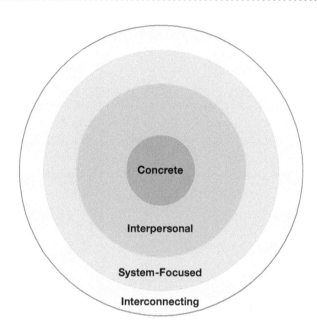

support others as they too journey along the continuum. Although, as noted in earlier chapters, many mainstream notions of leadership—and especially educational leadership—tend to favor more individualistic, self-authoring approaches and constructions (e.g., "Leaders should be strong and know all the answers"), our research supports the real value and promise of bringing more self-transforming, interconnecting capacities and orientations to leadership roles of all kinds.

Harder to find among the genuinely brilliant and generous leaders in our study—and less familiar, in our experience, in schools, districts, and educational organizations—an interconnecting approach to justice-centering leadership nonetheless echoes the wisdom of more collectivist leadership orientations and women of color feminisms.

By way of example, we point to the identity-expansive threshold theorizing of the trailblazing scholar of Chicana cultural theories and queer feminisms, Gloria Anzaldúa (2002, 2015). Speaking to both the paradoxes and possibilities of continuing to evolve into and beyond a self-transforming orientation, Anzaldúa's work—and that of her colleague, AnaLouise Keating (2013)—describes the transformational promise of an intellectual and theoretical humility that remains open to constant evolution and border crossing. As Keating explained, reflecting on the power of Anzaldúa's emphasis on fluidity and in-betweenness, "Threshold theories draw from numerous perspectives and offer no final destination, no permanent fixed truths" (p. 11). Keating also captures—in clear and powerful ways in her own writing—how a more self-transforming orientation to identity and relationships is about moving *beyond* opposition toward interconnection as a way to hold and be more. This is quite different from retreating or pulling back from conflict (a more socializing response). We quote her here at some length:

> Grounded in a framework of interconnectivity—a metaphysics of interconnectedness, as it were—threshold theories are relational. . . . Threshold theories are premised on a shared commonality (not sameness)—a complex commonality so spacious that it embraces difference—even apparently mutually exclusive differences. . . . This loosening of previously restrictive categories, perspectives, and beliefs—while incredibly painful—can create shifts in consciousness and new opportunities for change; we acquire additional, potentially transformative perspectives, different ways to understand ourselves, our circumstances, our worlds. (pp. 11–13)

Although we, of course, have not engaged in any developmental assessments with Keating or Anzaldúa, their scholarship nonetheless helps, in our view, give shape and voice to a way of knowing that is still relatively rare in the U.S. context. A constructive-developmental lens also helps illuminate one path toward such an interconnecting way of leading and making meaning, as it identifies the developmental "prerequisites" one must grow through on the way to a more self-transforming way of knowing and being.

For these reasons, we are especially excited to share stories and reflections from the leaders in our study who were moving toward and/or making meaning with elements of a self-transforming way of knowing. Although fewer leaders appear in this chapter than in the previous ones—and different leaders highlight different aspects of an interconnecting approach to centering justice—we hope that their different glimpses of practice, together, offer a mosaic depiction of this domain, rich with possibility. In the next sections, we explore leaders' experiences in the interconnecting domain, including their

- internal sensemaking (particularly as connected to self-transforming capacities as an entry point),

- interconnecting practices and approaches for centering justice, and

- growing edges and orientations to ongoing possibilities, paradoxes, and complexities.

As mentioned, we feature fewer leaders in this chapter, and some reappear in multiple places. Because of this, we include the fuller list of identifiers leaders shared with us when first introducing them in the chapter but gradually move away from reminders as individual leaders become more familiar. We also quote some leaders at greater length in this chapter than has been our practice so far, in order to really give space to the complexity of their thinking and leading.

Next, we start by exploring how interconnection—of systems and people—served as a front-of-mind priority for leaders making meaning in this way.

PRIORITIZING INTERCONNECTION

Although expressed less frequently by the participants in our study, educational leaders demonstrating elements of a self-transforming way of knowing spoke powerfully about the promise and complexity of leading with ever more holistic, interconnected understandings of justice, equity, leadership, identity, and positionality at the fore. As you may recall from Chapter 5, leaders with strong self-authoring capacities could absolutely hold a strong value for interconnection and collaboration—and many were beginning to stretch the edges of their own deeply cherished value systems through iterative reflection and thought partnership. That said, growing toward a more self-transforming way of knowing, being, seeing, leading, and thinking involved the qualitatively distinct and enhanced capacity for holding and being *more*—more inclusive, more connected, more than oneself alone. We think of this distinction as the difference between authentically *believing* something like interconnection is important, on the one hand, and more fully *embodying* it, intrinsically, on the other. For emerging self-transforming knowers, interconnection was more than a philosophical commitment or value stance. Rather (or in addition), and as we will explore throughout this chapter, it was an increasingly central, internalized *orientation*—and an integral part of their internal calculus as leaders and human beings.

As we will explore next, the leaders growing toward and within the interconnecting domain named three key shifts informing their practice:

- recognizing schools as one system amid many other, broader systems and histories;

- taking an ever-wider and more expansive view on these systems, themselves, and others; and

- honoring the intrinsic interconnection of people, communities, issues, (in)justices, and systems.

BEYOND SCHOOLS

One of the ways an orientation toward a more encompassing, interconnected view came into focus was through leaders' emphasis on schools as one system among many. Just as understanding schools as finite systems helped self-authoring leaders think and act strategically within the purview of their classrooms, teams, buildings, districts, and organizations (please see Chapter 5), zooming out even further—to understand education as one element in a larger constellation of systems—helped leaders take an even *greater* perspective on their work, as well as its challenges and potentialities. As Joyce—a consultant who identified as Caribbean African American—explained,

> We're in a really tough time in education. I think in the world. And we can't go about living as though education isn't connected to the social events of the world. So to treat them in isolation would be a disservice to the work I do.

Evan—a district-level curriculum leader who identified as a white, cisgender male—likened his experience of learning to look *beyond* school to stepping out of a particular frame of reference. As he put it,

> If I understand schools to be part of much larger systems . . . I can see that it's just a unit within a larger system. . . . It's as if I'm—I don't know if I can extend that metaphor—like looking at a framed picture. It's like, there's a lot in there, and there's a lot to understand and analyze. Whereas prior to that, I was inside of that frame and *in* that picture.

Stepping "outside" of the framed picture of school, Evan explained, helped him realize that "the school needs to understand itself and its relationship to other organized bodies of power." We think this metaphor—of carefully examining the details of experience within the "frame" of the education sector while also being able to step outside and see beyond it—is an apt one for the kind of perspective taking and internal capacity needed for a more interconnecting approach. As Shokry—a consultant who named his Dominican/Egyptian heritage as a key identifier—explained, when you grow this way, "You start to see that the world is much more interconnected and that schools are not isolated." Reflecting further about the necessity to extend justice efforts beyond the schoolhouse door, Shokry shared,

> Thinking about our world being interconnected, our businesses and our nonprofits and our schools all follow similar curricula because, really, school is meant to prepare you for career, college, and civic duty. So, I started thinking about it being a little futile to just do this kind of work where we're digging and uncovering and growing in schools. It's the world that our students and our teachers are part of that doesn't acknowledge that work or support it, right? It almost becomes counterintuitive. And I think I started seeing the world at large as a professional development space. I started seeing the world at large as a learning and development space. And it didn't feel that it was boxed within certain institutions anymore.

By developing a more aerial view and perspective, Shokry was able to see potential points of connection, synergy, and conflict within and across systems. Yet, as we shared earlier, it wasn't just a technical shift for

Shokry—like simply zooming out a lens on a camera or aiming the same lens at different elements of experience. Rather, seeing on these multiple levels actually required new capacity to take in and hold greater complexity and nuance—at all levels. Describing the *internal* changes that helped bring different dimensions of experience into focus while he was looking and seeing in new ways, Shokry said, "It feels almost like a full circle return in the sense that I get to view the work from a different perspective." "I guess my understanding of the work feels fuller," he continued. "My ability to hear people feels stronger, to some extent." It is these kinds of shifts of internal experience and meaning making—as well as their connections to practice—that we aspire to highlight in this chapter.

HOLDING EVEN BIGGER PICTURE VIEWS

Leaders demonstrating some elements of self-transforming capacity also named, as central to their thinking, a more generalized and internally realized commitment to holism and the "big, big picture." As Brooke—a head of school who identified as a white, cisgender, gay woman—explained, "Everything is bigger than us." Leading with equity and justice at the center, she explained, "continues to inspire me to see bigger and be bigger and do more beyond just, like, the insular me." Relatedly, Jean-Claude—a district-level coordinator of curriculum and teacher leadership who identified as Asian American—helped articulate why it was so important to him to always strive to see more and to look beyond himself. As he explained,

> I think just getting a larger three-sixty view, as close to a three-sixty view, *more* of a three-sixty view. To understand the complexity of it. I think it goes back to how I still have a limited view—all of us do—of this big puzzle that we're working with, right? I see X number of pieces and others see other pieces. . . . I have to get up and see the world from a different angle . . . and I think what helps me is to constantly go in and out of different layers of circles, concentric circles perhaps.

In a more literal anecdote that nonetheless helps illustrate the impact of seeing things from afar and anew, Dr. B—a teacher educator and former principal who identified as an African American woman—described how a skydiving experience helped her reframe her work as principal at the time and a leader for equity and justice:

> When we actually jumped out of the plane, it was the most exhilarating experience. . . . As I got closer to the ground, I saw a football field—saw two football fields in fact—and I saw a building, the sign of which for me was a school. And as I saw that school, it made me think of my school. And I landed on the beach, so I could see all the way out into the ocean. I could see all of these ships and barges, where I could just see vast amounts of water.

Then I could also see all the way to the [city] skyline and just all these highways and buildings and all these gazillion cars, and as I was falling from the sky, I'm thinking about all the gazillion situations and circumstances that all these people are dealing with. But as I got closer and I saw this school, I thought of my school and I said, "That school looks like a kernel of corn, about the size of a kernel of corn," and what it did for me, it put things in perspective. . . . I saw in the grand scheme of things, that school was a kernel of corn. . . . So my work, the work that I do [is] writ large and important, very important, but it was that small in the grand scheme of things. And so when I went back to work, my perspective was different.

With this new understanding, Dr. B explained, she was able to think differently about ways to contribute—to both hold onto the urgency of her commitments and to think more expansively about how she could be a part of the change she imagined. As she shared, "I find myself being a little more open to what my path is supposed to be. I know it's education, but [I'm] not being closed off to what I think it has to be, but kind of opening myself up to more possibilities."

Zooming out even further to a cosmic level in his reflections, Lee—a national-level nonprofit leader who identified as a white, cisgender, gay, Jewish male—reflected on how he works to balance the scope and vastness of the universe with the urgencies of up-close, lived realities. Both, he shared, are true—and mutually fueling:

You could look at it like, "Wow, we really, really don't matter because . . . we're just such a speck," and I'm just thinking that's a helpful perspective to remember sometimes because we do get so riled up and obsessed about every action that we take and whether or not it's making a difference. It's, like, at the end of the day, maybe you just need to put it all in the big perspective and recognize that this is just one moment in a much bigger scheme. And at the same time, you are experiencing this little moment, like, this is—for you, this is happening, and for the people around you, this is happening. So it matters because it's your life and you're living it. But you can also look at the total other end of the telescope and take a breath.

HONORING AND EMBRACING INTERCONNECTION

In addition to—or perhaps as an extension of—this growing capacity to see and navigate the world from multiple depths and heights, participants moving into or making meaning with a self-transforming way of knowing also expressed deep understandings of and yearnings for interconnection—of individuals, groups, social issues, and more. Lee, for example (the national-level nonprofit leader quoted above), confided, "I see myself in others, and I want others to see themselves in me." Achieving this, he explained, would be "like a spiritual reciprocity." Foundational, then, to his leadership orientation is the idea that, "We together are recognizing our common destiny, our common humanity, and I'm essentially putting a covenant with you, and that is a mutual covenant."

Shokry (consultant, Dominican/Egyptian) similarly centered interconnection in his approach to leadership, explaining, "I think when we start to see the connectivity between people, we start to understand that we're all inspirations to each other." "I think too often," he continued, "especially in our modernized life, we overlook how connected we are to each other's successes." Moreover, like many others, he recognized how the COVID-19 pandemic helped pull back the curtain on this fundamental interdependence:

> Whether I am at the top of an economic system in which I am very well off, or I am at the lower rungs of it in which I am worried about food and financial security, I am still impacted by the welfare of those around me. I think even our current circumstance with the pandemic has shown us that there are very few degrees of separation between our lives.

Recognizing this interconnection, according to Ladan Jahani—a social worker who identified as Iranian American—is key to social change. As she explained, "It is just about people being on this planet. I think the more you can show how we are connected, the better things become."

Essentially, for participants working to embrace and enact a more self-transforming, interconnecting approach to their justice-centering leadership, entering into the work meant asking, as Thea—a district-level leader and Black woman—poetically did, "How do we create a community where we are liberating ourselves as one another?" This grounding question and orientation was similarly echoed by Ella—a director of culture and language who identified as an African American woman:

> How do we encourage a world where people really see that they're connected with each other? How do we encourage a world where people see value and see that another person's suffering is not very distinct from their own? In a lot of ways, it could seem very philosophical and kind of existential, but social justice is, I think, making that practical—making the philosophical and existential practical. How does that then translate? And then become acts of social justice or movements of social justice? It's like we are all connected, so [we need] . . . to decide to be a part of that tapestry.

In the next sections, we dive more deeply into how participants worked to both see and be a part of the larger "tapestry" of life and change—and bring their interconnecting orientations to leadership practice. First, though, we invite you to engage with the following reflective questions as a way to tap into and connect with your own experiences.

1. What is top of mind for you right now?

2. What do you see as some of the borders of your own belief system and/or field of vision?

3. What perspectives and/or parts of justice are you most interested in learning more about?

4. What do you see as some of the more important influences (e.g., political, historical, cultural) on the education sector? How might these different systems intersect and overlap?

5. In what new ways, if any, might you want to foreground interconnection in your work?

6. How prepared do you feel to do so? What supports do you have—or might you need—to enhance this part of your leadership?

LEADERS' INTERCONNECTING APPROACHES TO CENTERING JUSTICE

Compassion and tolerance are not a sign of weakness, but a sign of strength.

—Dalai Lama XIV

In essence, bringing self-transforming capacities to leadership involved revisiting—and expanding—the relational and agentive capacities discussed in earlier chapters. Specifically, as we mentioned at the start of this chapter, a more self-transforming, interconnected orientation involved taking an ever-bigger perspective on the complexities, paradoxes, and possibilities of one's own identity and positionality (and those of others), and foregrounding more interconnected, interdisciplinary, and intra- and interorganizational approaches and understandings. That such an approach involves complex developmental capacities seems a particularly important learning given the emphasis placed on intersectionality, mutuality, and sustainable coalition building in the social justice literature (e.g., Allen, 2016; Bell, 2016; Keating, 2013; Magee, 2019). Here, we highlight particular strengths of practice shared by leaders growing toward and leading with self-transforming capacities, including

- continually and intentionally working to expand their own points of view and understandings,

- inviting coalition and collectivism,

- reframing anger as compassionate urgency, and

- building bridges through inquiry.

EXPANDING ONE'S VIEW

Although, as we discussed in Chapter 5, self-authoring leaders used their internally generated values and convictions to guide, align, and inform action toward greater equity—and spoke of the importance of exploring, with others who shared those values, the unintentional inconsistencies and "blind spots" in their leadership—leaders with emerging self-transforming capacities described the importance of not only holding oneself and others accountable to core values, but of continually interrogating and exploring those values in and of themselves. In other words, for self-transforming knowers, any particular set of ideas, perspectives, or beliefs is fundamentally and by definition partial—no matter how deeply felt—not because they are wrong per se, but because they could never encompass the entirety of experience. As Lee (national-level nonprofit leader, white, cisgender, gay, Jewish) explained, "I'm always interested in the counter narrative. Who would disagree with the point of view, and what is their point of view about that?" Shokry (consultant, Dominican/Egyptian) likewise explained,

> I'm trying to ground myself in this belief—and ground my actions in the belief—that my experience doesn't necessarily equate to the experience of others. And until I'm able to put my experience aside, I actually won't get to see another person's perspective as fully as I could. You know, this idea of being able to look through someone else's eyes doesn't work if we want to keep our own eyes on.

For leaders in our study who were growing into more self-transforming orientations, the work of balancing personal convictions and agency with a more expansive openness was a central tension and preoccupation. As Ella put it, "I want to naturally know how to be responsive and stay pliable and flexible . . . but also know and stand in my own space and voice in that." Reflecting on this tension at some length, Lee shared the following:

> I've seen a lot of quite assertive, opinionated leaders . . . in very prominent positions of leadership, where their vision, their perspective, their agenda governed the choices that they made for their community or their city, and it actually left out a lot of other voices that also ought to be part of the conversation. And I've come to realize that . . . no person has the full story, no person could internalize and be conscious of all of the different perspectives, interests, [and] values. Actually, what [leadership] requires is a collective approach. Any given leader, their strength can lie in simultaneously having a point of view—because you need a point of view in order to just move forward; otherwise, you're just going to stand still or constantly wait for someone else to tell you what to think, and who knows if what they're saying makes sense. You have to have a point of view and you have to be willing to hold it loosely enough to allow others in. And not just, like,

allow others in, but actually welcome them, to welcome the fact that you don't have the full story and that together you can create the full story. . . . So I have to be very thoughtful about how much of myself is part of the decision making versus how much of my facilitating [invites] others to come to a shared understanding. And that, to me, is one of the hallmarks of what I hope to embody and what I hope to teach others to do, which is to think about, "Where is your ego in all of this and when do you need to step forward?"

Making a similar point about starting with—but not stopping at—personal agency, Jean-Claude (district-level leader, Asian American) explained,

This work is about a better future. . . . I have to stand for something, and I have to decide for myself what that better future could look like. So I think I have to start there. But it's not the end of it, right? . . . My better future is not everybody else's better future. . . . Maybe we have a common better, but then the argument is over how we do it. . . . Sometimes I think these terms are used very ambiguously, right? I mean, when we say "better," what is that? What does that mean? Better for whom? . . . What else are we not thinking about? How else can we see this? How else, so that other people can have a wider, broader scope [and] purview to help them make their decisions? I think that's really how I see my role right now. . . . I do as much as possible to say, "Is there another way of looking at this? Before you make that decision, can we also think, should we also think about it this way?" So I think that's kind of how I place myself.

For leaders with self-transforming or emerging self-transforming capacities, a big part of letting go of the certainty of one's convictions involved the courage and vulnerability to look ever deeper within, to challenge even fundamental understandings of *who one was in the world* and what that meant, and to risk seeing the world and even oneself anew. Fighting the urge to seek "confirmation bias to make sure your own world makes sense," as Jean-Claude described it, was a constant commitment—and opportunity. As Shokry explained, "I uncover new biases within myself every single day. And it is both infuriating to find that they exist and exciting to be able to identify them because I can address them." Jean-Claude similarly described his lived experience of committing to intellectual and critical humility:

I think, like everybody else, I have blind spots. I defined social justice for you . . . the way I understand it, right? And I think that can change, and I think there are certain perspectives that I'm not including in my definition. So I think it's really understanding more ways—or a more expansive way—of thinking about social justice, and the ambiguities within that. So what could be "just" to one person might not be to another person. And to allow myself to go there—to share things, read things, and see things that may actually challenge the way I define it currently. . . . And sometimes, I don't know, it might be hard, and I might reject it. But in the end, I like to at least give myself an opportunity to say, "Oh, there's another way, a deeper way, a more expansive way of thinking about social justice." When you're advocating for social justice in one way, for example, are you thinking [about] injustice or inequity elsewhere that can't be seen immediately? So I think those are things I think a lot about and actually feel tormented about sometimes [laughs] because I think it's so fluid and there is no absolute "this is what I'm working towards" because just when you're working towards it, you learn something new, and you have to allow yourself to keep on defining how you understand this work.

In another powerful and related example, Luz—a principal of a high school dedicated to human rights, who identified as a Black, Afro-Latina, cisgender woman—described her experience re-seeing and reframing the work she had done for many years with young women of color in her care. "I didn't necessarily have women that were speaking with me and encouraging me to move beyond gender norms within the Latino community," she explained, reflecting on her experiences as a young person. "And so I just created my own—not on my own, but I did what felt right for me." Out of this yearning from her youth and the natural connections she built with the young women—especially young women of color—in her school community, Luz developed a series of ongoing groups and events for girls and young women that centered on interpersonal relationships, family histories, homeopathic remedies, aromatherapy, poetry, healing, development, and more. Yet, as impactful and defining as this work had been for Luz and those in the community, when one of Luz's own children shared that they identified as trans/nonbinary, she recognized the importance of thinking differently and even more expansively about gender—as a mother, teacher, leader, and person:

> That experience had me reflect on my work and wonder whether I was actually recreating more oppressive situations for young people who maybe didn't identify as young women or young men because it was so male-female. So that pushed me to grow and evolve.

Amid this ongoing learning and unlearning, Luz embraced "the process of becoming more humanized daily," and committed to helping more and more young people, like her own child, "figure out who they are in a world that doesn't [always] show them who they can be." Investing in youth development in this way, she explained, was a passion that both fueled her drive *and* demanded reexamination of formerly taken-for-granted certainties. As she put it—capturing the hallmark of a self-transforming stance—"I'm interested in continuing to evolve and grow . . . so that we may rise together."

INVITING COALITION

As the stories above suggest, leaders in our study who were operating with or developing self-transforming capacities recognized that to learn, grow, see, include, and build in ways that felt most needed and potential-filled, it was essential to look outside of and beyond oneself and to be in coalition with others. After all, if one's perspective is, by definition, limited and bounded, and if one's work as an educator is inherently influenced by many larger systems, leaders need others—not to validate the completeness of their personal values and beliefs, but to see into and beyond them, and to position them within a larger constellation of ideas, opportunities, and imperatives. As Luz put it,

> I think social justice requires . . . a sense of collective leadership, right? No one of us is more powerful than all of us, and in that sense, it's "How do we move strategically and powerfully to transform the community that we live in so there's a real ripple effect that allows us all to rise in love and freedom together?"

Developmentally speaking, then, and as we discussed in Chapter 2, growing toward a self-transforming orientation to leadership involves a return to the collective side of the helix/gyre—but with new, more complex capacities and heightened perspectives. Moreover, although relationships can and do still play a central role in self-transformational leadership approaches, those same relationships can hold, include, and encompass more. As Lee explained, "Relationships ultimately become a coalition, where you're building connections between various groups who may have a lot of differences between them, but may have some common interests that can form the basis of a really bold vision for what you're trying to accomplish." In other words, and as Lee's example helps illustrate, self-transforming knowers can very much nourish and appreciate individual, interpersonal relationships, yet they also demonstrate growing capacities to see the relationships (or potential relationships) that can exist among and between different stakeholders in their networks and across sectors.

Zora—the CEO and founder of a nonprofit with national reach, who identified as a heterosexual, married African American woman and mother who grew up in a low-income community but experienced economic mobility—likewise emphasized the transformational potential of relationships writ large through coalition. Despite the isolation that can accompany modern technological shifts, she explained, "Relationships matter mightily and relationships can be scaled . . . just like we've seen in other movements like the civil rights movement, the gay rights movement, the women's movement." Yet, distinct from important understandings about interest convergence (Bell, 2016)—wherein social progress is made only when it suits the needs and purposes of the dominant group—Zora layered the importance of deep regard and "heart change" atop the practical, transactional dimensions of coalition. As she explained, "When you're dealing in the world of people who have been marginalized, ideas have to come from within that community, and there also has to be allies . . . 'cause that's often where the heart change is, in the allies." Ultimately, Zora, shared, "it will be about whether or not we deeply care about our fellow man or woman or person who does not identify with either gender and their well-being that will make the biggest difference over time." Put another way, as Loile—a district-level leader who identified as an African American woman—phrased it, "When there is community, there is survival. And that is the world I'd like to live in."

Building Bridging Ties

Echoing arguments made by political theorist and professor Danielle Allen (2016), the leaders with emerging self-transforming capacities in our study spoke passionately about building *bridging ties*—or seeking out and honoring the ideas, perspectives, and priorities of people across roles, positionalities, and lines of both difference and similarity—within relationships, teams, organizations, and partnerships of all kinds. Like Allen (2016), participants recognized the capacity to work in such bridging ways as essential for moving toward more democratic, inclusive, responsive, and just systems and institutions. As Zora explained,

> [My organization] has an incredibly diverse team on purpose, like, we decided on a very diverse team in the field. In that diversity there's some things that are obvious in terms of the hue of people's skin, and then there's things that are not as obvious. We have white members of our team who grew up in rural America in low-income families. We have African American members of our team who ended up growing up in higher-income families. We have white members of our team who grew up in the most privileged households in their communities. And the collective, regardless of race and class, sexual orientation, etcetera, matters a lot to the work. And I always say I'm only as good as my team, like, I'm actually not that good as an individual. I'm only as good as my team.

With a focus on enhancing professional and economic opportunities for low-income, first-generation college students and students of color, Zora's organization takes a purposefully inclusive, collaborative, and cross-sector approach. As she explained, "There needs to be a lot of input coming from the ground and the people most close to the opportunity areas and the challenge areas." "Hearing those voices and making sure that their opinions and thoughts are definitely included in the direction of the organization," she shared, is essential. In this way, Zora told us, she can develop authentic partnerships with impacts greater than the sum of their parts. Offering a bit more about her approach to collaboration, she said,

> [Another] thing I'm super proud of is that we've done it in partnership with higher education institutions who really do feel we are partners with them. They don't feel like we've come in and said, "You're just awful and you don't know what you're doing, so let us do it." It's more like we're in partnership in order to do the right thing for this group of students in this particular city . . . even if it's trying to figure out, "How do we work together in a large bureaucracy?" I'm very proud of that. And I'm also very proud of the donors and the employer partners that have also said, "We have a role to play." . . . This is not only good for the university, for these students. It's actually good for our cities, and so we all need to come together around that.

Henrietta—the co-founder of an educational nonprofit focused on leadership development, who identified as white—likewise emphasized the importance of coalition and cross-sector work, both for the high school students she was engaging with in her region and the network of community partners she was trying to build. Part of the mission of her organization, she explained, was the development of diverse teams of young people working together to solve real-world problems. Bringing together different perspectives and experiences, she felt, would help make the teams more effective in the immediate sense, but it could also—more importantly and more broadly speaking—mirror the collective work she felt was needed to really move the needle toward greater justice, civic engagement, and coalition. "This isn't just about jobs," Henrietta explained. "This is, I think, a much larger issue." Further underscoring how powerful she felt authentic collaboration could be when diversity—of all kinds—was leveraged as a mutual strength and asset, Henrietta said,

> I just am so convinced that, you know, with the complex challenges that we face, we have got to figure out how to do that work collectively and leverage each other's strengths, or we won't be able to solve these complex problems. And again, I feel that that's sort of on an individual level but also [in relation to] what is happening in our country right now, and our world.

Reframing Leadership as Collective Wisdom

Although leaders adopting a more interconnecting approach recognized the great promise of authentic collaboration and coalition, they also acknowledged how their emphases on the collective generally stood in stark contrast with taken-for-granted understandings of leadership—and especially educational leadership. As educational leadership scholars are increasingly arguing (e.g., DeMatthews, 2018; Khalifa, 2018), most mainstream leadership practices, standards, and preparation programs aim their foci, primarily, at school-specific competencies and criteria (e.g., curriculum leadership, professional learning, assessment, data analysis, and operations). Such bounded skills and competencies are, of course, important for individuals stepping into leadership roles in schools and districts—and leadership standards and preparation efforts are increasingly moving to include more critical, culturally responsive, and even community-inclusive domains—yet a school-centric approach often fails to center the imperatives of working beyond "the silos of schools," as Henrietta called them, or to acknowledge the deep traditions of community leadership pioneered by Black principals and educational leaders of color and activists (DeMatthews, 2018; Gassaway, 2018; Khalifa, 2018).

Layering a developmental dimension atop these understandings—namely, that leading effectively with an interconnected approach requires complex internal capacities—adds new nuance to why it can be so hard for leaders to work both within and across schools and sectors, and perhaps also why it was so rare to find leaders with self-transforming capacities still working in brick-and-mortar schools. But what a missed opportunity! Making a powerful case, for instance, about how even just looking *across* schools could help break down traditional boundaries and jurisdictions, Shokry reflected,

> I think one of the most heartbreaking things I've seen working with—I think I worked with 63 schools this year—is that in every school building there's something that people are getting absolutely right. Whether that be in one person's class, in one grade, whether it be a curriculum, whether it be parent outreach, whether it be an approach. But there's still little conversation between schools about what that means for student experiences and how they grow and develop as adults.

Moreover, and as Lee explained, the normative understanding of educational leadership—and particularly the principalship—as a *solitary* endeavor (reified by popular understandings of there being *one* principal, as well as bureaucratic and organizational norms requiring the appointment of just one person in the role) limits, by nature, a more collective approach. As Lee shared,

> I think traditionally, leadership is thought of as a leader, as a person—often who has archetypal characteristics . . . [but] leadership ultimately requires collective energy. . . . Any individual doesn't have it all, and that's okay, and you don't have to. . . . As someone who's aspiring to make systems change, it is your charge to . . . build a broad, diverse coalition, which means you are actively going to seek out multiple perspectives and points of view. Because if you want to change, you're going to need a group of people to do it, and ideally a group of people who all have different stakeholders or constituents or networks in order to make the change that you're hoping to make.

MOVING TOWARD COMPASSIONATE URGENCY

The leaders in our study who were making meaning with some elements of, or growing toward, a self-transforming way of knowing were working, in different ways, to counter hegemonic understandings of leadership and enact their lived commitments to interconnection in schools and the outside world. However, they also described some of the *internal* shifts and orientations that helped them be more effective bridge builders and facilitators for change within their roles and communities. Specifically, themes around (a) reframing anger and judgment and (b) building connection through inquiry emerged as important through-lines for leaders with some elements of self-transforming capacity. Leading in these ways helped these leaders move closer to what we describe as *compassionate urgency*—meaning a fervor around the work heightened and enhanced, not lessened, by their deep commitment to valuing the fullness (and incompleteness) of human beings navigating complex, oppressive systems.

Reframing Anger and Judgment

As we have been exploring, leaders with self-transforming capacity were often interested in actively seeking out ideas and opinions different from—or even seemingly opposed to—their own, as a way to see more deeply into their thinking and others' experiences. As Brent—an assistant principal who identified as white and gay—explained,

> What makes us smarter and what makes us stronger is engaging in perspective-shifting discourse and engaging with others who are different from us. The more we segregate and homogenize, the less we're able to be stronger, better people. . . . Like, that is a core of our humanity—that we evolved to be able to collaborate and to make meaning with others.

Yet, as Brent and other leaders confided, living this commitment was hard and ongoing work, especially in a world replete with harm, misunderstanding, and even seemingly active not-knowing. Acknowledging the aspiration in the lofty sentiment he just shared, for instance, Brent added, "Now those are on good days. I've definitely had bad days." Indeed, "working not to be angry," as Brent phrased it, required ongoing practice and deep, humanizing patience—not to excuse or overlook harms perpetuated by others (or oneself), but to better understand, confront, and move beyond them. Reflecting further, he said,

> The work that we do has universal implications, and the choices that we make affect our world as a whole. And so just the weight of that. When I see people making choices that hurt others, which then continue to escalate or cascade in ripples of hurt, I get really angry about that. And I don't know that anger is about to stop those ripples of hurt. Compassion is probably a better answer. . . .

I want to hear their reasons . . . but I also want to be able to be heard by them, and I think that the emotion of anger, it gets in the way of that happening.

Shokry similarly described how he'd been working to think differently about and rechannel the very appropriate anger he'd understandably feel when confronted by resistance or manifestations of racism or oppression in his work and life. Describing this shift, he shared,

I think growing up I saw anger as being fuel, right? In ways that were positive. You know, being told you'll never accomplish something. Being angry and saying, "I'll prove them wrong." [But] that kind of feeling, I think, comes at a cost. I think it takes a toll on health, I do. . . . While it's natural to feel feelings of anger, processing them so that we can we can turn them into, in some cases, empathy, and in some cases personal reflection, and in some cases growth— but being able to actually change the composition of our feelings into something beneficial, I think, is a real important skill.

For Shokry, then, repurposing anger wasn't about letting others or even himself "off the hook"—or about "sucking up" limitless harm with saintly grace—but about more effectively building bridging ties for mutuality and reciprocity, while also prioritizing his own health and well-being. In other words, it was about recognizing and embracing anger as an important internal alarm system and signal of injustice, while simultaneously growing the capacity to hold out that anger as object, psychologically speaking—to channel and transmute it rather than be run by it or harmed by its impact. To help better capture the subtlety and tension in this internal shift, we quote Shokry next at some length:

I think I'm still exploring what anger may be for me at this point in my journey. I think about being a much younger man and feeling feelings of anger over very small occurrences, right? Someone cut me off on the road, or you know, my belief that I didn't get an opportunity because of my race—or seeing that a government institution hasn't done what I believe to be to the benefit of the people it's supposed to serve. I mean, there are lots of ways to be angry. But the anger has never helped me to resolve situations. In cases where I still reach my outcome, remaining angry did nothing but make me feel more isolated.

Although deeply committed to taking a bigger perspective on anger, Shokry— as Brent did earlier—recognized that navigating this tension was as hard as it was urgent for his own and others' healing and liberation:

I'm working to understand the mode to forgiveness. I think I approach what I interpret as being offense or offensive as someone else being trapped in an ideology that neither serves me nor them because it keeps us apart. I think about this when we talk about racism. I think about this when we talk about classism. I think about this—I think pretty much all the -isms, right? It harms two people. It harms us both in that we can't benefit from one another, or be in fellowship with one another, or be engaged in growing with one another, right? We have a whole slew of experiences that someone else has that you will not benefit from because you're acting on this -ism or in light of this -ism. I think I have to also do some searching to understand that, while I'm forgiving of the lots of others that make them oppositional, or cause them to see me as a threat, or hindrance, or someone who they see as unworthy of respect or care, I have to also acknowledge that . . . there is an emotional toll that it takes on me. And while I think I have been able to settle for myself the fact that my response is never one of anger or hatred insomuch as I can help it . . . I have to still recognize that, in terms of my energy and my capacity, they are impacted by the -isms that . . . tend to be very intersectional. And while I've learned at this juncture to not see the offender as an enemy, I still have to see the issue of racism and classism and ablism and I still have to be proactive in that.

Although difficult in its own right, balancing necessary and appropriate anger with compassionate urgency—or as Lee put it, having "the patience and the respect for people and their needs and their stories and their reasons and their fears and . . . not just be[ing] righteous and frustrated"—proved especially hard in a world not always receptive to such radically expansive approaches. Naming Reverend Martin Luther King Jr. as both a deep influence and a cautionary example in light of his murder, Kristina—an educational consultant who identified as a faith-driven, married Black woman and a native of a Southern city well-known for its civil rights history—shared,

> I recognized that there's something different about [Martin Luther King Jr.]—like his ability to connect with all different types of people and push an agenda, right? Or build empathy and connection and galvanize people. There's something to this. . . . I think I picked up cues around he's not angry. He does have a righteous anger about the cause and the work and injustice, but when he's speaking, he's calm, he's very poised, very graceful, he's a great listener. He's really able to build alliances and allies and all of these things, and at the same time he was assassinated—really for being a threat.

Navigating this tension was something Kristina both prioritized and struggled with—both in terms of her own practice and the responses from valued others around her. As she explained,

I think for me, it was internalizing that [balance of anger and compassion] and then enacting that in my own life, over and over again. And I think sometimes, you know, that came with a cost as well, of sometimes your own peers or members from your own community. Even someone like Dr. King [heard] like, "Oh, you're a sellout. You don't get it. You are afraid to speak truth to power, etcetera." And so I think for me, the older I get now, I kind of strike a balance between the two, like, definitely having this ability to bridge the gap and, you know, hear different opinions and do all this, but at the same time kind of speak truth to folks and positions of power in a way that I did when I was younger.

As we discussed in Chapter 2, and as Kristina's example helps reinforce, growing toward a self-transforming way of knowing does *not* mean that one loses the strengths of one's convictions or develops a kind of moral relativism. On the contrary, self-transforming leaders can *still* take a strong stand for what they believe in and can still very much uphold core beliefs and nonnegotiables. Rather, developing self-transforming capacities involves adding new layers of perspective and understanding to one's value systems—and to others'—so as to no longer be "run" by them in the psychological sense. When leaders can cherish and hold and yet *be more than* their values, others can be, too. As we explore in the next subsection, making room for mutual learning through inquiry is another way the leaders in our study with elements of self-transforming capacity worked to build bridges.

Inquiry as Bridge Building

Reflecting on how her growing capacity to enact compassionate urgency helped her span gaps and build bridges in her consulting work, Kristina explained,

You know, it's hard to kind of put it into words, but I . . . have the ability to hear a different or dissenting opinion and still try to understand and empathize, and then help someone understand your perspective in a way that's not accusatory, not judgmental. . . . I have the ability to do that often, and I think it makes people feel safe. You know, I think that the way a couple of other folks handle it [i.e., colleagues who take a more instructive approach]—even though what they say is absolutely true, [it] caused what they were saying to not be heard.

Luz (principal, Afro-Latina) also felt strongly that inclusivity was ultimately necessary for liberation because "it can't be done alone." "I'm not necessarily interested in hurting or losing anyone," she explained. "I'm interested in building a stronger, more liberated society or world or community."

Speaking even more explicitly about inquiry as a means for bridge building, Shokry explained that, when confronted by pushback, resistance, or ideas that feel counter to his understandings of the world, he seeks opportunities to more fully understand the gap. As he shared,

> Those are probably the instances in which I inquire the most. To me that's always a reason to give someone an ear or to make inquiry, right? People do that on their own timeline. Doesn't mean we can't provide the opportunity for it. I'm really trying to wrap my brain, [but] I haven't had any challenges that I can recall that weren't changed by genuine inquiry as a person. . . . I think that approach is probably one that hasn't been used largely with consultants in the education space.

Lee, too, underscored the power of really trying to understand where someone else was coming from—as a way of seeking, not necessarily common ground, but a shared way forward. "Everyone's position," he asserted, "comes from some moral instinct." Honoring this, he explained, was a path toward greater understanding and collaboration:

> It may not be the same moral instinct that you share. But if it is a moral instinct, then you can isolate that instinct, and you can have empathy about it, and share that empathy. It might enable you to have a mature dialogue.

Although, in this way, taking an inquiry stance could serve as means for advocacy and bridge building, it was just as important, Lee explained, to aim such inquiry within as without. "I'm not really trying to change anyone right now," he shared. "But you certainly cannot expect for people to change their view if you yourself aren't also willing to be changed."

Further emphasizing the importance of really seeking to understand while remaining open to learning, Jean-Claude (district-level leader, Asian American) explained, "We're not trying to get to the absolute truth. I mean, I don't think there is one. . . . I'm not trying to win anything, right? It's not a game or a contest where I have to come out the victor." Sharing more about how he tries to do this internally, he said,

> There are so many situations. So if it makes sense to somebody else, it makes sense to them. That's what it is. It somehow makes sense to them. I can articulate why it makes sense to me in a different way, but it ultimately makes sense to them. It's just how they make meaning of whatever the situation is. . . . I try to take sort of an empathetic view as well. So if I were that person, why would that person think X, Y, and Z? . . . Trying to be sort of that empathy, I suppose, getting into the person's head as best as I could. Knowing that presents limitations because I'm not that

person, but for a moment suspending myself from myself [laughs] and seeing, well, if I were that person, why would I come up with the conclusion that that person did? So I try to go through some of those exercises. . . . While exhausting at times, I do claim it as a responsibility to, in the sense of agency, build greater understanding between others, between myself and others, and you know, right or wrong, I think it's something that I feel as if I need to do. And that may change again with time, I don't know, but at this point, I feel that I can play a role and I do play a role.

Capturing, perhaps, the essence of the compassionate urgency the leaders in our study with elements of a self-transforming way of knowing were striving to articulate, embody, and enact in their bridge building, Jean-Claude shared the following, recognizing the hard and ongoing work *everyone* needs to engage in, in different ways, to undo the legacies of dehumanization, racism, and oppression still so strongly active in contemporary life:

You can't expect others to learn to think so differently from how they've learned, and how they've made sense of the world, in however many years, overnight. So it's a learning that takes a long, long time, and it's an unlearning process that takes a long, long time. And I think it's a lot. It's a huge ask, you know—for one to ask of another to make sense of the world even ever so slightly different from how you saw it yesterday. Because it's a lot of undoing in many different ways. This work is not easy because of who we grew up with, where we grew up, where we went to school, the values that were imparted to us, right? All that is within us, right? It's who we are and I hope that we are able to constantly transform ourselves through the learning, through how we make sense of things, because we [can] allow different inputs into our own thinking. So that takes time. Learning is not something that happens as a turnkey process. It's a constant reminding, a constant sort of chipping away at how we've been making sense of the world.

In the next two sections of the chapter, we explore the aspects of practice and meaning making that leaders with elements of a self-transforming way of knowing named as growing edges—and then land on the ways they're growing to manage and make sense of the ongoing complexity of their leadership and the imperatives and possibilities of justice.

DEVELOPMENTAL STRUGGLES AND GROWING EDGES: INTERCONNECTING LEADERSHIP AMID UNCERTAINTY

As we explored above, leading with interconnection and compassionate urgency at the fore came with its own implicit and ongoing tensions, but the leaders in our study demonstrating emerging self-transforming capacities named two distinct developmental challenges that sat just along their growing edges:

- working with few comparable leadership models, and
- turning back toward action amid competing options.

In the sections that follow, we share self-transforming leaders' ongoing explorations of life, justice, and the beauties and complexities of identities and interconnection as key supports for growing their practice, especially in bureaucracies and school systems that did not always seem designed with their ways of making meaning in mind.

INTO THE UNKNOWN: FEW MODELS

Reflecting on what felt most difficult about growing to employ a more interconnecting leadership style and orientation, a few participants with emerging self-transforming capacities named the challenge of leading in ways not readily understood or enacted within dominant systems and paradigms—in both the education sector and the world more broadly. As Lee put it, "I think I have very few role models who do what I imagine needs to be done, or that I wish to be done." Brent, too, struggled to envision a society that more readily prioritized inclusion over exclusion:

> When I study societal pain—and issues ranging from slavery to religious wars to segregation to things that lead to tangibly different worlds for people—I think that, to me, it seems really clear that exclusive principles can really cause a lot of that. And so the negation of that for me would be inclusion. And so what does that look like, feel like, sound like, smell like? I, I don't see lots of good examples of that. And so I think that the way I form [my thinking] is through the negative.

Clear on what he knew he wanted to move *away* from, Brent nonetheless found few examples of the world he wished to *see*, to help him find his way there. Although, as we touched on earlier in this chapter and also in Chapter 2, there have certainly been thinkers, theorists, and leaders advocating for interconnected mutuality and expansive perspective taking as paths toward greater justice and equity for decades, if not centuries (e.g., Anzaldúa, 2002, 2015; Harro, 2013; Keating, 2013; Magee, 2019; Merriam & Associates, 2007), the leaders in our study with elements of self-transforming capacity often found themselves feeling rather alone—epistemologically— in their schools, organizations, and communities. Ironically, despite these leaders' capacities to connect and build bridges, a loneliness often accompanied their work, as they lamented the human potential not yet realized in the world at large. In other words, often on their own, they struggled to reconcile the seeming simplicity of authentically coming together in fellowship with the arguably infinite barriers that can get in the way of human connection. As Brent shared,

> I think learning to live with that tension—that paradoxical understanding of reality—I think it's harder. I don't laugh as much as I used to, and I think that stems from that. I think that this tension is part of that.

Jean-Claude, too, expressed his sadness and frustration at what he perceived as a broader "inability for humans to see the grand view of everything, all the information that's needed" to make necessary changes to society and the world. As he shared,

> It's a certain sadness that makes me wonder . . . about the nature of humanity and, do we not learn from our own lessons? To what extent are we capable, able, to sort of see beyond ourselves? Beyond the immediate? Beyond what's in front of our eyes? . . . How do we learn from our past? How do we learn to see what's not immediately visible? How do we accept hard truths? How do we entertain possibilities that might contradict what we think we know? And I, I just keep going back to a belief, perhaps, that we have limitations as to how we can make sense of what we see around us. And that brings a certain sadness because I think . . . we could do better . . . in terms of how we make decisions, how we understand the world around us. But oftentimes, I think we somehow allow other factors to get in the way.

Eager to connect and understand, it was sometimes painful for leaders making meaning with elements of a self-transforming way of knowing to accept others' hesitancy to do the same while also hanging onto hope.

TURNING BACK TOWARD ACTION

In addition to struggling to accept the walls and resistances people put up, even against their own best and mutual interests, leaders making meaning with or growing toward a self-transforming way of knowing also shared the challenge of turning back toward definitive action in a landscape of competing possibilities and multiplicities. As Jean-Claude explained, "there are so many untruths, so many truths, that there is no one truth—and I don't know that we know how to get past that, I suppose." Taking it all in, he asked, "What's the entry point for all of this?" Although complicated and certainly messy, leaders making meaning in this way described how, in some ways, that complication was actually *the point*—and something needed for progress. Thinking about how he collaborated with his own team to further social justice issues in their curriculum work in the district, for instance, Jean-Claude shared,

> And so there was a lot of debate as to how we enter it and what's the right focus, what are we ready for? . . . I think I started out

with a lot of ideas, like how about this? How about if we did this? And a lot of times, it ended up that way, but then just as many times, I think, it also ended up as something else because somebody else had a better idea, or somebody else saw some pitfalls. And I think that's just the nature of this, and I think stepping back right now, it's all I can say is it was probably for the better that we had conflicts or different—I wouldn't say conflict at all—but just conflicting perspectives as to how to approach it.

Zora, too (nonprofit CEO and founder, African American woman), recognized the importance—and complexity—of staking out a territory or position, so to speak, while remaining mindful of the vast expanse of simultaneous work needed to really effect change toward justice. Yet, there was a comfort, she felt, in really digging into something that aligned well with her talents and dispositions—like carving out an area of expertise and contribution while still seeing it as part of a greater whole. As she explained, describing her decision to focus on higher ed and economic mobility,

> Knowing that there are a lot of other pieces and a lot of other things that intersect—like criminal justice, health care, education in K–12, etcetera—but really for me, this is the social justice issue that I happen to be working on, while absolutely acknowledging that the others are very important and we need people also passionately working on those to make our country and the world a better place. But I [decided I] should spend my time, for the rest of the time—which hopefully is very long on this earth—working on the issue that I started to realize I could play an outsized role in helping to right the arc towards justice.

Similarly grounding herself in what she could do as part of a constellation of efforts, Ella (director of culture and language, African American) described of her thinking,

> I have to take a step back and decide . . . kind of ground myself in what it is that I'm doing. What am I here to do? What have I committed to do? And I also have to lean very much into trust. Trusting other people are doing their best, will do their best. Trusting that it's okay that I'm one person, and I am where I am. I'm exactly where I need to be, doing what I need to do. Just take a deep breath and just allow myself to . . . as I said, ground into why I'm doing what I'm doing. And then, from that perspective, I'm being a little bit more objective, make the best decision I can in the moment, and trust that everything else will fall right into place, even though that's really hard sometimes.

In the end, leaders explained, it's really all connected, so doing good work in one domain—when mindfully aware of overlaps, gaps, and interrelationships—can influence change in others. As Lee reflected,

There are so many different ways to understand how you might make change on a system. You could advocate for charters, you could advocate for more money, you could advocate for a student takeover, you could advocate for a parent outreach program, you know, like there are so many different possibilities. And one of the keys to picking what you're going to focus on is recognizing how interconnected the different parts of the system are—so like pulling the thread of a sweater, it bunches up at different parts of that sweater.

Moreover, recognizing the multiple connection points in a system—or how the threads in the metaphorical sweater intersect—can allow leaders to engage multi-modally and on multiple fronts, both to influence change and to combat burnout and fatigue. Thinking, for instance, about how literature can serve as an act of resistance and transformation just as much as leading in the educational sector, Shokry explained,

> I saw James Baldwin and Ralph Ellison and Nella Larson as being, in my mind, the strongest advocates for justice and equity that I had come across. So, it was following those footsteps, and I guess what it's kind of brought me to realize is that there is some reprieve when you can do the work in different arenas. . . . It's saved me from burnout to some extent, to be able to switch mediums and switch tracks. And it feels as if when I've kind of burnt out in one medium, I'm able to recover and grow in another, and I don't know if that's the same for everyone, but it's something that I wish for everyone.

Christopher, too—a leader in a national philanthropic organization, who identified as African American—emphasized how freeing it could be to grow beyond the boundaries of prescribed systems and sectors and to take the action necessary in a moment while simultaneously honoring the complexity of the big picture. Describing his process of coming to know, feel, and understand how multiplicity could, in fact, co-exist with confident action, he shared an example from his own life:

> We talked about holding contradictory things in your head. I used to be an actor, not a great one. A hip-hop artist, not a great one. But a really good one of both [laughs]. But I always would think I have to either do this or do that. Do this or do that. And that's the illusion. Because the older I get, now I see that . . . everyone can be hyphenated. 'Cause they're just things within our identity. . . . So I had to, I thought, pick a thing—as opposed to opening myself to being *all* of these things because our identities are multiple. But again, I didn't have that language, and I didn't have that experience to know that was the truth, you know what I'm saying? . . . And so now, as I continue, I try not to do that anymore. If you say, "Oh,

well you're either this or that, or this or that." No, I'm all those things. The question is who do I need to be today?

Although certainly not easy, doing the very best of what you can when you can—as did Christopher and the leaders above—without losing sight of the bigger picture and the vast complexities of the challenges and imperatives at hand, can have ripple effects beyond one's immediate actions. Doing *something*—intentionally and purposefully, and in synergy with one's fullest and biggest capacities—is indeed a way to be a part, at least in small ways, of everything. We find it significant to recognize here, and hope you notice too, how developing self-transforming capacities once again marks a return of sorts on the developmental spiral/gyre/helix for these leaders—back toward the call to action described in Chapter 3, but this time with more holistic, inclusive perspectives and greater under-standings of themselves, others, and the multiple systems in which they live, learn, and lead.

LIVING THE QUESTIONS: MANAGING COMPLEXITY AND AMBIGUITY

In the end, leading with self-transforming capacities proved both painful and potential-filled for the leaders we learned from in our study. Although the capacity to see more of the system—and themselves—revealed for leaders just how much farther there is to go, taking an ever-wider view also allowed that much more beauty to seep into their everyday seeing: the precious fra-gility of human existence, the miracle of learning and connection, the eternal spring of hope. In this way, they shared, leading in interconnecting, self-transforming ways was really about living the questions as they came—about finding one's way, with others, through the messiness of the now, toward a future that could better hold us all. And even though that future is undefined, unknown, and uncertain, there rests in that not knowing a beckoning call for innovation, creativity, collaboration, contribution, and love. It is in the not knowing that the future is born.

To close out, for now, this section on self-transforming leaders, we share some of their reflections about finding joy in complexity. Because sometimes, as Zora shared with us, "Hard is good."

First up is Brooke (head of school, white, gay), who summed up her think-ing by sharing, "I just try to maintain an open mind for solving problems because the solution may not be what you think it is. Something I do know is nothing is easy or simple."

Shokry likewise shared, "I think every day I'm reminded of how little I know. And I think that's exciting. I think that is probably the beginning of any good learning experience—coming to terms with the fact that we don't know."

Brent, too, recognized uncertainty as something necessary and even powerful:

> The world should be messy. That's what diversity produces. That's what a truly inclusive community is—it has many unanswered questions and many, many confusions, and you're working together to try and understand the world better. . . . I think life is the realization of growth and of change, and change, while challenging, is what allows us to live.

And, finally, we end with Jean-Claude, who shared,

> I think what brings me a lot of joy is to see something differently, to see things differently. Revisiting a place . . . revisiting a piece of art, relistening to a piece of music—seeing it differently, hearing it differently. I would say that's probably what brings me the most joy. . . . And I think that understanding that complexity, like things are complex—being able to partake in that is wonderful. Like, I'm a part of it now, part of that complexity. Yeah, that makes me really happy, actually.

We wish you all such happiness as you travel ever-onward, toward greater justice, equity, freedom, and liberation. As we near full circle, we want to return to the enormous gratitude with which we began: for all in this work who have taught us so much and so generously shared of themselves and their passions. We thank all the leaders whose wisdom, dedication, and love infuses every page of this book. And, we thank *you* for all you are, all you give, and all you do each and every day to make the world a better place. Heartfelt gratitude from our hearts to yours.

In the next chapter, we look back on and bring together many of the different ideas we explored throughout this book and offer stories, metaphors, implications, activities, and tools for launching forward. First, though, we close with summative takeaways and a reflective opportunity.

CHAPTER SYNOPSIS AND KEY TAKEAWAYS

> *I would like to beg you, dear Sir, as much as I can, to have patience with everything unresolved in your heart and to try to love* the questions themselves *as if they were locked rooms or books written in a very foreign language.*
>
> —Rainer Maria Rilke (1934/1993)

Throughout this chapter, we shared reflections from leaders growing toward or leading with elements of a self-transforming way of knowing to offer a rare glimpse of what it looks like, sounds like, and feels like to lead with interconnecting orientations and approaches. Although still relatively rare in the world and in the education sector, the capacities and practices foregrounded in this chapter—we hope—invite us to *see around the bend* of the developmental staircase (so to speak) toward what could be, just up ahead.

Although, again, we do not see development as a panacea or cure-all for the world's ills, we do think, hope, and believe that helping adults see more deeply into themselves, others, the systems around us, and the intersections of all of these holds great promise for leveling up our shared readiness for change—and justice. We so hope that the ideas, practices, and stories we've presented in this chapter and book offer one small inroad into this very human project writ large.

Below, as you know is our practice, we list key takeaways from this chapter in Figure 6.3, as well as an overview of the interconnecting domain and its practices in Table 6.1.

FIGURE 6.3 CHAPTER TAKEAWAYS

- Leaders making meaning with elements of a self-transforming way of knowing described the importance of prioritizing *interconnection*—of schools and broader social systems, of people across roles and positionalities, and between themselves and others.

- Leaders foregrounding interconnecting approaches underscored the importance of working closely with others—to see more deeply and mutually into their self-systems *and* to build the coalitions needed to address the complexities and multiplicities of injustice.

- For leaders operating in this domain, looking further out and looking deeper within involved the continual renegotiation and reinterrogation of understandings and expertise. Although leaders could still have strong values and philosophies, they recognized that, as lone individuals, their range of vision was necessarily incomplete.

- Leaders in this chapter also spoke passionately about the power of compassionate urgency—and of, in some cases, reframing anger and building bridges as a means of developing greater understanding, connection, and effectiveness.

- Without many prominent, readily accessible examples of interconnecting leadership in schools or the world, leaders making meaning with elements of a self-transforming way of knowing sometimes felt alone or sought opportunities to contribute outside of school-based leadership.

- Yet, as the leaders in our study explained, embracing the tensions, complexities, and imperatives of leading, teaching, and living in ways that center justice—with great capacity but intellectual humility—can itself provide a kind of joy and hope. Embracing uncertainty—yet striving toward a horizon of justice—generates possibility.

TABLE 6.1 OVERVIEW OF LEADERS' PRACTICE—AND GROWTH—IN THE INTERCONNECTING DOMAIN

DOMAIN OF JUSTICE-CENTERING LEADERSHIP PRACTICE	PRIMARY FOCUS	PREREQUISITE INTERNAL CAPACITIES	FOREGROUNDED PRACTICES AND APPROACHES	EXPERIENCES THAT SUPPORT DEVELOPMENTAL STRETCHING AND GROWTH	REPRESENTATIVE QUOTES
Interconnecting	The broader constellation of systems that include the education sector and their intersections Opportunities for bridge building and coalition between individuals, groups, communities, and systems	Self-transforming	Seeing the interconnected pieces and elements of a system Continually expanding own view Seeking input from all—those with similar and different ideologies and values Building bridges Reframing anger, judgment Inviting coalition	Living the question, in company Exploring paradoxes and contradictions in leadership and identity Learning more about self, others, and social justice as an ongoing process Turning back toward action to move systems and work forward	"How can we help each other see more deeply into ourselves and the world around us?" "What might we help each other recognize and address with more conscious awareness?" "What parts of this issue, complexity, or imperative do I not yet understand?" "Everything is bigger than us." "You start to see that the world is much more interconnected and that schools are not isolated." "I think social justice requires . . . a sense of collective leadership." "I'm interested in continuing to evolve and grow . . . so that we may rise together." "I think what brings me a lot of joy is to see something differently, to see things differently."

We invite you to pause and consider the following questions, which are offered to give you a chance to reflect on yourself, your justice-centering leadership, and how, if at all, what we've shared is connecting for you and those in your care.

1. What is top of mind and top or bottom of heart for you after reading this chapter?

2. How, if at all, do the stories, ideas, and discussions in this chapter connect with your own experience and wisdom? Your own justice-centering leadership?

3. What are two or three of the larger insights you've had as you read this chapter? Who, if anyone, are you thinking about?

4. How, if at all, might you share some of the stories, ideas, and/or practices from this chapter? With whom? When? What's your next step?

5. After reading this chapter and considering leaders' stories about the interconnecting domain of the model, what, if anything, might you like to practice and/or do differently in general? For your justice-centering leadership?

6. Early in the chapter, Dr. B recounted an experience she had skydiving and how it helped her see her work from a new perspective. As she said, "The work I do [is] writ large and important, very important, but it was that small in the grand scheme of things." Who or what helps you put your important work into broader context? To see it differently? To see how it is connected to the work of others and other systems?

7. Throughout his interview, Lee emphasized the importance of coalition. As he explained, "As someone who's aspiring to make systems change, it is your charge to . . . build a broad, diverse coalition, which means you are actively going to seek out multiple perspectives and points of view." How, if at all, does this connect with your thinking and the work you are leading in your organization? What coalitions are you a part of? What coalitions would you like to be a part of? Support or create?

8. Shokry spoke at length about his efforts to think differently about and repurpose anger. Recognizing anger as both necessary and appropriate, he also explained that it "comes at a cost," and that he's been working to "change the composition" of that feeling "into something beneficial." How, if at all, does this idea resonate with you?

9. Jean-Claude described his commitment to continually revisiting and broadening his thinking about justice to make room for ideas and points of view he may not have considered or even welcomed earlier. "I like to at least give myself an opportunity to say, 'Oh, there's another way, a deeper way, a more expansive way of thinking about social justice,'" he explained. What people, experiences, resources, and ideas have helped you expand your thinking about justice? What might still be important to consider, explore, and include?

10. After reading this chapter, what is something you'd like to think more deeply about? Do differently? Get better at? Learn more about? What comes to mind and heart when you think about the questions you are holding? The "messiness of the now"? A future that could better hold us all?

11. What, if anything, would you like to think more about before turning to Chapter 7?

INTERLUDE II

······································

HOLDING MANY HORIZONS

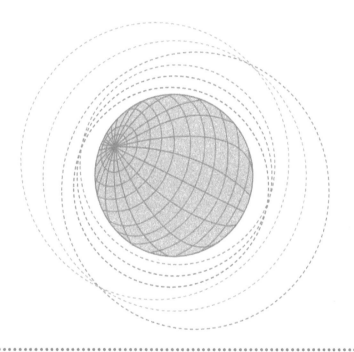

IMAGE SOURCE: Adapted from Tony Kirvan.

We've come, through our research, to understand justice as a beckoning horizon. Just up ahead, it calls forward all committed to freedom—with hints and glimpses of what could be, what *should* be. Yet, much like a visible horizon line, the justice a person is striving *toward*—and the injustice they are moving *away from*—are deeply influenced by the position they inhabit on earth and can shift as the movement brings different parts of the landscape and experience into focus.

Moreover, while any one person's unique vantage point—geographical, temporal, cultural, racial, developmental, intersectional—can provide directionality and purpose, a goal at which to aim one's actions and efforts, it is also the case that any *one* perspective is, by definition, limited and bounded. What of all the horizons not currently in sight? How might one's vision for justice grow to include the trajectories of others, even those moving in seemingly different directions, while still firmly advocating for what one feels to be most urgent and true? How might leaders—broadly defined—work not only toward the justice they recognize at the time, but in ways that also allow for heightened perspective taking and greater understanding of how people's many *different* horizons of justice intersect and overlap? How might they work toward a justice big enough to hold and honor this tremendous complexity?

We hope that, by adding a developmental dimension to the rich and robust conversations about justice and educational leadership, the previous chapters have helped you explore these very questions. We also hope that they have supported you in considering your own metaphorical lines of sight and those of the people in your care.

Before turning next, in Chapter 7, to summative ideas, implications, and launching points for action, we invite you to consider the following reflective questions—privately and/or with a partner or small group.

A REFLECTIVE INVITATION

1. What aspects of justice feel most firmly centered in your "line of sight"? Why do you think that is?

2. What steps are you taking to move closer to your horizon(s) of justice? With whom are you traveling?

3. What other aspects of justice are important to you, though perhaps more on the periphery of your vision and thinking?

4. Who or what might help you bring these areas of justice into greater focus?

CHAPTER 7

....

GROWING LEADERS FOR JUSTICE

A Call to Learning and Action

Hope is rooted in . . . incompletion, from which [people] move out in constant search—a search which can be carried out only in communion with others.

—Paulo Freire (1970/2000, p. 91)

Recently, we were talking with a sixth-grader who was describing his bursting full passion for learning to play the violin and guitar. At first, he explained, he thought he should *only* listen to music that featured those two particular instruments, and he spent countless hours watching YouTube videos about the history and craftsmanship of string instruments, as well as tutorials to help him learn to play the classical and rock songs he listened to and liked most. And learn he did! While we were impressed by his progress and initiative (and the mini concert he performed for us), we were perhaps most inspired when he shared what at first seemed like a casual addendum to his study plan. "I realized that in order to get really good at any kind of music," he explained, "I have to learn everything I can about *all* music. And appreciate all kinds and types and instruments and styles."

Because timing is everything, and coming as it did on the heels of completing the first drafts of this book, his insight struck us as particularly significant and symbolic. Yes! Finding one's way into something as big and beautiful as music—or social justice—can sometimes start with a specific interest or calling. And, importantly, that love and commitment, if we let it, can also spill over into and lead us to new connections and discoveries that reinforce, stretch, and redefine that initial spark. This expansive evolution *can* happen, especially if, as did this fortunate sixth grader, we have the necessary resources and supports. It's all part of growing the different and interconnected parts of ourselves, our relationships, our advocacy, and our world. And, as we've been emphasizing, this often involves returning to familiar questions and passions with *new* ways of seeing and understanding.

Throughout this book, we explored how a group of fifty educational leaders committed to centering justice in their work embarked on a trajectory of ever-more-inclusive learning and practice—individually and collectively. Sparked, in many cases, by a deep commitment to justice and the transformational potential of education, leaders worked to "fill up" in each of the four domains of practice outlined in our developmental model (i.e., the concrete, the interpersonal, the system-focused, and the interconnecting) and then, with appropriate supports and stretching, grew toward and into the ones that followed. In fact, as these leaders' powerful stories and reflections help illustrate, it is often the recognition of a growing edge—or bringing into more conscious awareness the boundaries of one's current meaning making and acting—that makes possible further growth. As the opening quote from Paulo Freire similarly argues, it is actually by embracing incompleteness that we can find hope, together. For when we acknowledge room for growth in ourselves and our systems, we simultaneously make room for change. And we need one another to make change possible. On the other hand, rigidity, certainty, inaction, and isolation cause us to stagnate.

In this chapter, we think back on leaders' layered stories and insights to revisit our developmental model as a whole. We also offer implications for practice and next steps and—most importantly—provide opportunities for you to connect big ideas with your own practice and action planning to step forward in your own noble practices. As always, we hope these bridges between theory and practice are helpful to you and those in your care—and to your efforts to center justice in contexts small and large.

REVISITING AND RECAPPING OUR DEVELOPMENTAL MODEL

Although the hope Freire speaks of in the chapter epigraph can feel hard to hold onto in these times replete with hurt, harm, tragedy, dehumanization, and catastrophe, we find bolstering, hope-full strength in the evidence from our research that educational leaders with any developmental way of knowing *can* commit to social justice. And they can find entry into and build capacity for the urgent work ahead. As Rana—an independent school head who identified as Egyptian American and Muslim—put it, reflecting on the fueling power of justice-centering leadership in her life, "This is the work of hope, you know?"

Indeed, a developmental lens helps us understand that leading on behalf of social justice isn't an either-or proposition, where someone's "in" or "out," but rather a lived-in commitment, enacted again and again in ever more complex, fluid ways. Understanding the trajectory of ways of knowing outlined by constructive-developmental theory—and how these ways of making meaning can inform on-the-ground leadership practice in the moment and over time—provides both a *language* and *roadmap* for differentiating the supports and challenges we offer others (and ourselves) as we strive to better meet the imperatives of now and dream new futures ahead. Everyone who chooses to can find an entry point into social justice, and everyone can grow right now—given the right, developmentally appropriate mix of challenge and support. As Harris—a principal of a high school for English language learners who identified as a forty-eight-year-old, white, gay, male—explained, there is something genuinely wondrous in this possibility:

> What I think is the most wonderful is that we're all on a spectrum, and we're all growing and we're all learning and we're all seeing things through different lenses. We all have places to grow and go, and it's what's fun and challenging to think about at the same time.

Cheryl—a district-level school improvement leader who identified as a white woman—also underscored in her interview with us how understanding development, like understanding one's positionality and identity, can really inform and infuse *all* of leadership and equity work. As she put it,

> Every conversation is an identity conversation. Like, race and privilege and identity come up pretty consistently in every interaction you have. And my belief is that so do ways of knowing; so do our styles of communicating and seeing.

Of course, as we've also discussed, growing one's internal capacity is not a *guarantee* of a commitment to social justice (i.e., people can bring different values systems and lived experiences to any of the ways of knowing). However, as we've also emphasized, development *can* equip us with greater readiness to center justice and more entry points to choose from. It is also not a 1-2-3 quick fix, but rather an investment (and continual reinvestment) in bridging the gap between our biggest selves today and the selves we aspire to grow into, tomorrow and every day hereafter. Although we are in no way proposing incremental change as a solution to urgent problems, imperatives, and dehumanizations, we recognize that the immediate steps people can and need to take today will, of necessity, be different and that transformation requires continual action and steady marching forward. As Jean-Claude—a district-level coordinator of curriculum and teacher leadership who identified as an Asian American male in his forties—further articulated this idea, growing as a social justice leader and advocate is a *process*, whether looking within or without. "It's lifelong work," he explained. "It's not going to happen with a snap of the finger. It is the work of a lifetime, if you will."

In quilting together the stories, reflections, confidences, and hopes of the fifty generous educational leaders featured in this book, we aspired to capture not a collection of "best practices," per se (although the leaders in this study are engaging in so many wonderful things!), but rather a composite portrait of some of the most foregrounded actions, initiatives, orientations, and entry points into justice in educational leadership today. We pay forward these leaders' treasured sharings as invitations to see yourself and your practice in some or even all of the chapters and to think—privately and/or with others—about alignments and divergences, strengths and growing edges, and possibilities and next steps.

We know, as you do, that there are so many *more* ways educators can, should, and *need* to center justice in schools, districts, organizations, partnerships, and coalitions, and that the mission is critical. The mission is now, living and breathing. There really is no time to waste. We hope that, in mapping along a continuum the practices and orientations that felt most important to different leaders at the time of our study, we have helped to tell a story not only of what some leaders *do*, but also of *how* they came to their actions, what they hope to do next, and the supports and challenges they need to get there.

Ultimately, as the leaders in our study helped us see, centering justice means bringing all of oneself and the biggest and best of our capacities to the table, every day. It also means engaging in the work with deep and vulnerable humility and with the openness to change, fail, reflect, and try again. And again. As so often tends to happen, there's a quote attributed to author, poet, and activist Maya Angelou that somehow perfectly captures this idea. Reflecting on the power of growth, learning, and change in her own life, she reportedly said, "I did then what I knew how to do. Now that I know better, I do better." We can think of no better mantra to frame the recap and synthesis of our developmental model for justice-centering educational leadership, which we present in Figure 7.1. As you can see, we have brought together examples of both strengths and developmental stretches for each of the four domains of practice for easy reference and side-by-side review.

Like a set of stairs, these domains of practice accumulate in a particular order, with movement "up" reflecting an increased capacity for introspection and perspective taking and an expanded field of vision—internally and externally— as well as an increased internal locus of control. Yet, just as in our original depiction of the developmental model (i.e., the interlocking cylinders pictured throughout the chapters), it is important to remember that what appear as "columns" in the figure actually overlap, flow together, and inform one another—and that *all* are needed. In other words, the goal isn't necessarily to reach the "top" step and stay there, leaving earlier approaches behind. Instead, it is to gain greater facility *across* all levels and domains, and to thus have more leadership tools at the ready to employ in fluid and responsive ways.

Toward this end, it may be helpful to think of the "steps" in this latest, incorporative visualization not as discrete boxes or platforms, but as an alternative view of the cylinders and domains of our model tipped on their sides, as shown in Figure 7.2. This way, you can think of them as another hidden

Concrete

Examples of Strengths:

Orienting to social justice as the "right" thing to do

Taking tangible action steps (e.g., contributing time, resources, and expertise)

Focusing on the measurable and technical (e.g., selecting equity-focused curricula, focusing on equitable representation)

———

Stretches for Growth:

Explicit learning about equity and identity

Making connections and building relationships across lines of difference

Interpersonal

Examples of Strengths:

Deep empathy and interpersonal connection

Embracing the fundamental value and holism of students, teachers, and families

Honoring diverse cultural capital and funds of knowledge

Caring for the social-emotional dimensions of equity work (e.g., listening, relationship and community building)

———

Stretches for Growth:

Engaging in necessary conflict and difficult conversations

Sharing one's authentic thinking, feeling, and experience

Receiving encouragement and support from valued others

System-Focused

Examples of Strengths:

Developing and communicating a school/district vision that foregrounds equity and justice

Thinking systemically and strategically to align practices across an organization in keeping with personal values

Advocating for students, families, and colleagues through necessary conflict, principled disruption, and boundary setting

Enhanced capacities for and commitments to reflection and self-awareness

———

Stretches for Growth:

Inviting others more fully into vision and mission work Critiquing own value system and understandings

Recognizing the incompleteness of one's expertise and perspective

Reaching beyond the educational system for allies and solutions

Interconnecting

Examples of Strengths:

Building coalitions for change across lines of difference and commonality

Embracing the fluidity and complexity of one's own and others' identities and experiences

Inviting and synthesizing multiple viewpoints and ideas

Building bridges

Reframing anger, judgment

Prioritizing interconnection on micro and macro levels

———

Stretches for Growth:

Continuing to explore the paradoxes and possibilities of justice work, in company

Turning back toward concrete action and policy amidst multiple, competing possibilities

Learning more about self, others, and justice as an ongoing, collaborative process

Navigating hierarchy and imposed boundaries

Carving out sustainable spaces for community and growth

---

staircase in the spiral of growth. And, as we all know, it generally takes stamina and much, much practice to move up and down stairs with agility and without losing one's breath.

With the entirety of the model now at your fingertips, we want to offer our deepest and most sincere gratitude to you for making time—and space in heart, mind, and soul—to consider the stories and lived experiences of the

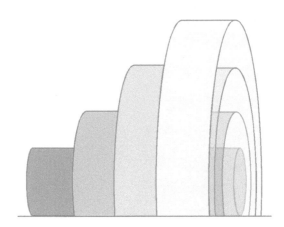

giving and insightful leaders featured throughout this book. We also want to thank each of them again—profoundly and always—for making this book possible with their courage, commitments, generosity of heart and mind, and vulnerability. They, like you, are inspirations. And we hope they've given you sparks and ideas to carry forward and nurture, as they have for us.

With this in mind, and as you now know is our intentional practice, we invite you next to pause and engage with a few reflective opportunities designed to help you think more about the model as a whole and your own leadership development. As always, you are welcome to consider these questions privately and/or to use them as discussion prompts with close colleagues. We begin with an opportunity to connect with and reflect on your own experiences as a justice-centering leader.

CONNECTING WITH AND REFLECTING ON SELF

1. What, after reading this book and reviewing the full model in Figure 7.1, is top of mind for you? Top or bottom of heart?

2. In which domains of practice do you feel most confident and experienced? Least?

3. What do you currently see as your biggest strengths as a justice-centering leader, teacher, and/or colleague?

4. What do you see as your growing edge(s)?

5. What would you like to grow about yourself? Your practice? The ways in which you support others in your care?

6. After reading and deepening your understanding of ways of knowing and constructive-developmental theory, how, if at all, do these ideas connect with other frameworks, theories, or lenses you employ to understand yourself and those in your care? How, if at all, might you employ this framework to support your own social justice practice? Your own growth? The growth of those in your care? What is your next step on any of these fronts?

7. What, if anything, makes it challenging for you to push forward in your justice-centering work? What would help you to do so at this time?

8. What would you like to celebrate right now about the justice-centering work you are leading? Engaging in?

In addition to reflecting privately about self, leaders often find it useful to ask trusted colleagues and supervisors about what *they* see, from the outside, as next steps for their personal growth and development—in general and with respect to justice-centering leadership in particular. Below, we offer a series of questions you can ask of others who know you and your practice well.

INFORMAL SURVEY QUESTIONS FOR SOLICITING FEEDBACK ON YOUR JUSTICE-CENTERING LEADERSHIP

1. What are some aspects of my work with you, our collaboration, and/or my justice-centering leadership that you appreciate?

2. What are some aspects of my work with you, our collaboration, and/or my justice-centering leadership that you wish I could do better or more effectively, or that you find are less helpful to you?

3. What are some aspects of my justice-centering leadership that you think are less helpful to our team/group/district/system/organization?

4. Is there anything you would suggest, wish for, or recommend that could help me to create conditions that would be more meaningful for and supportive of you?

5. Do you have any additional comments or suggestions that you think would be helpful for me to understand?

DEVELOPING IMPLICATIONS FOR PRACTICE AND NEXT STEPS

> *Diversity is about all of us, and about us having to figure out how to walk through this world together.*
>
> —Jacqueline Woodson, American author

As we have been exploring, supporting leadership development and growing justice-centering educational leaders calls for more than knowledge and skills. It also calls for *capacity*—and, in many ways, both the patient and the impatient love and care of a gardener. We are all gardeners, aren't we? Just as a gardener needs to cultivate and nurture individual plants—from seedling to flower bloom—within diverse ecosystems and climates so, too, do we need to curate differentiated and personalized holding (and growing) environments that support development in ourselves and those in our care. Just as the most successful gardeners draw from knowledge of both individual plants and their interactions and conditions across a landscape, leaders who most effectively center justice—according to our research—have grown the capacity to see both the big picture and the small and to navigate between them with dexterity and intuition.

While we believe that the stories and experiences shared with us by the leaders in our study, as well as the trajectory synthesized in this book, hold many important implications, we share here three key, summative takeaways and hopes for next steps. We offer these as jumping-off points for new inquiries, explorations, and investments of self and heart.

1. With ever-expanding expertise, sensitivity, self-knowledge, and relational capacity, *justice-centering leaders—according to our research—need to know themselves and others well and to differentiate supports and challenges for growth accordingly.* Holding, caring for, and loving people in this way can, in and of itself, be an act of justice, we've learned. And this stance can also serve as a foundational orientation to leadership enriched by practice and intentionality. Understanding adult development (broadly defined) and the layered domains of practice featured in this book can help leaders better recognize the qualitatively different ways adults make meaning of justice, their experiences, and the world, and thus meet them where they are without relinquishing the urgency for growth.

2. Our research also suggests that *justice-centering leaders need to continually hone their capacities for perspective taking, both within and without.* As the recollections from the leaders in our study helped bring into even greater focus, growing along the continuum of justice-centering leadership involved expanding one's scope of vision and locus of control. With enhanced capacities to zoom in and out—and to see how the parts of a system make up larger wholes (within individuals and across the arcs of history)—leaders who think and see from more inclusive, expansive vantage points have more tools at their disposal to support growth at the individual and organizational levels and beyond. To revisit the gardening metaphor, addressing inequity is never as simple as pulling weeds as they pop up. Rather, when a gardener understands the soil and the climate and the encompassing conditions *as interactive and interconnected*, they are better able to encourage wanted growth, provide essential fertilizer,

and nurture conditions for thriving. Even if that sometimes means still pulling weeds.

3. Finally, this connects to the big idea that *justice-centering leadership requires the prioritization of interconnection.* While we admire gardeners' capacity to care for the smallest of buds while enriching the entirety of a flower bed, we remain moved and struck, too, by recent discoveries about how plants—and trees in particular—are actually connected to and communicate with one another across vast expanses of terrain (Simard, 2016). Although sometimes invisible to human perception, the interconnection of life within and beyond the flower bed, and indeed across the whole of the earth, parallels the ways leaders emphasized cross-sector work and coalition as necessary for social change. On the macro and micro levels, it's all interdependent, just as the freedom of any one person is intimately connected to the freedom of all. That the capacity to authentically think and see in such interconnecting ways is tied to development feels like a particularly important learning foregrounded in our study because developmental theory provides a map of sorts for getting us there.

These implications for practice both converge with and diverge from conventional understandings of leadership—in schools and broader society—particularly paradigms of individualism and rigid hierarchical systems that can limit possibilities for authentic collaboration. As Irene—an independent school director of admissions and enrollment who identified as a fifty-six-year-old, white, Jewish mother—lamented, collaboration and real conversation about inequity isn't the norm in most educational contexts. "As leaders, even as teachers," she explained, "we don't get to have the kind of conversations we should be having nearly often enough."

What might it be like, we wonder, if more schools and systems valued, welcomed, and nurtured interconnecting approaches and capacities? If, for instance, more adults making meaning with elements of a self-transforming way of knowing could find the supports and connections they need to feel well-held, psychologically speaking, within schools? We think it's significant that most of the leaders in our study who demonstrated some element of a self-transforming way of knowing chose to contribute to education *outside* of brick-and-mortar schools (i.e., as consultants, district-level leaders, philanthropic or nonprofit leaders, or in higher education). Others confided that they were considering leaving in-school leadership soon. What might it take to conceptualize and operationalize an educational leadership big enough to hold these educators and advocates—in community with students, colleagues, and families? Especially since the literature on social change points so clearly to the importance of these connections.

For example, as described in Chapters 1 and 2—and particularly in our discussions of critical consciousness and liberatory action—research underscores the importance of looking beyond one's sphere of influence to connect and align with others and to recognize the interwoven nature of being and transformation. Social justice scholar and Professor Emerita Lee Anne Bell (2016) likewise described, albeit indirectly, how self-transforming capacities coincide with wider educational and societal imperatives for social justice:

> As individuals and groups, our visions can only be partial. Coalitions bring together multiple ways of understanding the world and analyzing the oppressive structures within it. Specific skills of perspective taking, emphatic listening, and self-reflection are critical. Furthermore, since all forms of oppression are interactional and co-constitutive with each other, alliances among people from diverse social locations and perspectives may perhaps be the only way to develop interventions muscular enough to challenge systemic oppression. (p. 20)

By illustrating how such an interconnecting orientation to leadership requires sophisticated developmental capacities, our research joins and builds upon important conversations about mutuality and sustainable coalition building in the social justice literature and beyond (e.g., Bell, 2016; Keating, 2013; Magee, 2019). It points us back, too, to the importance of looking *across* theories and paradigms and to the wisdom of bodies of thought not always centered in education (e.g., women of color feminisms, decolonizing efforts, BlackCrit, DisCrit, Indigenous theories, queer theory, translanguaging, and Critical Race Theory). What other lenses or implications come to the fore for you as we inch closer to the end of this book?

Next, we invite you to engage with a reflective opportunity aimed at considering even more deeply your own professional context and practice. We hope, as always, that these questions are helpful for you.

REFLECTING ON YOUR PROFESSIONAL CONTEXT AND PRACTICE

A garden is a grand teacher. It teaches patience and careful watchfulness; it teaches industry and thrift; above all it teaches entire trust.

—Gertrude Jekyll, British horticulturist and garden designer

1. What different entry points, supports, and contexts for ongoing learning exist in your workplace for you? How, if at all, might some of the ideas in this chapter and this book inform and/or influence how you are thinking about supporting yourself and your growth? Supporting those in your care? Enhancing the structures in your workplace with even more developmental intentionality?

2. How might you apply any of the ideas discussed in this book to your own practice and justice-centering leadership? Who could help you? What is your next step?

3. After reading this book, what kinds of practices and structures do you want to build into or enhance in the contexts in which you serve to help adults engage in conversations about justice? About development? About justice and development?

4. How does the research presented in this book—or pieces of it—apply to working with those in your care? What kinds of supports would you like to add to those you offer to others? Who can help you with all of this? What is your next step?

5. In what ways, if any, do the ideas, frameworks, images, and metaphors discussed in this book help you with reconsidering how you might enhance conditions for justice-centering conversations with educators—whether these occur in your team, in your cabinet, in your classroom, in your faculty meeting, or in any kind of learning conversation?

6. What kinds of justice-centering conversations would you like to add to your practice? With whom would you like to have these? Are there ways in which you would like to connect these to development? Other frameworks? What is your next step?

7. What questions/challenges/dilemmas seem especially important for you to consider in terms of implementing these practices for others and for yourself?

JUSTICE-CENTERING LEADERSHIP, INTERNAL CAPACITY, WISTERIAS, AND HOPE

> *"Hope" is the thing with feathers that perches in the soul and sings the tune without the words and never stops at all.*
>
> —Emily Dickinson, "'Hope' Is the Thing With Feathers (314)"

As human beings, and as leaders and advocates for justice, we can continue to grow our practice and ourselves throughout our lives. Throughout this book we have shared moments of life—of heart, mind, struggle, and hope—from dedicated leaders' justice-centering work and highlighted the internal capacities needed to lead in the ways they do. We have worked to illuminate their powerful, inspiring, and painful stories, their commitments to and practices on behalf of justice-centering leadership, and the roots and inspirations of their dedication—what guided them to where they are, what sustains them there now, and what they need to continue forward. Their hearts, minds, and spirits—as well as their capacities and growing edges— enliven the pages of this book. They have opened themselves to us and for us so that we could learn from and share their wisdom, as well as their experiences with the complexities (inside and out) of leading for justice in schools and the world today.

In sharing examples from leaders' lives, we have tried to highlight the internal capacities that animate and enable their most effective practices. In so doing, we have explored the similarities and differences in their strengths, orientations to justice, and developmental growing edges. Great internal capacity is needed to lead in our ever-changing, diverse, complex context and world. This speaks in every page of this book.

It also, poetically, reminds us of the multifaceted beauty, resiliency, and diversity of the wisteria plant. Native to Asia, the stunning wisteria spends a few vulnerable years building a root system, but then can quickly grow ten to twenty feet before offering a burst of blossoms and romantic flowering—some rather quickly and some after nearly twenty years of building readiness. In this way, the wisteria is a powerful reminder of the varied pace, complexity, and majesty of development and growth.

A twining vine, the wisteria also reminds us of the importance of just-right supports. Some wisteria, on their own, can grow into lovely treelike plants. Yet, most varieties like to climb trellises, arbors, fences, walls, and trees. They grow by climbing into, onto, and around a safe, reliable, encouraging, and *sustainable* support structure. It is the external support that helps them spread and reach outward. In a similar way, developers of adults need to create holding environments that nurture and guide adult learning, growth, and leadership in ways that meet people where they are *and* provide scaffolding for stretching beyond the safe and familiar. Like wisterias, people need different kinds of careful holding as they grow through the layers and experiences of life. Each one so beautiful. Each one unique.

Also like human beings, the wisteria has many visible and invisible similarities to and important—distinctive—differences from other relatives in its family: different root systems, various healing properties, and beautiful blossoms offering a rainbow of colors. The shapes of wisteria leaves vary, too, as do their textures. This diversity—like all diversities—needs to be appreciated, acknowledged, embraced, respected, admired, and loved. Appreciating how our many commonalities, differences, stories, gifts, histories, wisdoms, traditions, and values drive thinking, feeling, behaviors, and possibilities is essential. Likewise, understanding more about our internal capacities can help us hold one another with greater tenderness, support each other in our growth, and tend to more fertile ground, together. We cradle the future in our hearts and hands.

Like the beautiful wisteria, which can continue to grow, become more complex, and evolve over its lifetime of, in some cases, centuries—so, too, can we. Although we cannot, of course, quite grow for centuries as *individuals*, the gifts we give and receive now can be generative gifts for the future—gifts that live in us and live on after us. As an example of this tenacity and longevity, we share in Figure 7.3 a photograph of a wisteria vine taken around 1908 at Wave Hill—a famous public garden and cultural center that runs alongside the Hudson River in the Bronx, New York. Having had the pleasure of facilitating professional learning sessions for educators at Wave Hill multiple times, we find it remarkable and inspiring to see this very same vine flourishing today, nearly 150 years after it was planted, even after surviving a fire (Brey, 2021).

FIGURE 7.3 WISTERIA VINE AT WAVE HILL GARDENS C. 1908

SOURCE: © Wave Hill, 1908.

On a related note, it's a common sentiment among advocates that the work they do today may not bear fruit until long after they are gone. But in dreaming forward—and investing with hope and love—they help lay the foundation for a better world. Making a similar point, there was an anecdote that President John F. Kennedy was fond of telling. In fact, he used it at least five times in 1962 alone—in reference to conservation efforts, in conversation with auto workers, and in speeches and addresses from the east coast to the west. It was a recounting of the story of a French Marshal who asked his gardener to plant a tree. The gardener, as the story goes, objected that the tree was slow growing and would not reach maturity for a hundred years. According to Kennedy, the Marshal replied, "In that case, there is no time to lose. Plant it this afternoon!"

Like the Marshal's tree—and like justice—development takes time. And, as was Kennedy's point, there's no better time than *now* to begin such long, hard, and necessary work. Even though the blossoms may be a bit further away—in each of us and in society—building internal capacity for justice-centering leadership is vital and urgent today. It is also, we think, one of the most important and pressing ways leaders can apply developmental theory in education and beyond. As Thea—a district-level leader focused on teacher leadership who identified as a Black woman—put it, "This work is *the* work, right? It's not an initiative. It is not a new thing we're going to do now for a time. But this is *the* work, and it's social justice."

We hope that you've experienced this book—and the developmental trajectory it describes—as an invitation to walk and think forward together. We hope that the stories throughout—from leaders like you who have given their time, expertise, and very selves to their efforts to center justice—inspire you to see possibility and forge new paths ahead. May we step forward together with love and care and hope. And may our roads be lined with wisteria to guide the way.

STEPPING FORWARD AND ACTION PLANNING

As we close our time together, we thank you again and sincerely for reading this book. We hope you've found it a meaningful support for your justice-centering leadership and a resource for supporting those in your care. We hope, too, that you will take a few minutes to pause and consider two final reflective invitations. First, we offer an opportunity to consider next steps in relation to a pressing justice-related challenge you are currently facing. We close, after that, with a reminder to care for yourself as you engage in the heavy and beautiful work of centering justice in your classrooms, schools, teams, districts, organizations, communities, and beyond. We send our loving gratitude—and lifting wishes—to you for all you carry and do.

NEXT STEPS FOR A MOST PRESSING CHALLENGE

1. What is your most pressing justice-oriented dilemma or challenge at this time?

2. Who is involved? Do you have a sense of their ways of knowing?

3. What, for you, is the pain point? In other words, what's the hardest part of the challenge for you right now?

4. How are you handling it?

5. What would you like help with at this time?

6. How, if at all, might any of the experiences, thinking, and wisdom shared by the leaders in this research—or the developmental model presented in this book—help you with meeting your pressing challenge, addressing your dilemma, and/or soothing your pain point?

7. Who could you share this with? What kinds of support would be helpful to you?

8. What is one concrete (action) step you will take to help yourself with this difficult situation?

MAKING A PROMISE TO YOURSELF: CENTERING SELF-CARE

1. How do you support and care for yourself?

2. What kinds of strategies and practices do you employ right now to care for your own renewal?

3. What is one thing that you will do to care for your renewal over the next month? Two months? Three months?

4. Please make a promise to yourself about how you will care for and sustain yourself as you engage in the vital and emotional work of caring for others and leading for justice. You may also want to share this promise with a colleague and check in with them regularly about how you're doing and how they are doing with their self-care.

REFERENCES

Adams, M. (2014). Social justice and education. In M. Reisch (Ed.), *The Routledge international handbook of social justice* (pp. 249–268). Routledge.

Adams, M., Blumenfeld, W. J., Castañeda, C., Hackman, H. W., Peters, M. L., & Zúñiga, X. (Eds.). (2013). *Readings for diversity and social justice* (3rd ed.). Routledge.

Allen, D. (2016). Toward a connected society. In E. Lewis & N. Cantor (Eds.), *Our compelling interests* (pp. 71–105). Princeton University Press.

Almeida, P. (2019). *Social movements: The structure of collective mobilization.* University of California Press.

Anzaldúa, G. (2002). Now let us shift . . . the path of conocimiento . . . inner work, public acts. In G. E. Anzaldúa & A. Keating (Eds.), *This bridge we call home: Radical visions for transformation* (pp. 540–576). Routledge.

Anzaldúa, G. (2015). Geographies of selves—Reimagining identity. In G. Anzaldúa & A. Keating (Eds.), *Light in the dark/Luz en lo oscuro: Rewriting identity, spirituality, reality* (pp. 69–73, 79–81). Duke University Press.

Apple, M. A. (2018). *The struggle for democracy in education.* Routledge.

Au, W. (2018). *A Marxist education: Learning to change the world.* Haymarket.

Ayers, W. (2008). *Social justice and teaching.* https://billayers.wordpress.com/2008/05/07/social-justice-and-teaching/

Barnum, J., & Kahane, A. (2011). *Power and love: A theory and practice of social change.* ReadHowYouWant.

Basseches, M. (1984). *Dialectical thinking and adult development.* Ablex.

Baxter-Magolda, M. B. (1992). *Knowing and reasoning in college: Gender-related patterns in students' intellectual development.* Jossey-Bass.

Baxter-Magolda, M. B. (2009). *Authoring your life: Developing an internal voice to navigate life's challenges.* Stylus Publishing.

Belenky, M. F., Clinchy, B. V., Goldberger, N. R., & Tarule, J. M. (1997). *Women's ways of knowing: The development of self, voice, and mind* (10th anniversary ed.). Basic Books.

Bell, J. (n.d.). The four I's of oppression. Retrieved from https://drive.google.com/file/d/11qe0RduQ1-NWsvHyNjSiAMgleYMTqdwd/view

Bell, L. A. (2016). Theoretical foundations for social justice education. In M. Adams & L. A. Bell (Eds.), *Teaching for diversity and social justice* (3rd ed., pp. 3–26). Routledge.

Berea College. (n.d.). *The power of Sankofa: Know history.* Carter G. Woodson Center. https://www.berea.edu/cgwc/the-power-of-sankofa/

Bonilla-Silva, E. (1997). Rethinking racism: Toward a structural interpretation. *American Sociological Review, 62*(3), 465–480.

Bonilla-Silva, E. (2010). *Racism without racists: Color-blind racism and racial inequality in contemporary America.* Rowman and Littlefield.

Brey, J. (2021, May 27). Blooming wisteria. *Wave Hill.* https://www.wavehill.org/discover/garden-journal/blooming-wisteria

Bridwell, S. D. (2013). A constructive-developmental perspective on the transformative learning of adults marginalized by race, class, and gender. *Adult Education Quarterly, 63*(2), 127–146.

Brooks, D. (2020). Seeing each other deeply. *Brigham Young Magazine*, Winter. https://magazine.byu.edu/article/seeing-each-other-deeply/

Brooks, J. (2016, November). *White privilege and educational leadership: Interrogating research and policy related to preparation and practice* [Paper presentation]. Annual Meeting of the University Council of Educational Administration, Detroit, MI.

Castagno, A. E. (Ed.). (2019). *The price of nice: How good intentions maintain educational inequity*. University of Minnesota Press.

Cherng, H. Y. S., & Halpin, P. F. (2016). The importance of minority teachers: Student perceptions of minority versus white teachers. *Educational Researcher*, 45(7), 407–420.

Cisneros, S. (1991). Eleven. In *Woman hollering creek: And other stories* (pp. 6–9). Vintage Contemporaries.

Collins, C. (2018). What is white privilege really. *Teaching Tolerance*, 60, 1–11.

Collins, P. H. (2022). *Black feminist thought: Knowledge, consciousness, and the politics of empowerment* (30th anniversary ed.). Routledge.

Crenshaw, K. (1989). Demarginalizing the intersection of race and sex: A Black feminist critique of antidiscrimination doctrine. *University of Chicago Legal Forum*, 1989: 139–167.

Crenshaw, K. (1991). Mapping the margins: Intersectionality, identity, and violence against women of color. *Stanford Law Review*, 43(6): 1241–1300.

Crenshaw, K. (2013). Demarginalizing the intersection of race and sex: A Black feminist critique of antidiscrimination doctrine, feminist theory and antiracist politics. In K. J. Maschke (Ed.), *Feminist legal theories* (pp. 23–51). Routledge.

Crenshaw, K. (2017, June 8). *Kimberlé Crenshaw on intersectionality, more than two decades later*. https://www.law.columbia.edu/news/archive/kimberle-crenshaw-intersectionality-more-two-decades-later

Cross, W. E., Jr. (1995). The psychology of Nigrescence: Revising the Cross model. In J. G. Ponterott, J. M. Casas, L. A. Suzuki, & C. M. Alexander (Eds.), *Handbook of multicultural counseling* (pp. 93–122). SAGE.

Crowley, R. M. (2016). Transgressive and negotiated white racial knowledge. *International Journal of Qualitative Studies in Education*, 29(8), 1016–1029.

DeMatthews, D. E. (2018). *Community engaged leadership for social justice: A critical approach in urban schools*. Routledge.

DiAngelo, R. J. (2010). Why can't we all just be individuals? Countering the discourse of individualism in anti-racist education. *InterActions: UCLA Journal of Education and Information Studies,* 6(1). https://escholarship.org/uc/item/5fm4h8wm#page-4

DiAngelo, R. (2018). *White fragility: Why it's so hard for white people to talk about racism*. Beacon Press.

DiAngelo, R. (2021). *Nice racism: How progressive white people perpetuate racial harm*. Beacon Press.

Diem, S., Welton, A. D., Walters, S. W., & Clark, S. P. (2022). Companion article: Understanding the politics of race, equity, and neoliberalism in everyday leadership. In R. O. Guillaume, N. W. Arnold, & A. F. Osanloo (Eds.), *A companion guide to handbook of urban educational leadership: Theory to practice* (pp. 103–106). Rowman & Littlefield.

Donaldson, G. A. (2008). *How leaders learn: Cultivating capacities for school improvement*. Teachers College Press.

Dover, A. G. (2013). Teaching for social justice. *Perspectives*, 15(1), 3–11.

Drago-Severson, E. (1996). *Head-of-school as principal adult developer: An account of one leader's efforts to support transformational learning among the adults in her school* [Unpublished doctoral dissertation]. Harvard University.

Drago-Severson, E. (2004a). *Becoming adult learners: Principles and practices for effective development*. Teachers College Press.

Drago-Severson, E. (2004b). *Helping teachers learn: Principal leadership for adult growth and development*. Corwin/SAGE.

Drago-Severson, E. (2009). *Leading adult learning: Supporting adult development in our schools*. Corwin/SAGE and Learning Forward.

Drago-Severson, E. (2012). *Helping educators grow: Strategies and practices for leadership development*. Harvard Education Press.

Drago-Severson, E. (2016). Teaching, learning, and leading in today's complex world: Reaching new heights with a developmental approach. *International Journal of Leadership in Education, 19*(1), 56–86.

Drago-Severson, E., & Blum-DeStefano, J. (2016). *Tell me so I can hear you: A developmental approach to feedback for educators.* Harvard Education Press.

Drago-Severson, E., & Blum-DeStefano, J. (2017). The self in social justice: A developmental lens on race, identity, and transformation. *Harvard Educational Review, 87*(4), 457–481.

Drago-Severson, E., & Blum-DeStefano, J. (2018). *Leading change together: Developing educator capacity in schools and systems.* Association for Supervision and Curriculum Development.

Drago-Severson, E., & Blum-DeStefano, J. (2019). A developmental lens on social justice leadership: Exploring the connection between meaning making and practice. *The Journal of Educational Leadership and Policy Studies, Special Issue #1 on Educational Leadership and Social Justice, 3*(1).

Drago-Severson, E., Blum-DeStefano, J., & Asghar, A. (2013). *Learning for leadership: Developmental strategies for building capacity in our schools.* Corwin.

Drago-Severson, E., Blum-DeStefano, J., & Brooks Lawrence, D. (2020). Connections bring us closer to equity and justice. *The Learning Professional, 41*(5), 32–40.

Drago-Severson, E., Blum-DeStefano, J., & Brooks Lawrence, D. (2021, November). *Toward a research-based, developmental continuum of social justice educational leadership* [Paper presentation]. Annual Convention of the University Council of Educational Administration 2021, Columbus, OH.

Drago-Severson, E., Blum-DeStefano, J., & Brooks Lawrence, D. (2022, April). *Supporting leaders' practices for diversity, equity and inclusion: The promise of a developmental continuum of social justice educational leadership* [Paper presentation]. Annual Meeting of the American Educational Research Association, San Diego, CA.

Drago-Severson, E., Roy, P., & von Frank, V. (2015). *Learning designs.* Corwin and Learning Forward.

Frank, A. (1959). *The works of Anne Frank.* Doubleday.

Fraser, N. (2019). *The old is dying and the new cannot be reborn.* Verso.

Freire, P. (1970/2000). *Pedagogy of the oppressed* (30th anniversary ed.). Bloomsbury.

Gassaway, B. (2018). *Helping principals build partnerships: A principal's guide to healthy and sustainable school-community relationships.* Gassaway Alg.

Gay, G. (2010). *Culturally responsive teaching: Theory, research, and practice* (2nd ed.). Teachers College Press.

Gay, G. (2013). Teaching to and through cultural diversity. *Curriculum Inquiry, 43,* 48–70.

Gill, J. (2019, October 22). Keeping current on the state of knowledge about principals and APs: Scholars dig into latest research on three crucial topics in school leadership. *WALLACE Blog.* https://www.wallacefoundation.org/news-and-media/blog/pages/keeping-current-on-the-state-of-knowledge-about-principals-and-aps.aspx?

Giroux, H. A. (2016). Beyond pedagogies of repression. *Monthly Review, 67*(10), 57–71. https://doi.org/10.14452/MR-067-10-2016-03_6

Goleman, D. (1988, June 14). Erikson, in his old age, expands his view of life. *The New York Times.* https://archive.nytimes.com/www.nytimes.com/books/99/08/22/specials/erikson-old.html

Gooden, M. A., & O'Doherty, A. (2015). Do you see what I see? Fostering aspiring leaders' racial awareness. *Urban Education, 50*(2), 225–255.

Grant, C. A. (2012). Cultivating flourishing lives: A robust social justice vision of education. *American Educational Research Journal, 49*(5), 910–934. https://doi.org/10.3102/0002831212447977

Grissom, J., Egalite, A., & Lindsay, C. (2021). How principals affect students and schools: A systematic synthesis of two decades of research. *The Wallace Foundation.* https://www.wallacefoundation.org/knowledge-center/Documents/

How-Principals-Affect-Students-and-Schools.pdf

Guo, W., & Vulchi, P. (2019). *Tell me who you are: A road map for cultivating racial literacy*. TarcherPerigee.

Guskey, T. R. (1999). *New perspectives on evaluating professional development* [Paper presentation]. Annual Meeting of the American Educational Research Association, Montreal, Canada.

Harro, B. (2013). The cycle of liberation. In M. Adams, W. J. Blumenfeld, C. Casteñeda, H. W. Hackman, M. L. Peters, & X. Zúñiga (Eds.), *Readings for diversity and social justice* (3rd ed., pp. 618–625). Routledge.

Helms, J. E. (2020). *A race is a nice thing to have: A guide to being a white person or understanding the white persons in your life*. Cognella.

Holvino, E. (2012). The "simultaneity" of identities. In C. L. Wijeyesinghe & B. W. Jackson III (Eds.), *New perspectives on racial identity development: Integrating emerging frameworks* (2nd ed., pp. 161–192). New York University Press.

Immordino-Yang, M. H. (2015). *Emotions, learning, and the brain: Exploring the educational implications of affective neuroscience*. W. W. Norton & Company.

Immordino-Yang, M. H., Darling-Hammond, L., & Krone, C. (2018). *The brain basis for integrated social, emotional, and academic development: How emotions and social relationships drive learning*. Aspen Institute. https://www.aspeninstitute.org/wp-content/uploads/2018/09/Aspen_research_FINAL_web.pdf

Immordino-Yang, M. H., & Knecht, D. R. (2020). Building meaning builds teens brains. *Educational Leadership, 77*(8), 36–43.

Irby, D. (2021) *Stuck improving: Racial equity and school leadership*. Harvard Education Press.

Jean-Marie, G., Normore, A. H., & Brooks, J. (2009). Leadership for social justice: Preparing 21st century leaders for a new social order. *Journal of Research on Leadership Education, 4*(1), 1–31. https://doi.org/10.1177/194277510900400102

Johnson, A. L. (2022, March 22). *Zull's model of the connection between brain function and human learning*. Adapted visually by Amy Leigh Johnson based on descriptions in "How the brain learns" by James Zull, 2006. https://www.flickr.com/photos/amyleighjohnson/5231686111/

Jones, K., & Okun, T. (2001). *Dismantling racism: A workbook for social change groups*. ChangeWork.

Keating, A. (2013). *Transformation now! Toward a post-oppositional politics of change*. University of Illinois Press.

Keenan, H. B. (2017). Unscripting curriculum: Toward a critical trans pedagogy. *Harvard Education Review, 87*(4), 538–556.

Kegan, R. (1982). *The evolving self: Problem and process in human development*. Harvard University Press.

Kegan, R. (1994). *In over our heads: The mental demands of modern life*. Harvard University Press.

Kegan, R. (2000). What "form" transforms? A constructive-developmental approach to transformative learning. In J. Mezirow and Associates (Eds.), *Learning as transformation* (pp. 35–70). Jossey-Bass.

Kegan, R., & Lahey, L. L. (2009). *Immunity to change: How to overcome it and unlock the potential in yourself and your organization*. Harvard Business Press.

Kegan, R. (2013, January). Keynote address. 22nd Annual Conflict Resolution Symposium, Ottawa, Canada.

Kegan, R. (2018). What "form" transforms? A constructive-developmental approach to transformative learning. In K. Illeris (Ed.), *Contemporary theories of learning* (pp. 29–45). Routledge.

Kegan, R., Broderick, M., Drago-Severson, E., Helsing, D., Popp, N., & Portnow, K. (2001). *Toward a new pluralism in ABE/ESOL classrooms: Teaching to multiple "cultures of mind."* Executive Summary. NCSALL Report #19a. National Center for the Study of Adult Literacy and Learning.

Kegan, R., & Lahey, L. L. (2009). *Immunity to change: How to overcome it and unlock the potential in yourself and your organization*. Harvard Business Press.

Kegan, R., & Lahey, L. L. (2016). *An everyone culture: Becoming a deliberately developmental organization*. Harvard Business Review Press.

Kendi, I. X. (2019). *How to be an antiracist.* One World.

Khalifa, M. (2018). *Culturally responsive school leadership.* Harvard Education Press.

Khalifa, M. A., Gooden, M. A., & Davis, J. E. (2016). Culturally responsive school leadership: A synthesis of the literature. *Review of Educational Research, 86*(4), 1272–1311.

King, M. L. (1965). *Remaining awake through a great revolution.* Oberlin College Archives.

Knefelkamp, L. L., & David-Lang, T. (2000). Encountering diversity on campus and in the classroom: Advancing intellectual and ethical development. *Diversity Digest, 4*(3), 12–19.

Kohlberg, L. (1969). Stage and sequence: The cognitive-developmental approach to socialization. In D. A. Goslin (Ed.), *Handbook of socialization theory and research* (pp. 347–380). Rand McNally.

Kohlberg, L. (1984). *Stage and sequence: The cognitive developmental approach to socialization: The psychology of moral development.* Harper & Row.

Kumashiro, K. K. (2015). *Against common sense: Teaching and learning toward social justice.* Routledge.

Ladson-Billings, G. (1995a). But that's just good teaching! The case for culturally relevant pedagogy. *Theory Into Practice, 43,* 159–165.

Ladson-Billings, G. (1995b). Toward a theory of culturally relevant pedagogy. *American Educational Research Journal, 32,* 465–491.

Ladson-Billings, G. (2014). Culturally relevant pedagogy 2.0: a.k.a. the remix. *Harvard Educational Review, 84,* 74–84.

Ladson-Billings, G., & Tate, W. F. (1995). Toward a critical race theory of education. *Teachers College Record, 97*(1), 47–68.

Lahey, L., Souvaine, E., Kegan, R., Goodman, R., & Felix, S. (1988/2011). *A guide to the subject-object interview: Its administration and interpretation.* Minds at Work.

Leithwood, K., & Louis, K. S. (2012). *Linking leadership to student learning.* Jossey-Bass.

Lensmire, T., McManimon, S., Tierney, J. D., Lee-Nichols, M., Casey, Z., Lensmire, A., & Davis, B. (2013). McIntosh as synecdoche: How teacher education's focus on white privilege undermines antiracism. *Harvard Educational Review, 83*(3), 410–431.

Lewis, A. B. (2022). Dreaming out loud: Four music educators dream for the future of music education. *Bulletin of the Council for Research in Music Education, 232,* 64–80.

López, I. F. H. (2000). Institutional racism: Judicial conduct and a new theory of racial discrimination. *The Yale Law Journal, 109*(8), 1717–1884.

Love, B. (2019). *We want to do more than survive: Abolitionist teaching and pursuit of educational freedom.* Beacon Press.

MacDonald, E. (2011). When nice won't suffice. *Journal of Staff Development, 32*(3), 45–47.

Magee, R. V. (2019). *The inner work of racial justice: Healing ourselves and transforming our communities through mindfulness.* TarcherPerigree.

Maxwell, J. A. (2013). *Qualitative research design: An interactive approach* (3rd ed.). SAGE.

McIntosh, P. (1989). Unpacking the invisible knapsack. *Peace and Freedom, 49,* 10–12.

McIntosh, P. (2015). Extending the knapsack: Using the white privilege analysis to examine conferred advantage and disadvantage. *Women & Therapy, 38*(3–4), 232–245.

McIntosh, P. (2018). White privilege and male privilege. In M. S. Kimmel & A. L. Ferber (Eds.), *Privilege* (pp. 28–40). Routledge.

Merriam, S. B. & Associates. (2007). *Non-Western perspectives on learning and knowing.* Krieger.

Milner, H. R. (2020). *Start where you are, but don't stay there: Understanding diversity, opportunity gaps, and teaching in today's classrooms.* Harvard Education Press.

Milton, B. E., & Brooks Lawrence, D. (2022). *Inherited wisdom: Drawing on the lessons of formerly enslaved ancestors to lift up Black youth.* Cognella Academic.

Mizell, H. (2007). Students learn when adults learn. *The Learning System, 3*(3), 2.

Mosley, A. J., & Heiphetz, L. (2021). Integrating social and moral psychology to reduce inequality. *Psychological Inquiry, 32*(3), 173–177.

Muhammad, G. (2020). *Cultivating genius: An equity framework for culturally and historically responsive literacy.* Scholastic.

Muhammad, G. E., Dunmeyer, A., Starks, F. D., & Sealey-Ruiz, Y. (2020). Historical voices for contemporary times: Learning from

Black women educational theorists to redesign teaching and teacher education. *Theory into Practice, 59(4)*, 419–428.

Nieto, S. (2010). Foreword. In T. Chapman & N. Hobbel (Eds.), *Social justice pedagogy across the curriculum: The practice of freedom* (pp. viii–x). Routledge.

Officer, D. R. (2018). An everyone culture: Becoming a deliberately developmental organization. *The Innovation Journal, 23(3)*, 1–6.

Osterman, K. F., & Kottkamp, R. B. (1993). *Reflective practice for educators: Improving schooling through professional development.* Corwin.

Paris, D. (2012). Culturally sustaining pedagogy: A needed change in stance, terminology, and practice. *Educational Researcher, 41(3)*, 93–97.

Paris, D., & Alim, H. S. (Eds.). (2017). *Culturally sustaining pedagogies: Teaching and learning for justice in a changing world.* Teachers College Press.

Perry, W. G. (1970). *Forms of intellectual and ethical development in the college years.* Holt, Rinehart and Winston.

Perry, S. P., Skinner-Dorkenoo, A. L., Wages, J. E., III., & Abaied, J. L. (2021). Systemic considerations in child development and the pursuit of racial equality in the United States. *Psychological Inquiry, 32(3)*, 180–186.

Piaget, J. (1952). *The origins of intelligence in children.* International Universities Press.

Pollock, M., Deckman, S., Mira, M., & Shalaby, C. (2010). "But what can I do?": Three necessary tensions in teaching teachers about race. *Journal of Teacher Education, 61(3)*, 211–224.

Price-Dennis, D., & Sealy-Ruiz, Y. (2021). *Advancing racial literacies in teacher education: Activism for equity in digital spaces.* Teachers College Press.

Reisch, M. (Ed.). (2014). *The Routledge international handbook of social justice* (pp. 249–268). Routledge.

Rilke, R. M., & Burnham, J. M. (1934/1993). *Letters to a young poet* (M. D. Herter Norton, Trans.). WW Norton & Co.

Rock, D. (2010). Your brain at work: Strategies for overcoming distraction, regaining focus, and working smarter all day long. *Journal of Behavioral Optometry, 21(5)*, 130.

Rock, D., & Grant, H. (2016). Why diverse teams are smarter. *Harvard Business Review, 4(4)*, 2–5.

Rock, D., & Page, L. J. (2009). *Coaching with the brain in mind: Foundations for practice.* John Wiley & Sons.

Rogers, C. R. (1961). *On becoming a person: A therapist's view of psychotherapy.* Constable.

Rogers, F. (1997, May 21). *Lifetime Achievement Award acceptance address at the 24th Annual Daytime Emmy Awards Ceremony* [Speech]. Radio City Music Hall, New York.

Rorty, R. (1998). *Truth and progress: Philosophical papers* (Vol. 3). Cambridge University Press.

Rubie-Davies, C. M. (2008). Teacher beliefs and expectations: Relationships with student learning. In C. M. Rubie-Davies & C. Rawlinson (Eds.), *Challenging thinking about teaching and learning* (pp. 25–39). Nova.

Sen, A. (2009). *The idea of justice.* Belknap/Harvard.

Simard, S. (2016). *How trees talk to each other* [Video]. TED Conferences. https://www.ted.com/talks/suzanne_simard_how_trees_talk_to_each_other#t-6260

Singh, A. A. (2019). *The racial healing handbook: Practical activities to help you challenge privilege, confront systemic racism, & engage in collective healing.* Harbinger.

Singleton, G. (2014). *Courageous conversations about race: A field guide for achieving equity in schools.* Corwin.

Sleeter, C. (2016). Wrestling with problematics of whiteness in teacher education. *International Journal of Qualitative Studies in Education, 29(8)*, 1065–1068.

Smith, A. D. (2006). *Letters to a young artist.* Anchor.

Staggenborg, S. (2016). *Social movements* (2nd ed.). Oxford University Press.

Sue, D. W. (2010). *Microaggressions in everyday life: Race, gender, and sexual orientation.* John Wiley & Sons.

Tatum, B. D. (2013). The complexity of identity: "Who am I?" In M. Adams, W. J. Blumenfeld, C. Casañeda, H. W. Hackman, M. L. Peters, & X. Zúñiga (Eds.), *Readings for diversity and social justice* (3rd ed.) (pp. 6–9). Routledge.

Tatum, B. D. (2017). *Why are all the Black kids sitting together in the cafeteria? And other conversations about race* (20th anniversary ed.). Basic Books.

Thoma, B., Caretta-Weyer, H., Schumacher, D. J., Warm, E., Hall, A. K., Hamstra, S. J., Cavalcanti, R. Chan, T. M., & ICBME Collaborators. (2021). Becoming a deliberately developmental organization: Using competency based assessment data for organizational development. *Medical Teacher, 43*(7), 801–809.

Vulchi, P., & Guo, W. (2017). What it takes to be racially literate. *TED Talk.* https://www.ted.com/talks/priya_vulchi_and_winona_guo_what_it_takes_to_be_racially_literate

Wagner, T. (2007). Leading for change: Five 'habits of mind' that count. *Education Week, 26*(45), 29–32.

Welton, A. D., & Diem, S. (Eds). (2022). *Strengthening anti-racist educational leaders: Advocating for racial equity in turbulent times.* Bloomsbury.

Wijeyesinghe, C. L., & Jackson, B. W., III. (Eds.). (2012). *New perspectives on racial identity development: Integrating emerging frameworks* (2nd ed.). New York University Press.

Winnicott, D. W. (1965). *The maturation processes and the facilitating environment.* International Universities Press.

Yosso, T. J. (2005). Whose culture has capital? A critical race theory discussion of community cultural wealth. *Race Ethnicity and Education, 8*(1), 69–91.

Young, M. D., O'Doherty, A., & Cunningham, K. M. W. (2022). *Redesigning educational leadership preparation for equity: Strategies for innovation and improvement.* Routledge.

Zembylas, M. (2010). Teachers' emotional experiences of growing diversity and multiculturalism in schools and the prospects of an ethic of discomfort. *Teachers and Teaching: Theory and Practice, 16*(6), 703–716.

INDEX

Continue learning...

Ellie Drago-Severson
drago-severson@tc.edu
dragoseverson.wordpress.com

Jessica Blum-DeStefano
jblumdestefano@bankstreet.edu

Deborah Brooks Lawrence
deb2155@tc.columbia.edu

Contact us for more information about workshops and institutes!

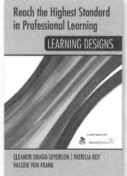

EQ22137952

CORWIN

CORWIN HAS ONE MISSION: to enhance education through intentional professional learning.

We build long-term relationships with our authors, educators, clients, and associations who partner with us to develop and continuously improve the best evidence-based practices that establish and support lifelong learning.

THE PROFESSIONAL LEARNING ASSOCIATION

Learning Forward is a nonprofit, international membership association of learning educators committed to one vision in K–12 education: Equity and excellence in teaching and learning. To realize that vision, Learning Forward pursues its mission to build the capacity of leaders to establish and sustain highly effective professional learning. Information about membership, services, and products is available from www.learningforward.org.